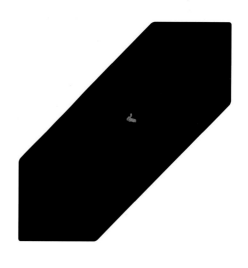

30

The One Show
Advertising's best print, radio, television and innovative media

First published in the United States
of America by
One Club Publishing
21 E. 26th Street
5th floor
New York, NY 10010
Telephone: (212) 979-1900
Fax: (212) 979-5006
www.oneclub.org

Distributed in the US
and Internationally by
Rockport Publishers, a member of
Quayside Publishing Group
100 Cummings Center
Suite 406-L
Beverly, Massachusetts 01915-6101
Telephone: (978) 282-9590
Fax: (978) 283-2742
www.quaysidepublishinggroup.com

ISBN-13: 978-0-929837-36-9
ISBN-10: 0-929837-36-3

10 9 8 7 6 5 4 3 2 1

**Books are to be returned on or before
the last date below.**

28.9.2012.

Contents

The One Club Board of Directors

This book is dedicated to all of you who worked the late nights, missed the fun weekend trips with friends, explained to your young children, wives, husbands, girlfriends, boyfriends, why you had to stay late at work, ate cold pizza yet again in the conference room because there was no time to go out, sat in airport boarding areas to wait for delayed flights to your clients and then endured the same thing on the way back, slept on the couch in your office, slept on the couch in someone else's office, wrote, rewrote and then re-rewrote everything, voraciously argued, cajoled and otherwise shepherded an idea that only you cared about and finally, when it was all done, started on your next project with the same vigor.

All in the service of creating work that was a little funnier, a little more powerful, that worked a little harder out in the world than it might have if you hadn't given everything you had to make it so.

You know who you are. And now with this book, so does everyone else.

David Baldwin
Raleigh, NC

One Show Judges

Chris Adams
TBWA\Chiat\Day/Los Angeles

Andy Azula
The Martin Agency/Richmond

Robert Baird
Mother/New York

Bob Barrie
Barrie D'Rozario Murphy/Minneapolis

Paul Belford
This is Real Art/London

Mike Byrne
Anomaly/New York

Glenn Cole
72andSunny/El Segundo

Marty Cooke
SS+K/New York

Adriana Cury
McCann Erickson/São Paulo

Joe DeSouza
Fallon/London

Andy Greenaway
Saatchi & Saatchi/Singapore

Paul Hirsch
Hirsch Denberg/Chicago

Matt Ian
Bartle Bogle Hegarty/New York

Paul Keister
Goodness Manufacturing/Los Angeles

Arno Lindemann
Lukas Lindemann Rosinski/Hamburg

Elspeth Lynn
Zig/Toronto

Steve Mapp
Butler, Shine, Stern & Partners/Sausalito

James McGrath
Clemenger BBDO/Melbourne

Filip Nilsson
Forsman & Bodenfors/Stockholm

Masako Okamura
Dentsu/Tokyo

Ian Reichenthal
Y&R/New York

Kai Roeffen
TBWA\Germany/Dusseldorf

Ted Royer
Droga 5/New York

Beth Ryan
Bartle Bogle Hegarty/New York

Eric Silver
BBDO/New York

Nick Spahr
Goodby, Silverstein & Partners/San Francisco

Rob Strasberg
Doner/Southfield

Norman Tan
BatesAsia/Shanghai

Monica Taylor
Wieden + Kennedy/Portland

Nancy Vonk
Ogilvy & Mather/Toronto

Todd Waterbury
Wieden+ Kennedy/New York

Yang Yeo
JWT/Shanghai

One Show Radio Judges

Mike Sweeney
Freelance/New York

Ginger Robinson
Wieden + Kennedy/Portland

Roger Baldacci
Arnold/Boston

Doug Adkins
Hunt Adkins/Minneapolis

Laura Fegley
Freelance/New York

Isaac Silvergate
Droga 5/New York

Warren Cockrel
Heat/San Francisco

Austin Howe
Freelance/Portland

Steve Dildarian
Freelance/San Francisco

Josh Denberg
Hirsch Denberg/Chicago

A

David Abbott
Chris Adams
Doug Adkins
Rachel Adler
Daniel Ahearn
Isami Akasaka
Mauricio Alarcon
Patricia Alvey
Ralph Ammirati
Magnus Andersson
James Andrews
David Apicella
Mathias Appelblad
Marcelo Aragao
Gil Arevalo
Jimmy Ashworth
Brian Avenius
Hisako Awaya
Andrew Ayad
Andy Azula

B

Ron Bacsa
Chris Baier
Rob Baiocco
Rob Baird
Larry Baisden
Roger Baldacci
Sam Ball
Fabrizio Ballabeni
Brenda Ballard
Antonio Banos
Marian Bantjes
Jane Barber
Kevin Barclay
Jonathan Barco
Gail Barlow
Bob Barnwell
Ann Barrick
Bob Barrie
Lars Bastholm
Jeffrey Batson
Paul Belford
Pilar Belhumeur
Juliana Bellini
Benjamin Bensimon
Abbey Bentley
Daniel Berenson
Nicke Bergstrom
David Bernstein
Beverly Bethge
Tara Biek
Arthur Bijur
John Bilas
Samantha Birchard
Jill Bonk
Eric Boscia
Peter Bossio
Jeff Bowman
Michael Boyce
Mark Braddock
Robert Braden
Tim Braybrooks
Henry Brimmer
Robert Brothers

Mark Brown
Justin Brubaker
Elinor Buchler
Jiri Bures
Heather Buscho
Brian W. Button
Mike Byrne

C

Jorge Calleja
Bridget Camden
Karena Cameron
Xavi Caparros
Josephine Carey
Valerie Carpender
Kimball Carter
Pete Case
Isabella Castano
Mark Chalmers
Alexander Chamas
Sue Won Chang
Claire Chapman
Luke Chess
Christine Chi
Ka Chin
Annie Chiu
Angela Cho
Chris Choi
Chris Clark
Bart Cleveland
Warren Cockrel
Peter Cohen
Christopher Cole
Glenn Cole
Carol Collins
Brian Collins
Mark Collis
Mark Conachan
Andy Conroy
Marty Cooke
Jake Cooney
John Cooper
Fabio Costa
Susan Cotler-Block
Jac Coverdale
Jeremy Craigen
Jay Cranford
Jonathan Cranin
Juan Cravero
Sherri Cumberbatch
Hillman Curtis
Adriana Cury

D

Deborah Dachis-Gold
Paul Daigle
Rick Dalbey
Nigel Dawson
Tyler Deangelo
Rich Degni
Eduardo Del Fraile
Tom Delmundo
Josh Denberg
Tres Denton
Anil Deorukhakar
Hiren Desai

Joe Desouza
Sarah Di Domenico
Aurora Diaz
Barb Dickey
Steve Dildarian
Bob Dísilva
Joe Dobbin
Tommy Donoho
Michael Duckworth
Ricardo Duran
Jim Durfee

E

Lee Earle
Catherine Eccardt
Mark Edwards
Leslie Edwards
Jenny Ehlers
Randy Elles
Chris Elliott
Elaine Ellman
Emily Engelson
Maureen Enright
Ken Erke
Dirk Eschenbacher
Denise Esterkyn
Stephen Etzine
Gwynne Evans

F

Jordan Farkas
Stephen Fechtor
Laura Fegley
Svetlana Fehretdinov
Natalie Ferguson
Sergio Fermin
Daniele Fiandaca
Dan Fietsam
Michael Fiore
Julie Flannery Allen
Cameron Fleming
Peter Foubert
Cliff Freeman
Kevin Freidberg
Andrew Frith
Calley Frith
Toshiya Fukuda
Gabrielle Fulginiti

G

Tom Gabriel
Jesse Gadola
Nanette Gaffin
Chris Garbutt
Ermelyn Garcia
Amil Gargano
Mario Paolo Garofano
Preston Garrett
Stephen Gates
Anne Geri
Pia Ghosh Roy
Kent Gilbert
Jeff Gillette
Andrew Glafcke
Jason Glassman
Ken Gleason

Dan Goldgeier
Adam Goldstein Goldstein
Jeff Goodby
Robyn Goodman
Kara Goodrich
Mitch Gordon
Brian Grabell
Jeff Graham
Steven Graham
Ian Grais
R. Vann Graves
Andy Greenaway
Adam Greenhood
Alex Grimm
Matt Grogan
Frank Grosberger
Philip Growick
Scott Grubb
Theresa Gutridge

H

Sungkwon Ha
Lori Habas
Nicki Hallenberg
Natalie Hammel
Sangeun Han
Rhea Hanges
Sascha Hanke
Lisa Harper
Mark Harricks
Stuart Harricks
Ellen Harwick
Jessica Hatchett
Jackie Hathiramani
Jim Haven
Kiel Hawkins
Mark Hayden
John Hegarty
Thomas Helms
Brendan Hemp
Ralf Heuel
Helmut Himmler
Keiko Hirano
Paul Hirsch
Keith Ho
Brad Hochberg
Rob Hoffman
John Hofmeister
Bjorn Hoglund
Heather Hollis
Dave Holloway
Alita Holly
Kevin Honegger
Austin Howe
Paul Howell
Mike Hughes
Francisco Hui
Richard Hundley

I

Matt Ian
Sun-Bin Im
Rei Inamoto
Brenda Innocenti
Naoki Ito
Masashi Ito

Raisa Ivannikova

J

Harry Jacobs
Chris Jacobs
John Jay
Anne-Marie Jeffrey
Andrew Jeske
Jennifer Johnson
Anthony Johnson
Erin Johnson
Derek Johnson
Jeffrey Johnson
Erik Joiner
Stephen Jones
Ed Jones
Laura Jordan Bambach
William Jurewicz
Stephenx Jurisic

K

Stephen Kamsler
Adris Kamuli
Scott Kaplan
Jeremi Karnell
Woody Kay
Peter Kehr
Paul Keister
Jessica Keller
Carol Lee Kelliher
Marcus Kemp
David Kennedy
Matthew Ketchum
Jerry Ketel
Kris Kiger
Joanne Kim
Eugina Kim
Joyce King Thomas
Greg Knagge
Joe Knezic
Jay Ko
Andy Kohman
Gabriela Kopernicky
Anders Kornestedt
Brandon Kos
Stan Kovics
Dennis Koye
Mike Kriefski
Nao Kumagai
Laura Kunkel
Denny Kurien

L

Brittney Lacoste
Lauren Lafranz
Merav Lahr
Ming Lai
Sean Lam
Stephen Land
Robin Landa
Bryan Landaburu
Augusto Landauro
Steve Landsberg
Jim Lansbury
Alessandra Lariu

Anne Larribau
Michael Lebowitz
Hosan Lee
Won Cheol Lee
David Lee
Nattavut Leekulitak
Adam Leighton
Dany Lennon
Kerry Lennon
Jim Lesser
Nelson Leung
Kate Levin
Rachel Levin
Ted Lim
Julio Lima
Sofia Limpantoudi
Rui(Asam) Lin
Arno Lindemann
Sophia Lindholm
Paul Little
Jason Little
Dave Loew
George Lois
Lyndon Louis
David Lubars
Elspeth Lynn
Ethan Lyon

M

Travis Mabrey
Leo Macias
Sam Maclay
Steven Majure
Karen Mallia
Mark Manion
John Mannion
Hope Manville
Jan-Till Manzius
Rankin Mapother
Steve Mapp
Nadav Markel
John Marques
Eric Martz
John Matejczyk
Kim Mathers
Mauricio Mazzariol
Cal McAllister
Ed McCabe
Joe McDonagh
Nicole McDonagh
Emma McDonald
Will McGinness
Jack McGoldrick
James McGrath
Chris McGroarty
Kevin Medlyn
Gourlain Mèlanie
Alex Melvin
Thomas Mendes
Jamie Meriwether
John Merrifield
Melinda Mettler
Stephanie Meyers
Brett Michael
Raphael Milczarek
Burke Miles
Linda S. Miller
Graham Mills
Stephen Minasvand

Laurence Minsky
Brittney Mitchell
David R. Mitchell
Noah Miwa
Sarah Moffat
James Mok
Clement Mok
Sakol Mongkolkasetarin
Younghwa Moon
Milind More
John Moses
Jim Mountjoy
Zak Mroueh
Jacob Murphy

N

Yuto Nakamura
Rebecca Naul
Jeff Neely
Enric Nel-Lo
Arun K. Nemali
Jessie Nemergut
Patrick Niebrzydowski
Filip Nilsson
Jacqueline Nolan
Laura Novack
William Novak

O

Coby O'Brien
Frank O'Brien
William O'Connor
Brendan O'Flaherty
Derek O'Leary
Emily Oberman
Jesse Oberst
Colin Ochel
Matthew R. Ogelby
Masako Okamura
Martin Olinger
Richard Oliver
Jeff Olsen
Chantal Olson
Lauren Omanoff
Takashi Omura
Hollie Ontrop
Krittayot Opassatavorn
Simone Oppenheimer
Kristen Opsal
Ron Ordansa
Jen Orser
Mikio Osaki
Keith Otter
Arve Overland
Akira Oyama

P

Ben Pagel
Jack Palancio
Rob Palmer
Benjamin Palmer
Alfred Park
Charles Parr
Ciaran Parsley
Jeff Parson
Todd Paulson
Stan Pearlman
Andy Pearson

B. Martin Pedersen
Rchard Pels
Larry Perera
Theresa Petri
Fabio Pinto
Matt Powell
Kevin Proudfoot

Q

Sara Quint

R

Doug Raboy
Alan Rado
Bjorn Ramberg
Anselmo Ramos
John Rankins
Alvaro Rego
Ian Reichenthal
John Reider
Michelle Reitblat
Nancy Rice
Rob Rich
Allen Richardson
Alexander Ridore
Jason Ring
Chris Robb
Tracie Roberson
Phyllis Robinson
Kate Robinson
Ginger Robinson
Kai Roeffen
Jason Rogers
Meg Rogers
Nick Roope
Jeremiah Rosen
Laurie Rosenwald
Laurel Rossi
Damian Royce
Ted Royer
Roger Ruegger
Alan Ruthazer
Luis Ruvalcaba
Dr. Bill Ryan
Timothy Ryan
Beth Ryan

S

Dalit Saad
Jessica Sachs
Nicole San Filippo
Steve Sandstrom
Nathan Sansom
Stephanie Sarnelli
Sara Sarshar
Ruth Sauvageau
Robert Saxon
Marc Schaad
Ian Schafer
Jonathan Schoenberg
Joe Schrack
Ashley Schurott
Michael Schwabenland
Jaime Schwarz
Andrew Seagrave
Tod Seisser
Ariel Severino
Adrianne Shapera

Jon Sharpe
Jessica Shaw
Glen Sheehan
Bill Shelton
Hee Kyung Helen Shin
Marie Shirato
Dan Sicko
Alyssa Siegel
Mark Silber
Eric Silver
Isaac Silverglate
Rich Silverstein
Todd Simmons
Michael Simon
Michael Simon
Robert Skwiat
Pat Sloan
Rachel Smith
Jason Smith
Jade Snyder
Taylor Snyder
Mo Solomon
Rafa Soto
Nick Spahr
Rebecca Spring
Susan St Laurent
Arne Stach
Joe Staluppi
Kate Stankis
Russ Stark
Reuben Steiger
Hillary Steinberg
Sasha Stern
Lorna Stovall
Rob Strasberg
Thomas Stringham
Wade Sturdivant
Luke Sullivan
Steve Swartz
Manoj Swearingen
Mike Sweeney

T

Nancy R. Tag
James Talerico
Norman Tan
Koichiro Tanaka
Matthew Tarulli
Monica Taylor
Mike Tesch
Tony Thielen
Renny Tirador
Rodrigo Torres
Brian Torsney
William Tran
Ezequiel Trivino
Chuck Tso
Roman Tsukerman
Guy Tucker
Miles Turpin
Mark Tutssel

U

Drew Ungvarsky
Fehmi Mahir Uraz

V

Robert Valentine
Peter Van Bloem
Damion Van Slyke
Dirk Vandeman
Tanya Vanriel
Ana Velasco
Paul Venables
Michael Ventura
Larry Vine
Megan Voepel
Nancy Vonk

W

Graham Warsop
D.C. Washington
Todd Waterbury
Steve Wax
Robin Webb
Craig Welsh
Ben Welsh
Robert Shaw West
Patrick West
Kailey Wheaton
John White
Richard White
Dan Wieden
Liam Wielopolski
Jace Wietzikoski
Mattias Wikman
Scott Wild
Tim Williams
Katie Williams
Kianga Williams
Dominique Wilson
David A Wong
Ray Wood
Jennifer Wowk
Bill Wright
Jiashan Wu
Yu Hui Wu
Stephen Wyatt

Y

Betsy Yamazaki
Lo Sheung Yan
Fariida Yasin
Yang Yeo
Jeseok Yi
Jeongjyn Yi
Forest Young

Z

Mark Zapico
Jeffry Zavala
Richard Zeid
John Zhao
Pamela Zuccker
Mat Zucker

GOLD

Bartle Bogle Hegarty > New York

BBDO > New York

Blattner Brunner > Pittsburgh

Butler Shine Stern & Partners > Sausalito

Carmichael Lynch > Minneapolis

Cliff Freeman & Partners > New York

Cline Davis & Mann > New York

Crispin Porter + Bogusky > Boulder

davidandgoliath > Los Angeles

DDB > New York

Dentsu > Tokyo

Draft FCB > New York

Euro RSCG > New York

Fallon > Minneapolis

Goodby, Silverstein & Partners > San Francisco

GSD&M > Austin

JWT > New York

Leo Burnett > Chicago

Lowe > New York

McCann-Erickson > New York

McKinney > Durham

Ogilvy & Mather > New York

Publicis > New York

Saatchi and Saatchi > New York

School of Visual Arts > New York

TBWA\Chiat\Day > New York

TBWA\Chiat\Day > Los Angeles

Team One Advertising > El Segundo

Wieden + Kennedy > New York

Young & Rubicam > New York

SILVER

Arnold Worldwide > Boston

DDB > Chicago

DDB Canada > Vancouver

DeVito/Verdi > New York

Hill Holliday > Boston

KraftWorks > New York

la comunidad > Miami

Loeffler Ketchum Mountjoy > Charlotte

Ogilvy & Mather > Chicago

Publicis in the West > Seattle

Publicis Mid-America > Dallas

The Richards Group > Dallas

Venables Bell and Partners > San Francisco

Wieden + Kennedy > Portland

Young & Rubicam > Chicago

BRONZE

BooneOakley > Charlotte

Cactus > Denver

Conill Advertising > New York

The Creative Circle > Johannesburg

Hakuhodo > Tokyo

Marc USA > Pittsburgh

Publicis & Hal Riney > San Francisco

Publicis Lado C > Madrid

The Republik > Durham

The Richards Group > Dallas

Sarkissian Mason > New York

TBWA Media Arts Lab > Los Angeles

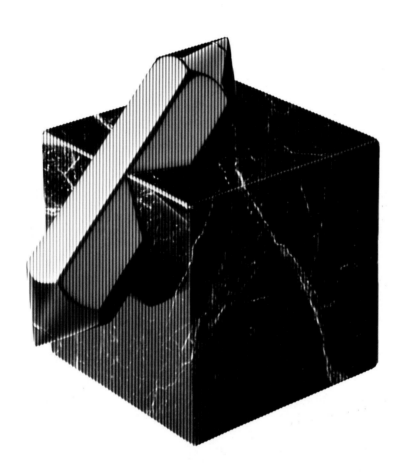

Creative Hall of Fame

Whatever the weather, this is always the warmest night of the year.

It is not a night for the cynics and the churlish; it is a night for the believers.

It is a night for three men who believed in the primacy of great work and had the grace and guts to produce it over a lifetime.

It is a night to be proud of our profession, for we work in an industry where our rivals are also our friends, and we always turn out to support them.

But best of all, this is a night that leaves a mark.

When we and our campaigns are long forgotten, there will still be a list of names in the Creative Hall of Fame.

It's not Mount Rushmore, but who wants that?

Better by far this kindly roster, this pat on the back from those who really knew.

David Abbott
2007 Creative Hall of Fame Chairman

Phil Dusenberry

You could well describe Phil Dusenberry as opinionated, stubborn, intolerant, demanding, and driven. In some people, such qualities might be nothing to celebrate. But for others, they can be hallmarks of a great leader. And Phil Dusenberry was indeed one of the truly great creative leaders in the history of advertising.

Phil didn't just have opinions. He always knew what was good, bad, or indifferent creative work. He had an unerring instinct for the insight that elevates even a good advertising idea to an emotional and human experience that would make a product relevant to what consumers thought and felt. He saw it as his mission to turn a product into a part of people's lives—certainly the defining characteristic of a successful brand.

Phil was very stubborn and intolerant. He couldn't abide by any creative compromise that would lessen the impact of the insight that drove a campaign. He'd battle with clients and agency people alike over sometimes seemingly small issues—a few words here or there, or a single scene among many—because he fervently believed that everything counted. It didn't matter who you were. When Michael Jackson refused to remove his sunglasses while filming the Pepsi campaign, Phil told him, "The glasses come off or we're outta here." The glasses came off.

Phil was demanding and driven—a requirement for a perfectionist. Someone at BBDO once quipped that with Phil running creative, the agency initials stood for "bring it back and do it over." Or as another advised, "If you eat with Phil, don't order a salad. He'll re-mix it." But as much as it has become a cliché, it is nonetheless true that Phil pushed no one harder than he drove himself.

Yet these characteristics alone would not necessarily have resulted in Phil's success. A piece of advice once given to me perfectly summarized a critical human component of our business—at the end of the day, you won't succeed if the people around you don't want you to. We all worked with and for Phil because we wanted to.

Even when Phil argued with you or turned down your work, you never believed there was any ego or motive other than his passion for doing better. He made us care more about everything we did because he cared more. He made us laugh with a sharp sense of humor that he willingly and often aimed at himself. He made it BBDO's business to celebrate every award, every sales or share increase, every brand-building success. Phil made it a point to share the credit with everyone who contributed, not only from creative but also from research, planning, account management, and yes, even media. And he made it his continuous commitment to champion the careers of the creative people who, as he always acknowledged, did the work.

And those are the two words—the work—on which Phil always focused all his talent and energy. The work was what consumed him, excited him, enthralled him, and sometimes bedeviled him. When the inevitable politics of the business undercut a major campaign and threatened his ability to protect it, Phil, many more times than

once, stormed into my office to resign, always with the same preface —"I can't take this crap any more." But happily for us, he could and did.

The work became the clarion call for the agency and our stated reason for being. He established "The Work, The Work, The Work" as the literal motto by which we would judge ourselves and promote the agency to clients and prospects. While all disciplines other than creative made essential contributions, their value was measured by their impact on the work. It wasn't our process or how we organized or our networking capabilities or any other algorithm by which we served clients as much as the creative product that became, under Phil's guidance, the defining identity of the agency and the critical differentiation between BBDO and our competitors.

And what brilliant work it was! The high entertainment of "mini-movies" for Pepsi; the humanizing of a corporate monolith by bringing "Good things to life" for GE; the fierce competitiveness of being "everywhere you want to be" for Visa; the business-building assurance to business people that they could "Relax, it's FedEx;" and the hilarious moments when the answer to hunger was to "grab a Snickers"; the star-studded parodies that raised a city's spirit with the hopes and dreams of "The New York Miracle" just after 9/11; and so much more for so many others that delivered the rationality and insight of strategy with the creativity that reached minds and hearts with logic and emotion. Phil never accepted what has today become too often the case in advertising—difference for its own sake, producing advertising without any understandable message. For him, no matter how the creative might titillate, if it didn't make sense, it didn't make it.

It was work that turned BBDO into arguably the most creative global network by raising the New York headquarters to new levels of creativity, which in turn made our network an attractive and desired partner for other creative agencies internationally and set the standard that BBDO agencies around the world sought to match in their own markets. So while Phil worked predominantly in New York, the work produced there had a profound impact on BBDO everywhere.

The only thing Phil ever feared was losing. He hated with a passion to lose an account or a new business pitch. He took it hard—viscerally and personally—which no doubt explains why it didn't happen too often. And the only thing I have to forgive him for is the work he produced for President Reagan. As a lifelong Democrat, I certainly didn't appreciate how effective it was.

I've written here about the great things Phil did for BBDO. But his place in the Creative Hall of Fame surely recognizes that his work lifted our entire industry. I think advertising, no matter how it changes in response to globalization and new technologies, will always need a big dose of Dusenberry.

— Allen Rosenshine

Paul Rand

"A salesman from a graphic arts house was in the other day with nothing apparently on his mind. Queried, he said, 'My boss says the great Paul Rand works here, and I thought I might get a look at him.' Just then Rand swept through the room. Asked if he was impressed, the salesman said, 'But he's so young.' " —*The Insider, Sept. 1939.*

When in 1941 William Weintraub left the Esquire-Coronet magazine company to start an advertising agency at Rockefeller Center, Paul Rand left with him. As art director of the Wm. H. Weintraub Agency he was given license and power, and within a short period Rand was working on campaigns for Dubonnet, Shenley liquors, Lee Hats, Disney Hats, Revlon, Hilbros Watches, El Producto Cigars, Stafford Fabrics, Kaiser Corporation and Auto Car. He hired a relatively large staff, but by his own admission, he never acted like a traditional art director; he would rarely delegate, but instead he'd design everything himself, except for certain illustrations by the likes of Ludwig Bemelmans, William Steig or Richard Lindner. Most of the time he would only come into the office for half of the week, sometimes only for half a day. The other time he attended to freelance projects for such companies as Smith Klein and French and Orbachs (where he worked with Bill Bernbach as copywriter). His keen ability to use design to sell quotidian products was earning him a considerable reputation.

Rand's importance at this period was the modernization of advertising design. Before he came to Mad Ave in the '40s, very little American advertising was really designed, but rather simply laid out by board men. Conversely, Rand was intimately involved in the entire design and typographic process. He brought to advertisements his unique appreciation of Modernist collage, which underscored his playful use of type and image. Rand was also influenced by Jan Tschichold's *New Typography*, the Modern typographic bible, and accepted the dogma—"I took it literally," he once said. "You don't do illustration, you use photography; you don't do handmade things, you do it by machine. I did it that way because that's how one learns. Even if you disagree you do it that way and then later throw it away." But Rand being Rand inevitably took liberties. Although he never studied calligraphy—because it was unnatural and stuck in time—he used his own informal handwriting whenever he could. Handwriting, he said, "is the most natural form of communicating." His advertising was also a blend of modernist economy and American wit. Of his work at the time he says: "You don't imitate anything. Collages are important, because they are not imitations of reality, but rather juxtaposed pieces of different realities."

What made Rand's work so extraordinary was the fact that they were ads for common products, produced in uncharacteristically witty, imaginative and memorable ways. Of this shirt-sleeve style he said, "I knew that not too many other guys were doing this in the US, but I never claimed that this was original stuff, because other guys were doing it in Europe."

His campaigns were never cookie cutter; they showed range and versatility. Moreover, they proved how Rand's intelligent application of abstract form was highly successful in a competitive market. About this he wrote: "For an advertisement to hold its own in a competitive race, it must be led off the beaten path by some more interesting device: the abstract symbol. If this symbol is too obscure in itself, it should be balanced with universally recognized forms."

While his newspaper ads for Orbachs and El Producto were unique in their day, the promotional brochure for Auto Car Corporation was a masterpiece of design erudition. Auto Car wanted a promotion that would show the public how they supported the war effort through the efficient manufacture of armored trucks and personnel carriers. For this they wanted to show off their plant in Ardmore, Pennsylvania. Rand hired photographer Andreas Feininger to shoot the plant in action—the assembly line, the welders, etc. When developed, however, the images were lackluster. The deadline was tight, so relying on his sharp wits and scissor he proceeded to collage the essential images, placing them with studied serendipity on the top of the page. On the bottom half of each page, he left space for text and then handed the layouts to Bill Bernbach who wrote the copy. By the way, contrary to myth, Bernbach did not teach Rand everything he ever knew about advertising; rather it is safe to say that Rand taught the golden boy a few lessons.

While making silk purses from found materials was not new to Rand (and was certainly in keeping with modernist tradition), it was unusual in the agency environment, where copywriters reigned supreme and usually give layouts to art directors who would make them pretty. To the consternation of many a copywriter, Rand took great pleasure in tearing up their layouts, particularly those that he thought were "lousy," and would often rewrite the headline. Rand was not known for his patience in such matters. "I was not going to let myself be treated like a job printer on Pitkin Avenue," he recalled.

Incidentally, Rand was the first to sign his work, which at the time (and even today) was no mean feat. When one day Weintraub called him into his office and demanded that he take his name off an ad, Rand said "this is your agency and I'll take it off, but then take my name off your door, because I'm leaving." The signature stayed on almost all his ads. But he admits that if a client had asked, he would have acquiesced. No client ever made such a request.

Rand didn't sign his ads because he believed they were art, but rather for self-promotion. Since he never took out ads in the Art Director's annuals, nor sent around flyers soliciting work, the signature was all the personal advertising he needed. For a similar reason, yet with a decidedly different result, he agreed in 1946 at the age of 32 to write a book about his work, entitled *Thoughts on Design*, published by Wittenborn the following year. Sharing his knowledge and insight with students and professionals was not the primary reason: He logically thought, "If ever there were a fire, at least I'd have all my samples in one place." But as the book took shape a more significant purpose became evident. In the preface he wrote: "This book attempts to arrange in some logical order certain principles governing advertising design. The pictorial examples used to illustrate these principles are taken from work in which I was directly engaged. This choice was made deliberately, and with no intention to imply that it represents the best translation of those principles into visual terms. There are artists and designers of great talent whose work would be perhaps more suitable. But I do not feel justified in speaking for them, nor secure in attempting to explain their work without any possibility of misrepresentation. This is not to say that this book is purely the result of my efforts alone. I am indebted to many people—painters, architects, designers of the past and present—for many theories and concepts."

Thoughts on Design was evidence that Rand, the street-smart kid from Brooklyn, who altered the way advertising was created, was also a vigorous design thinker with lots to say.

— Steven Heller

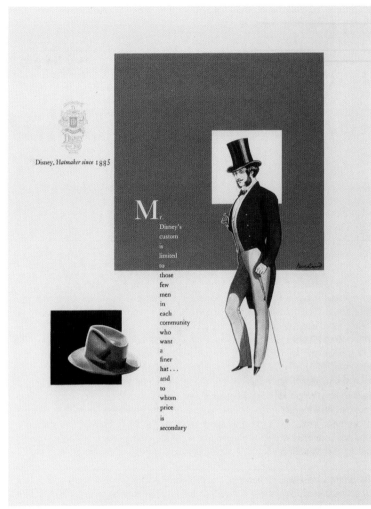

Tim Delaney

This is what I know about Tim.

He is tall.

He likes to talk.
He really likes to talk.

He's a bloody good writer,
but you know that already.

Tim's other name is
Deadline Delaney. Past the
Deadline Delaney would be
more accurate.
His copy is always late.

Tim possesses child-like wonderment.

Tim is a tad competitive,
he would have given
Carl Lewis a run
for his money.

When he's angry, he
looks like this.

When he's happy, he
looks like this.

He's not too bothered
about taking holidays.

He's a friend.

Tim is celebrating over
60 years of hair loss.
Bang goes another friend.

As its President,
he shook up D&AD when
it needed shaking up.
In fact, if ever you needed
anything shaken up, he
is definitely the right man for
the job.

In his early 20s, Tim
became the Managing
Director of BBDO London,
making him the youngest MD
in the history of MD's.
As he had never run a company
before, he rang up the MD's
of all his clients to find
out how they did it.

Tim once fronted his own
rock band, regularly playing
alongside no-hopers,
The Rolling Stones.
I've never heard Tim
sing but I suspect
advertising was a better
bet.

Tim once said, "Everything
has a story to tell and I want
to write it."
This tells us
1. Tim likes writing.
2. Tim has a big appetite
for work.

3. Tim is unnaturally curious.

His stories could fill the
New York Public Library.

He showed the BBC how
to advertise with mould-breaking
work.

Adidas was on its knees when
Tim took over the account.
Just look at them now.

For Hyundai, Tim wrote a
passionate campaign against
British prejudice towards
Koreans. The commercials were
genuinely profound.

His work for Harrods
is as famous as Harrods itself.

Sitting opposite Tim is like
sitting opposite an automatic
tennis ball machine. Ideas, opinions,
verbal abuse fly everywhere.

Tim was advisor to British Prime
Minister Jim Callaghan.

Tim has won everything going
except the Nobel Peace Prize.
Surely an oversight.

Tim is a generous man, especially
with sharing ideas. He's the Mother
Theresa of advertising.

Tim's brand essence wheel
includes words like integrity,
fearless, energetic, honest,
stubborn. There are other words
best left out.

This is Tim's big night.

Tim has a swear word perfect
tongue. Being dropped into a
tank full of angry piranhas would
be a more pleasurable experience
than one of his tongue lashings.

When we worked together, I
laughed my socks off.
When we talk on the phone,
I laugh my socks off.
When we have dinner,
I laugh my socks off.
Send more socks, Mother.

The dog of doubt has never
gnawed at the leg of Tim Delaney.

TIM DEALS WITH THE DOG OF DOUBT.

I could go on, Tim usually does.
What I do know is that in a time
when it's unfashionable
to take risks, when we are all
swimming around in a sea of beige,
the world needs Tim Delaney
more than ever.

— Martin Galton

R A L E O V N

YOU LOSE WATER FROM YOUR SKIN. WHY DOES REVLON REPLACE IT WITH ALMONDS, HONEY AND HERBS?

Every day your skin loses 20 fluid ounces of moisture. To reduce this loss, Revlon Research has created Dry Skin Relief, a quickly-absorbed non-greasy body lotion, which moisturizes and softens while forming a protective barrier against the elements that dry and wrinkle your skin. Made with silicone and natural oils, including almond oil, Dry Skin Relief also replenishes your skin with other natural ingredients. Honey and protein for their moisturizing and softening effects. And a mix of herbal extracts to soothe. Use it all over your body, particularly after sun-bathing, to restore your skin's natural feel and elasticity and to improve the tone and appearance. Available at larger Boots stores, other leading chemists and department stores in Original, Extra Dry and Fragrance Free formulas.

Dry Skin Relief.

REVLON

WHERE
I GO WHEN I RUN.
AND I DON'T mean the route.

adidas

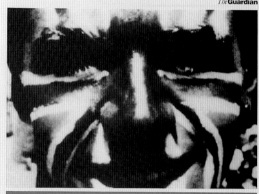

Is the mistrust of our European partners bigotry? Party politics? Or historically justified? And what effect will it have on our ability to negotiate a beneficial deal in Maastricht? Every day next week, the Guardian reports on events leading up to the summit and analyses the stance of key politicians, while Guardian Europe this Friday will bring you comment and opinion on the issue from all of Europe's leading newspapers.

The **Guardian**

Britain **has nothing against Europe. It's just the Italians, Germans and French we don't like.**

Another carpenter who promised to come back one day and finish the job.

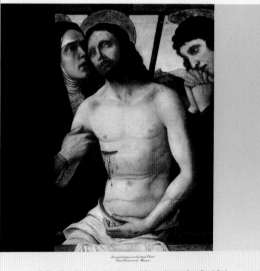

The Courtauld Institute Galleries' priceless collections of paintings can finally be seen in their entirety at Somerset House, the Strand. 10am–6pm Monday to Saturday, and 2pm–6pm Sunday. Also 6pm–8pm on Tuesdays, July to September. Admission £3.50. Concessions £1.

Courtauld Institute Galleries

WE DON'T LINE OUR BOOTS WITH FUR. WE LINE OUR BOOTS WITH BOOT.

Timberland

THIS VALENTINE'S DAY, PROVE THE BEATLES WRONG.

Jerry Della Femina

In the summer of 2008, a special exhibition celebrating 40 years of Jerry Della Femina's work was held in the One Club Gallery. It coincided with his induction into the Creative Hall of Fame.

The year was 1966.

The Wall Street Journal ran a front-page story entitled "The Rich Kids." They were talking about Jerry Della Femina, and a bunch of us young creative people who were hauling in huge salaries anywhere from $30,000 to $50,000 a year.

If that were today, we'd all need food stamps to supplement those salaries.

Four of us—Jerry, Frank Ziebeke, Ned Tolmach and myself—decided to take advantage of these staggering salaries by taking a job at Ted Bates for one year with the expressed idea of starting our own agency.

This, for those of you who remember, was right in the middle of the creative revolution and the Ted Bates people decided they wanted some of this new "Creative Stuff".

They stuck us in a corner of the building shut off from the rest of the agency. From time to time, they would waltz their new clients over to our area, open the door and point to us and quickly shut the door.

One year later, on October 10th 1967, we actually opened up our own agency in the Gotham Hotel on Fifth Avenue. Mind you, other than Jerry, none of us had ever been in a meeting with a client. We certainly had never been near a new business presentation. Collectively speaking we may have created two or three TV commercials...and we had little or nothing to do with the post-production...

We knew nothing about the business of business or even how to go about renting space...

What we were known for was some award-winning print ads that we had done over the years...

All we knew was that we wanted to do great advertising and do it our own way.

It was with this impressive experience and knowledge and about $100,000 in backing from friends and relatives that we launched our own agency.

Well, most of you know the story.

After about three months, with about four-thousand dollars left in the bank, Frank and Ned decided to go their own way, leaving Jerry and myself to fend for ourselves.

I'll never forget it. Jerry and I, while walking up 57th Street stopped in the middle of the block. We were upset to say the least.

Jerry turned to me and said, "What about you?"

I said without so much as a pause, "I am in all the way... even if I have to sell my house and move in with my mother-in-law."

Now, you know I must have been serious to make a commitment like that.

It was at that moment—that very moment—that Jerry and I created the context for success, and it was at that moment that the agency was truly started.

Well, we managed to pick up a couple of small accounts and Jerry said in a moment of total insanity, "Let's take the last four-thousand dollars and throw a party so everyone will see how well we're doing."

I said, "Are you crazy? Let's do it!"

Well it worked! Advertising and publicity actually can make a difference... what a concept!

We began to have new business meetings every day, sometimes two and three a day. I remember getting to one of the meetings having completely forgotten which one we were at. I whispered to Jerry, "What meeting is this?"

He laughed and said, "I'm not telling you."

We always had a lot of fun... mostly at my expense, I might add.

By the third month, we actually began to have the billing that we had been lying about up until then.

Our financial records were done on the back of manila envelopes. We called it "The ins and the outs." If the "ins" were more than the "outs," we knew we were still in business.

One Christmas, I actually had one of those financial reports framed as a gift for Jerry. Before the anniversary of our first year, Jerry wrote his book, *From those Wonderful Folks Who gave us Pearl Harbor*.

He became an icon overnight... an absolute living legend... and the agency began to grow like wildfire.

There are not many people, other than his family, that know Jerry as well as I do and I must tell you I thought this day of recognition might never come.

I was always concerned that his publicity was overshadowing the fact that he is one of the best writers this business has ever produced.

I felt that his persona as advertising's "Peck's Bad Boy" would prevent anyone from recognizing that he was far more than that image portrayed.

I, and all who know him well are excited to see him finally get the recognition that he so deserves.

I would like to congratulate a man of great integrity, the funniest man I have ever known, my favorite partner and my friend... Jerry Della Femina.

—Ron Travisano

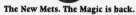

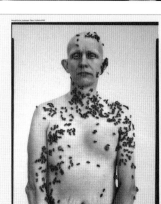

19

Best of Show / Client of the Year

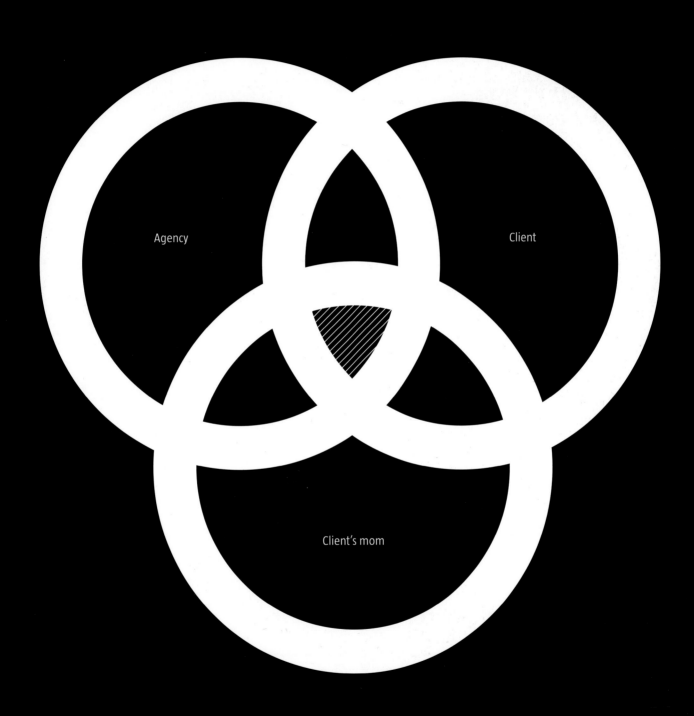

Agency

Client

Client's mom

Best of Show

Xbox *Halo 3*

With the biggest entertainment launch in history, Xbox needed a big advertising campaign. What they got was a world where fiction and reality became one. War veterans from the future were filmed in a Museum of Humanity. A battle scene was recreated in a diorama and shot. A photo exhibit was created from figurines. And all the parts made everyone believe that this was more than just a shoot-em-up videogame. Which is why it was this year's overwhelming choice for the One Show Best of Show.

Art Directors Nate Able, Tim Steir, Ben Wolan, Kevin Hsieh, Erin Wendel, Elliot Harris
Writers Mat Bunnell, Rick Herrera, Joel Kaplan, Keith Hostert, Lauren McCrindle, Cameron Mitchell
Agency Producers Hannah Murray, Vince Genovese, Nancy Cardillo, Larry Ewing, David White
Production Companies MJZ, GO Film, T.A.G.
Directors Rupert Sanders, Simon McQuoid
Creative Directors Scott Duchon, Geoff Edwards, John Patroulis, Rei Inamoto, John Jakubowski
Client Microsoft Xbox Halo 3
Agency McCann Worldgoup SF & T.A.G./AKQA/San Francisco
Annual ID 08085G

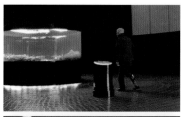

Client of the Year
Burger King

Gold	Silver	Merit
08084G	08066T	08222A
08060T		08406T
		08417T

WHOPPERFREAKOUT.COM

Crispin Porter + Bogusky approached Burger King with a risky idea: What would happen if the restaurant took its signature product, the Whopper, away for a day? And what if the customers' reactions were filmed? Thus was born the "Whopper Freakout" campaign. It took a bold client to agree to it, which is why Burger King is our Client of the Year. From the *Simpsons* campaign to the King and various print work, the familiar brand is always turning out fresh, new ideas.

Gold / Silver / Bronze

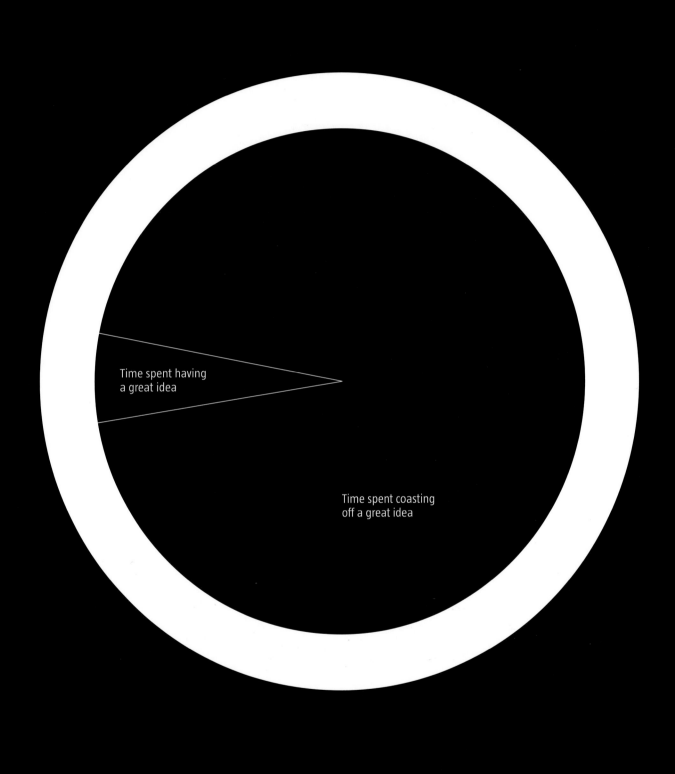

Gold

Newspaper Full Page or Spread, *Single*

Art Director Mark Voehringer
Writer Jake Benjamin
Designer Aaron Padin
Illustrator Simon Danaher
Creative Directors Tony Granger, Jan Jacobs, Leo Premutico, Audrey Huffenreuter
Client Procter & Gamble - Tide
Agency Saatchi & Saatchi/New York
Annual ID 08001A

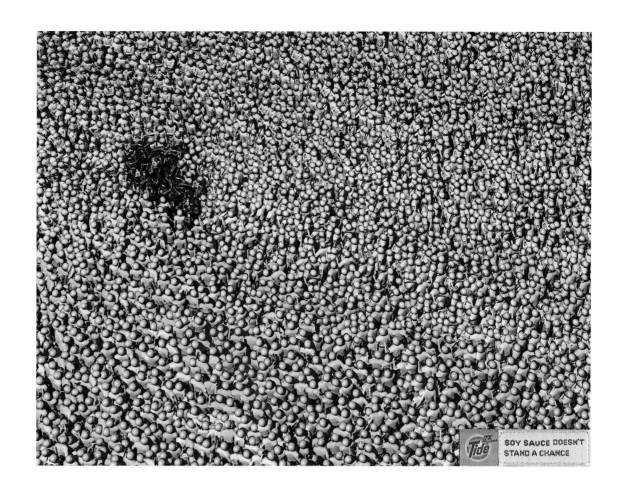

Silver

Newspaper Full Page or Spread, *Single*

Art Director Mark Voehringer
Writer Jake Benjamin
Designer Aaron Padin
Illustrator Simon Danaher
Creative Directors Tony Granger, Jan Jacobs, Leo Premutico, Audrey Huffenreuter
Client Procter & Gamble - Tide
Agency Saatchi & Saatchi/New York
Annual ID 08002A

Bronze

Newspaper Full Page or Spread, *Single*

Art Director Adrian Chan
Writer Eugene Cheong
Illustrator Adrian Chan
Creative Director Eugene Cheong
Client The Economist
Agency Ogilvy/Singapore
Annual ID 08003A

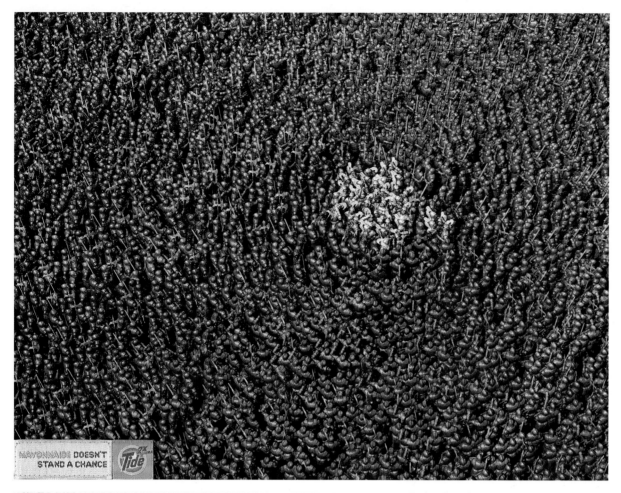

Gold

Consumer Newspaper Full Page or Spread, *Campaign*

Art Director Mark Voehringer
Writer Jake Benjamin
Designer Aaron Padin
Illustrator Simon Danaher
Creative Directors Tony Granger, Jan Jacobs, Leo Premutico, Audrey Huffenreuter
Client Procter & Gamble - Tide
Agency Saatchi & Saatchi/New York
Annual ID 08004A

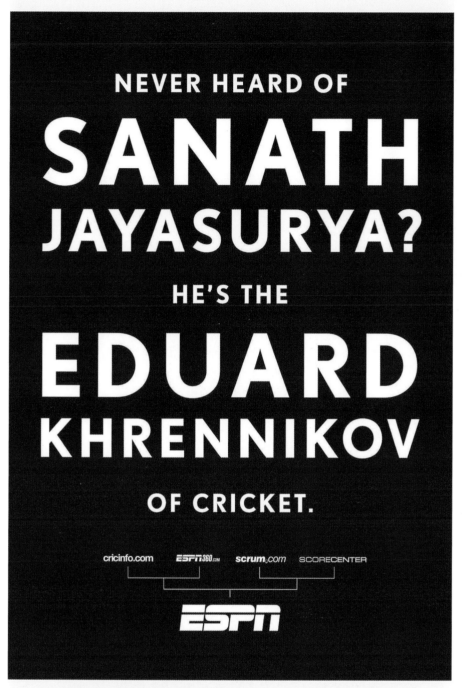

NEVER HEARD OF **SANATH JAYASURYA?** HE'S THE **EDUARD KHRENNIKOV** OF CRICKET.

cricinfo.com   ESPN360.com   scrum.com   SCORECENTER

ESPN

ESPN HAS ACQUIRED THE "HOME OF CRICKET," CRICINFO.COM, THE WORLD'S #1 CRICKET SITE. ANOTHER BIG STEP TOWARD THE FOREFRONT OF INTERNATIONAL DIGITAL SPORTS. (AND TOWARD MAKING HOUSEHOLD NAMES OUT OF EVERYONE FROM SRI LANKAN CRICKETERS TO RUSSIAN SKI CHAMPS.)

FOOTBALL PLAYERS USE **TAPE** TO KEEP THEIR PADS ON. **RUGBY PLAYERS** USE TAPE TO KEEP THEIR EARS ON.

scrum.com   ESPN360   cricinfo.com   SCORECENTER

ESPN

ESPN HAS ACQUIRED SCRUM.COM, THE WORLD'S #1 RUGBY SITE. JUST ONE MORE WAY THAT ESPN IS LEADING IN WORLDWIDE DIGITAL SPORTS. AND MAKING THE SEARCH FOR INTERNATIONAL SCORES RELATIVELY PAIN FREE.

USUALLY WHEN YOU GET THIS MANY **COUNTRIES TOGETHER** IT'S FOR **SOMETHING BORING**

SCORECENTER   ESPN360   scrum.com   cricinfo.com

ESPN

SPORTS FROM MORE THAN 180 COUNTRIES HAVE A NEW HOME IN 2008: ESPN SCORECENTER.COM. SCORES AND COVERAGE FOR EVERYTHING FROM SOCCER AND CRICKET TO HOOPS AND HOCKEY. FURTHER PROOF THAT ESPN IS LEADING THE WAY IN WORLDWIDE DIGITAL SPORTS. EXCITING NEWS.

Merit

Silver

Newspaper Full Page or Spread, *Campaign*

Art Director Ralph Watson
Writers Roger Baldacci, Mark St. Amant, Wade Devers
Creative Directors Pete Favat, Roger Baldacci, Mark St. Amant, Ralph Watson
Client ESPN
Agency Arnold Worldwide/Boston
Annual ID 08005A

ALSO AWARDED

Merit Newspaper Full Page or Spread, *Single*

Bronze

Newspaper Full Page or Spread, *Campaign*

Art Director Brian Bainbridge
Writer Simon Lotze
Creative Directors Kirk Gainsford, Alistair Morgan
Client Independent Newspaper
Agency Lowe Bull/Cape Town
Annual ID 08006A

YOUR MOM WASN'T YOUR DAD'S FIRST

He went out. He got two numbers in the same night. He drank cocktails. But they were whisky cocktails. Made with Canadian Club. Served in a rocks glass. They tasted good. They were effortless. **DAMN RIGHT YOUR DAD DRANK IT**

Canadian Club.

IN THE HISTORY
OF REPAIRS,
RED TAPE HAS YET
TO FIX ANYTHING.

YOUR ARM'S BROKEN.
YOUR BACK'S WRENCHED.
AND ALL YOU CAN THINK IS
"GETTING MY CAR FIXED
IS GONNA BE PAINFUL."

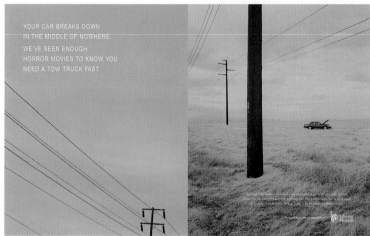

YOUR CAR BREAKS DOWN
IN THE MIDDLE OF NOWHERE.
WE'VE SEEN ENOUGH
HORROR MOVIES TO KNOW YOU
NEED A TOW TRUCK FAST.

WHOEVER HIT YOU
SHOULD'VE LEFT A NOTE.
THOUGH WE DO APPLAUD
THE LACK OF PAPERWORK.

Bronze   Merit

Silver

Magazine, Color Full Page or Spread, *Campaign*

Art Director **Kevin Daley**
Writer **Tim Cawley**
Photographer **Nadav Kandor**
Creative Directors **Ernie Schenck, Kevin Moehlenkamp**
Client **Liberty Mutual**
Agency **Hill Holliday/Boston**
Annual ID **08010A**

ALSO AWARDED
Bronze Magazine, **Full Page or Spread,** *Single*
Merit Magazine, **Full Page or Spread,** *Single*

Bronze

Magazine, Color Full Page or Spread, *Campaign*

Art Directors Julia Ziegler, Lisa Rienermann
Writers Jan-Florian Ege, Ron Kanecke, Jan Geschke, Stefan Fockenberg, Bjoern Ingenleuf
Photographer Lisa Rienermann
Creative Directors Oliver Voss, Deneke von Weltzien, Goetz Ulmer, Fabian Frese
Client Daimler
Agency Jung von Matt/Hamburg
Annual ID 08011A

ALSO AWARDED

Merit Outdoor, Campaign

Gold

Outdoor, *Single*

Art Directors Kangwook Lee, Chaehoon Lee, Yooho Lee, Sanghun Yoo
Writers Jungho Hwang, Sua Lee
Creative Director Yooshin Lee
Client Samsung Tesco
Agency Cheil Worldwide/Seoul
Annual ID 08012A

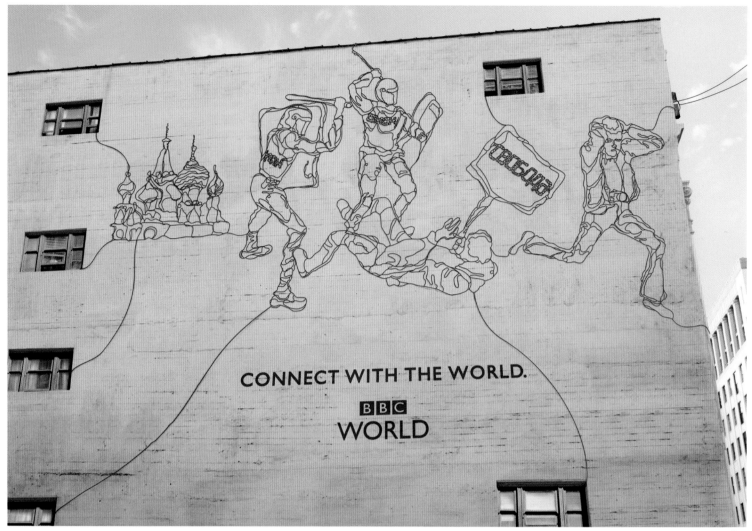

CONNECT WITH THE WORLD.

BBC WORLD

CONNECT WITH THE WORLD.

BBC WORLD

CONNECT WITH THE WORLD.

BBC WORLD

Silver

Outdoor, *Campaign*

Art Director Chuck Tso
Writer Scott Kaplan
Illustrator Elizabeth Berrien
Creative Directors David Lubars, Bill Bruce, Eric Silver, Jerome Marucci, Steve McElligott
Client BBC World
Agency BBDO/New York
Annual ID 08014A

ALSO AWARDED
Silver Outdoor, *Single*

unlimited use:
royalty free images from

photolibrary

www.photolibrary.com

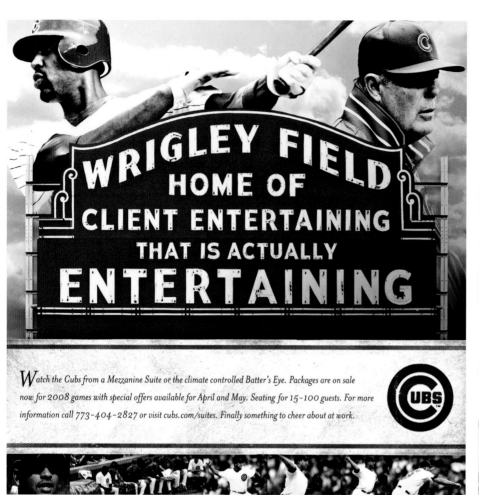

Silver

Trade Full Page or Spread, *Campaign*

Art Director Grant Simpson
Writer Scott Maney
Photographer Stephen Green
Creative Directors Scott Maney, Dan Madole
Client Chicago Cubs
Agency Jones/Chicago
Annual ID 08017A

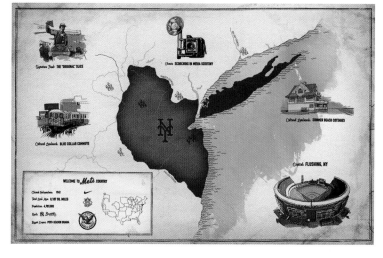

Bronze

Collateral P.O.P. and In-Store, *Campaign*

Art Director **Todd Derksen**
Writer **Mike Tuton**
Designer **Todd Derksen**
Illustrator **David Reinbold**
Creative Director **Todd Grant**
Client **Nike/MLB**
Agency **Cole & Weber United/Seattle**
Annual ID **08019A**

Bronze, Merit

Bronze

Collateral P.O.P. and In-Store, *Campaign*

Art Directors Bernardo Hernandez, Cristina Davila, Gonzalo Vergara
Writers Cesar Olivas, Pablo Farres, Vicente Rodriguez
Photographers Diego Dominguez, Inaki Domingo, Gonzalo Puertas
Creative Directors Guillermo Gines, Juan Sanchez, Montserrat Pastor
Client Sony Playstation
Agency TBWA\España/Madrid
Annual ID 08020A

ALSO AWARDED

📎 Bronze Collateral P.O.P. and In-Store, *Single*
📎 Merit Magazine Full Page or Spread, *Single*
📎 Merit Outdoor, *Single*

Bronze

Collateral Posters, *Campaign*

Art Directors Vikash Chemjong, Basab Tito Majumdar
Writers Basab Tito Majumdar, Vikash Chemjong, Ajay Gahlaut
Designer Basab Tito Majumdar
Creative Directors Vikash Chemjong, Basab Tito Majumdar, Ajay Gahlaut
Client GlaxoSmithKline
Agency Ogilvy & Mather/New Delhi
Annual ID 08021A

Original catalogue   Personalized catalogue

Gold

Collateral Promotion

Art Director Joanna Swistowski
Writers Caroline Ellert, Tom Hauser
Designers Matthias Grundner, Julia Jakobi
Creative Directors Tom Hauser, Soeren Porst, Arno Lindemann, Bernhard Lukas
Client IKEA Deutschland
Agency Jung von Matt/Hamburg
Annual ID 08022A

ALSO AWARDED

Silver Innovation in Marketing and Advertising, *Single*
Silver Branded Content, *Single*

HONDA
The Power of Dreams

Wouldn't it be nice if after reading a letter
you could plant it in your garden to grow some flowers?

We thought so.

That's why if you soak this letter in water, you can plant it in your garden
and it'll grow a lovely row of wildflowers.

We've got a lot of nice things for your garden.

From award winning mowers and lawn tractors to innovative tillers, brush cutters and more.

All designed to be as friendly to the environment as you are.

If you're looking to upgrade, we'd very much like to hear from you.
You can find us at honda.co.uk or call us on 0845 200 8000.

We love gardening and think that just like this letter,
we'd make a lovely addition to your garden.

Yours sincerely,

Iain Radcliffe
Marketing Communications Manager.

Honda (UK), 470 London Road, Slough, Berkshire SL3 8QY www.honda.co.uk 0845 200 8000

This letter is infinitely recyclable. When planted, it joins the environment to help
make trees that help make more paper to make more trees to make more paper.

Bronze
Collateral Promotion

Art Directors Ben Kaberry, Paul Nowilkowski
Writer Jaime Diskin
Designer Mark Bennett
Creative Director Malcolm Caldwell
Client Honda
Agency Inferno/London
Annual ID 08023A

Silver
Collateral Self-Promotion

Art Directors Tim Chai, Kah Yong Ong, Kevin Lim
Writer John Merrifield
Designers Tim Chai, John Merrifield
Creative Directors John Merrifield, Tim Chai, Tracey Fox
Client TBWA\Asia Pacific
Agency TBWA\Asia Pacific/Singapore
Annual ID 08024A

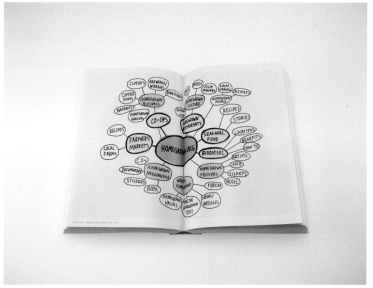

Silver

Collateral Self-Promotion

Art Director **Jelly Helm**
Writers **W+K 12**
Photographer **Chris Hornbecker**
Client **Wieden+Kennedy**
Agency **Wieden+Kennedy/Portland**
Annual ID **08025A**

Gold

Public Service/Political Newspaper or Magazine, *Single*

Art Directors Gumpon Laksanajinda, Wisit Lumsiricharoenchoke, Nopadol Srikieatikajohn
Writers Kulvadee Doksroy, Khanitta Wichitsakonkit
Photographer Anuchai Secharunputong
Creative Directors Wisit Lumsiricharoenchoke, Nopadol Srikieatikajohn
Client WWF Thailand
Agency Ogilvy & Mather/Bangkok
Annual ID 08026A

ALSO AWARDED

Merit Outdoor, *Single*

All this to put out just one cigarette.

Don't let Cape Town burn again. Please be more careful with your cigarette butts.
www.capefires.com

Bronze

Public Service/Political Newspaper or Magazine, *Single*

Art Director **David Malan**
Writer **Aaron Harris**
Photographer **Patrick Ryan**
Creative Directors **Anton Crone, Leon Jacobs**
Client **Volunteer Wildfire Services**
Agency **Saatchi & Saatchi/Cape Town**
Annual ID **08028A**

We're the reason
people have laps.

adopt a new life.

Studies show that my
sleeping all day improves
your life expectancy.

adopt a new life.

You don't need more
drama in your life.
You need string.

adopt a new life.

Change a life.
Or nine.

adopt a new life.

I am an excellent
source of outside.

adopt a new life.

Silver

Silver

Public Service/Political Newspaper or Magazine, *Campaign*

Art Directors Anthony Chelvanathan, Monique Kelley
Writers Steve Persico, Marcus Sagar
Designer Caio Oyafuso
Illustrator Monique Kelley
Creative Directors Judy John, Israel Diaz
Client Toronto Humane Society
Agency Leo Burnett/Toronto
Annual ID 08029A

ALSO AWARDED

Silver Public Service/Political Newspaper or Magazine, *Single*

50

6 million people in South Africa are living with HIV

Van der Vyv

Man acquitted of murd

By DIANNE HAWKER

Former actuary Fred van der Vyver celebrated his acquittal for murder with a bottle of champagne at the end of a costly, marathon trial.

On Thursday he left the Huguenot Chambers next to the Cape High Court with a spring in his step. While a crowd gathered outside the window of Castello's Restau-

also relied on the testimony o four international forensi experts and one local exper who successfully discredit evidence given by police.

On Thursday, Judge D van Zyl found the state failed in all respects to p Van der Vyver guilty of the der of his Stellenbosch student girlfriend Inge L

He also slammed th mony of several poli nesses who had given e on key forensic evidenc

8 % of adults around the world have never heard of hepatitis, HIV/AIDS or syphilis.   **NEWS**

NEWS   The percentage of people living with HIV in the Western Cape in 2006 was **15**

22 -The percentage of people who say they have had an extramarital affair.   **LIFE**

LIFE   The percentage of women who claim to have casual sex purely for the pleasure of it, is **25**

NEWS   The average percentage of women who are virgins when they go to university is **5**

26 -The percentage of HIV-infected South African females aged 3-34 in 2005.   **LIFE**

6 million people in South Africa are living with HIV.   **NEWS**

36 % of South African youth felt there was no risk of them contracting HIV in 2003.   **SPORT**

Bronze

Public Service/Political Newspaper or Magazine, *Campaign*

Art Director Rachel Brown
Writer Jabulani Sigege
Creative Directors Paige Nick, Karin Barry, Alistair King
Client Independent Newspapers
Agency King James/Cape Town
Annual ID 08030A

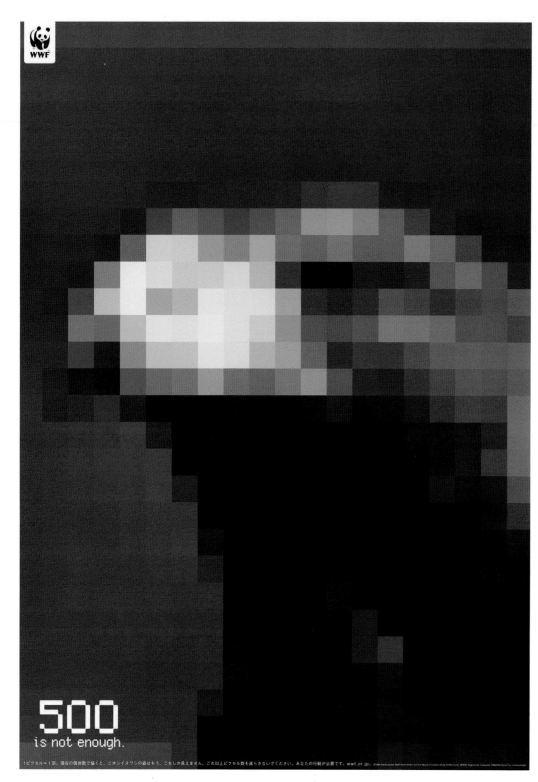

500
is not enough.

1ピクセル＝1羽。現在の個体数で描くと、ニホンイヌワシの姿はもう、これしか見えません。これ以上ピクセル数を減らさないでください。あなたの行動が必要です。www.wwf.or.jp。

1600
is not enough.

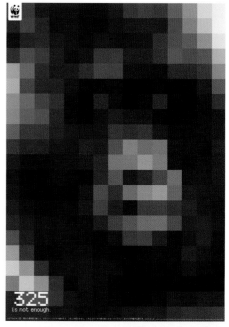

325
is not enough.

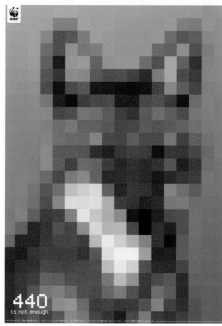

440
is not enough.

Gold

Public Service/Political Outdoor and Posters, *Campaign*

Art Director Yoshiyuki Mikami
Writer Nami Hoshino
Designer Kazuhiro Mochizuki
Creative Directors Nami Hoshino, Yoshiyuki Mikami
Client WWF Japan
Agency HAKUHODO Architect/Tokyo
Annual ID 08032A

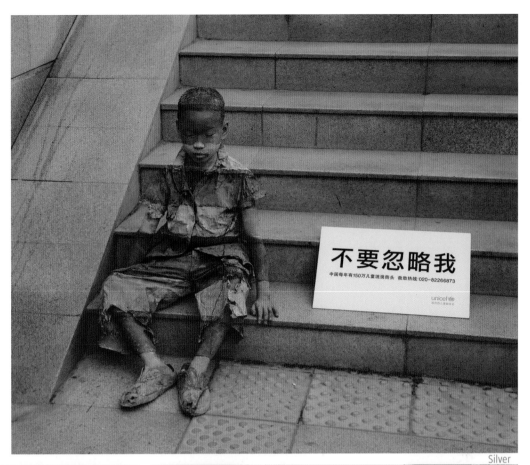

Silver

Merit

Merit

Silver

Public Service/Political Outdoor and Posters, *Campaign*

Art Directors Kevin Lee, Haibo Huang, Phoebe Liao, Stephen Zhong, Robin Wu
Writers Adams Fan, Derek Huang, Raymond Yung, Andrew Lok
Illustrators Haohui Zhou, Bin Liu, Spring Zhu, Chaowen Wu, Jinghua Pan
Creative Directors Kevin Lee, Fan Ng
Client Unicef
Agency Ogilvy & Mather/Shanghai
Annual ID 08033A

ALSO AWARDED

Silver Public Service/Political Outdoor and Posters, *Single*
Merit Public Service/Political Outdoor and Posters, *Single*
Merit Public Service/Political Outdoor and Posters, *Single*
Merit Innovation in Marketing and Advertising, *Campaign*

53

Merit

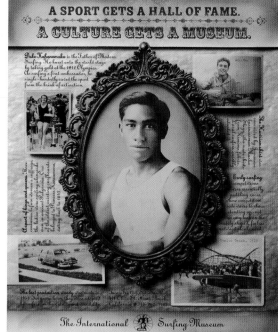

Merit

Merit

Bronze

Public Service/Political Outdoor and Posters, *Campaign*

Art Director **Christopher Gyorgy**
Writer **Dave Horton**
Photographer **Graphic Industries**
Creative Director **Christopher Gyorgy**
Client **International Surfing Museum**
Agency **DraftFCB/Chicago**
Annual ID **08034A**

ALSO AWARDED

✎ Merit Public Service/Political Outdoor and Posters, *Single*
✎ Merit Public Service/Political Outdoor and Posters, *Single*
✎ Merit Public Service/Political Outdoor and Posters, *Single*

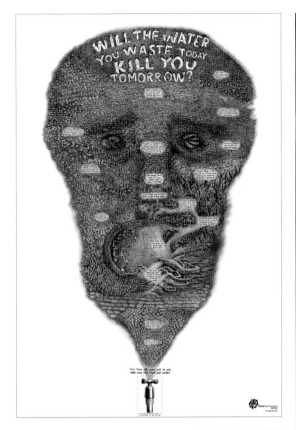

Bronze

Public Service/Political Outdoor and Posters, *Campaign*

Art Directors Jules Tan, Sonny Low, T T Ho, Kam-Wei Fong, See-Lok Ng
Writers Pamela Song, Samantha Hepburn, Allison Kiew, Szu-Hung Lee
Designers Kam-Wei Fong, See-Lok Ng, Ka-Kin Mah, T T Ho, Yien-Keat Wong, Jules Tan, Sonny Low
Photographer Studio Rom
Illustrators Jules Tan, Sonny Low, Kam-Wei Fong, Yien-Keat Wong, See-Lok Ng, Ka-Kin Mah, Peng-Hwee Terng
Creative Directors Hwa, Szu-Hung Lee
Client Global Environment Organization
Agency McCann Erickson/Kuala Lumpur
Annual ID 08035A

[We see a man wearing a black shirt and pants and hat sitting in an office, talking with an accent.]

MAN: I think I was always misunderstood. People just didn't seem to like me.

[We see him walking up to a woman and lifting her dress, at a playground throwing sand at kids, tousling a woman's hair, knocking plastic bottles off of a shopping cart.]

MAN: I think I annoyed them. I got on their nerves. I don't know why. It's just the way it was. Yeah. Maybe I was too intense. Maybe I came on too strong. I don't know. I really can't say. Yeah, it was lonely, very lonely. But you get used to it after a while.

And then one day everything changed. Someone finally accepted me for what I am. Since I've gotten this job, life is completely different. I finally feel useful, good at something.

SUPER: The Wind. Let's put his energy to good use.

LOGO: Epuron. Investing in wind energy.

Gold
Public Service/Political Television, *Single*

Art Directors Bjoern Ruehmann, Joakim Reveman
Writer Matthew Branning
Production Companies Paranoid Projects/Paris, Paranoid US/Los Angeles
Director The Vikings
Creative Director Lars Ruehmann
Client Epuron/German Ministry for the Environment
Agency Nordpol+ Hamburg
Annual ID 08036T

[This film illustrates graphically how a simple signature on a petition can provide real help to victims of torture, abuse or arbitrary imprisonment. At every stage of this film, signatures appear and victims grab them and use them to escape.]

SUPER: Your signature is more powerful than you think.

LOGO: Amnesty International.

Silver

Public Service/Political Television, *Single*

Art Directors Stephane Gaubert, Stephanie Thomasson
Writers Stephane Gaubert, Stephanie Thomasson
Director Philippe Grammaticopoulos
Production Company Curious Pictures
Creative Director Erik Vervroegen
Client Amnesty International
Agency TBWA\Paris/Boulogne-Billancourt
Annual ID 08037T

[We see slow-motion video of a bullet hitting several objects such as an egg, glass of milk, apple, bottle of ketchup, water bottle and a watermelon. Then we see a child's head as a bullet approaches it but then the bullet turns to text.]

SUPER: Stop the bullets. Kill the gun.

LOGO: ChoiceFM. Peace on the Streets.

Bronze

Public Service/Political Television, *Single*

Art Director Huw Williams
Writer Gary Walker
Agency Producer Yvonne Chalkley
Production Company Therapy Films
Directors Malcolm Venville, Sean De Sparengo
Creative Director Paul Brazier
Client CHOICE FM
Agency Abbott Mead Vickers BBDO/London
Annual ID 08038T

57

[We see two young boys at school being interviewed.]

SUPER: How do you spell Dinosaur?

BOY 1: OK...DINOSARU

INTERVIEWER: Dinosaur-u? OK, Sharu, how do you spell Dinosaur?

BOY 2: OK...DINOSORE.

INTERVIEWER: Dinosor-e? OK, who's your best friend?

[The young boy points to the other boy.]

INTERVIEWER: OK, if he's your best friend, what is his race?

BOY 1 and 2: What's race?

BOY 1: Race like race car.

BOY 2: Race, I forget, what's race?

BOY 1: Race is like race car.

SUPER: Our children are colour blind. Shouldn't we keep them that way?

Selamat Menyambut Hari Kemerdekaan ke 50.

LOGO: Petronas

Merit

Silver

Public Service/Political Television, *Campaign*

Art Director Tan Yew Leong
Writer Yasmin Ahmad
Agency Producer Sheikh Munasar @ Moon
Production Company MHz Films
Director Yasmin Ahmad
Creative Director Yasmin Ahmad
Client Petronas Nasional Berhad
Agency Leo Burnett/Kuala Lumpur
Annual ID 08039T

ALSO AWARDED

Merit Public Service/Political Television, *Single*

[We see soldiers and a battle scene frozen in time to a piano playing Chopin. On closer inspection we realize that the figures are not real and are miniatures made from plastic. The camera zooms in and makes its way through the scene in the middle of an intense battle against aliens. We finally zoom in on a figure of Master Chief, who is clutching a glowing ball. He looks up.]

SUPER: **Believe**

LOGO: **Halo 3. XBOX 360 Live.**

SUPER: **Jump in.**

Gold

Television Over :30, *Single*

Art Directors Nate Able, Tim Steir
Writer Mat Bunnell
Agency Producer Hannah Murray
Production Company MJZ
Director Rupert Sanders
Creative Directors Scott Duchon, Geoff Edwards, John Patroulis
Client Microsoft XBOX Halo 3
Agency McCann Worldgroup SF & T.A.G./San Francisco
Annual ID 08045T

[A couple from 1873 crash through the door of a room and slam it shut behind them. They're wearing early Levi's work wear, top to bottom. Our hero pulls his top off to reveal a shorter haircut from the 1950s. He fumbles desperately with the buttons of his fly and yanks his jeans down. Strangely there's another pair of Levi's underneath—slightly more modern ones. She grabs her blouse and pulls it open and down to reveal the same girl, but now a peroxide blonde from the '50s. They quickly yank each their tops over their heads again... she is now a brunette (with long '70s hair and beads) and he's got long '70s hair, stubble and a big-collared shirt. On the bed, she pulls off his jeans to reveal '80s-style ripped 501s. She playfully jumps onto the bed and straddles him. There's a flurry of feverish undressing as we see more and more layers of jeans, tops, blouses and shirts getting pulled off in quick succession. They roll across the bed onto the floor. They both strip down to outfits from the latest Levi's collection. They pull off this final layer and finally are partly naked. They kiss.]

SUPER: LEVI'S. New Spring 2007 Collection
LEVI'S. From the original.

Silver
Television Over :30, *Single*

Art Director Steve Wakelam
Writer Dean Wei
Agency Producer Davud Karbassioun
Production Company Rattling Stick
Director Ringan Ledwidge
Creative Director Caroline Pay
Client Levi's
Agency Bartle Bogle Hegarty/London
Annual ID 08352T

[We see two people walking over to an older colleague.]

GIRL: Hey Tim, show Joel how everything you touch turns to Skittles.

[Tim touches a stapler and it falls apart into Skittles.]

JOEL: That's awesome.

TIM: Is it awesome, when you can't hold your newborn baby boy in your arms? Did you feed and dress yourself this morning? I didn't. I met a man on the bus today. I shook his hand. He'll never see his family again. I guess it's pretty awesome.

[The phone rings.]

TIM: Excuse me.

[He picks up the phone and it turns to Skittles. In frustration, he pounds his fists on his desk which also turns to Skittles.]

SUPER: Touch the rainbow. Taste the rainbow.

Silver
Television Over :30, *Single*

Art Director Craig Allen
Writer Eric Kallman
Agency Producer Nathy Aviram
Creative Directors Gerry Graf, Ian Reichenthal, Scott Vitrone
Client Mars Snackfood - Skittles
Agency TBWA\Chiat\Day/New York
Annual ID 08046T

[We see a man wake up in the morning in bed.]

MAN: Oh, I can't do this anymore.

[Then we see his wife lean over, who is actually him in a wig.]

WIFE: I wish you would just quit that job.

[Then we see him as a broadcaster on TV, as a paramedic, as a man with an Afro, as an old file clerk and as a pregnant woman telling him that he needs a new job.]

SUPER: Self-help yourself.

LOGO: Start building. Careerbuilder.com

Silver

Television Over :30, *Single*

Art Director Eric Baldwin
Writer Jason Bagley
Agency Producer Jeff Selis
Production Company The Directors Bureau
Director Mike Mills
Creative Directors Mark Fitzloff, Monica Taylor
Client CareerBuilder.com
Agency Wieden+Kennedy/Portland
Annual ID 08047T

[We hear "In the Air Tonight" by Phil Collins as the camera is zoomed in on a gorilla's face. As it zooms out, we notice that it is sitting at a drum set. The drum solo in the song begins and the gorilla drums along with it.]

SUPER: A glass and a half full of joy.

Bronze

Television Over :30, *Single*

Art Director Juan Cabral
Writer Juan Cabral
Agency Producer Nicky Barnes
Production Company Blink Productions
Director Juan Cabral
Creative Directors Juan Cabral, Richard Flintham
Client Cadbury's Dairy Milk
Agency Fallon/London
Annual ID 08050T

[We see a shot of New York City and a drain where a ball of Play-Doh rolls out and turns into a rabbit. Several more balls of Play-Doh come out of manholes and sewer grates and turn into different colored rabbits. They hop around the city to the tune of "She's like a Rainbow" by the Rolling Stones. Hundreds of them congregate at a plaza where they turn into a huge Play-Doh wave and then into a giant rabbit and eventually into different colored cubes.]

SUPER: Colour. Like no other.
Bravia. New LCD Television.

LOGO: **Sony**

Bronze
Television Over :30, *Single*

Art Director Juan Cabral
Writer Juan Cabral
Agency Producer Nicky Barnes
Production Company Gorgeous
Director Frank Budgen
Creative Directors Juan Cabral, Richard Flintham
Client Sony Bravia
Agency Fallon/London
Annual ID 08049T

[The scene opens with a shot from above of Central Park and New York City. It's the Macy's Thanksgiving Day Parade and giant floats are making their way down the street. A Coke bottle float is in the middle of Underdog and Stewie floats and they begin to try and grab it. They bounce off of buildings and the Coke bottle keeps evading them. Then suddenly out of nowhere, a Charlie Brown float appears and finally gets the bottle.]

LOGO: **The Coke Side of Life**

Bronze
Television Over :30, *Single*

Art Director Hal Curtis
Writer Sheena Brady
Designer Robb Buono
Agency Producer Matt Hunnicutt
Production Company MJZ
Director Nicolai Fuglsig
Creative Directors Hal Curtis, Sheena Brady
Client Coca-Cola
Agency Wieden+Kennedy/Portland
Annual ID 08051T

VO: Meanwhile at the League of Evil...

[Seated at a table are a three-eyed villain and blob-like creature.]

VILLAIN: Agent...agent...a-gent...oh, hello, uh, Barry, I'm fine, how are you? Any-hoo...I'd like to cancel my cell phone service. What?! 175 dollars just to cancel!

[Motions to people at a large weapon to fire it up.]

VILLAIN: You know I could totally death ray your headquarters...I'd still be under contract??

[Motions to his people to turn off the machine.]

VILLAIN: Oh, you guys are evil...oh, you're welcome...

VO: Is your cell phone company more evil than evil? Net10 has no cancellation fees. Switch to Net10. No bills. No contracts. No evil.

Gold
Television Over :30, *Campaign*

Art Director Alex Lea
Writer Kevin Brady
Agency Producer Robin Feldman
Production Company World Leaders
Creative Directors Ted Royer, Duncan Marshall
Client TracFone
Agency Droga5/New York
Annual ID 08052T

[We see a man at night about to walk into his house. A crowd has gathered inside and are waiting to surprise him. They all hide and wait with a birthday cake with lit candles. He checks his mail and then walks up the stairs. The phone rings just as we hear him reach for his keys.]

PHONE: Hey Dan, this is Al from work...

[Just then everyone jumps out and yells surprise. Then the screen goes blank with static and we see what looks like a replay from the beginning. He reaches for his mail in the mailbox but then drops it. Meanwhile, upstairs the phone rings.]

PHONE: Hey Dan, this is Al from work. We need to talk. I just saw the security camera footage and it's clearly you masturbating in the conference room. Come see me in the morning, please?

[Just then the door opens and everyone says surprise but in a much more subdued, uncomfortable way.]

SUPER: There are stories. And there are stories you talk about.

LOGO: It's HBO.

Bronze   Merit

Silver

Television Over :30, *Campaign*

Art Director Matt Vescovo
Writer Colin Nissan
Agency Producer Rachel Seitel
Production Company RSA Films
Director Sam Mendes
Creative Directors David Lubars, Bill Bruce, Don Schneider
Client HBO
Agency BBDO/New York
Annual ID 08053T

ALSO AWARDED

Bronze Television Over :30, *Single*
Merit Television Over :30, *Single*

[We see the car scene from *Pulp Fiction* where Vincent and Jules are talking. A strange man is sitting in the back seat.]

VINCENT: You know what the funniest thing about Europe is?

JULES: What?

VINCENT: It's the little differences. They got the same shit over there as we got here, it's just there it's a little different.

JULES: Example?

VINCENT: Alright, you can walk into a movie theater in Amsterdam and buy a beer. And you know what they call a Quarter Pounder with Cheese in Paris?

JULES: They don't call it a Quarter Pounder with Cheese?

VINCENT: They got the metric system over there, they wouldn't know what the fuck a quarter pounder is.

GUY IN BACK SEAT: What the fuck is the matter with the French? Anyway, what do they call it?

VINCENT: They call it the Royale with Cheese.

JULES: Royale with Cheese. What do they call a Big Mac?

VINCENT: Big Mac's a Big Mac but they call it Le Big Mac.

GUY IN BACK SEAT: Hey, what do they call a Whopper?

VINCENT: I don't know, I didn't go into Burger King.

GUY IN BACK SEAT: You never been to Burger King? You never worn the crown, eh?

VINCENT: You know what they put on French fries in Holland instead of ketchup?

JULES: No, what?

VINCENT: Mayonnaise.

SUPER: If you don't see anything weird, that's weird.

LOGO: TCM. The films you should have seen by now.

Bronze

Television Over :30, *Campaign*

Art Directors Francisco Cassis, Santiago Saiegh
Writers Francisco Cassis, Santiago Saiegh
Agency Producer Guzmán Molín-Pradel
Director Dionisio Naranjo
Creative Directors Rafa Antón, Javier Alvarez
Client Turner Classic Movies
Agency Vitruvio Leo Burnett/Madrid
Annual ID 08054T

[A young man is sitting in an office across from an older man behind a desk. It soon becomes apparent that the young man is on a job interview.]

OLDER MAN: **So tell me about yourself.**

YOUNG MAN: **Well...**

[As soon as he starts talking, a stain on his shirt begins to shout gibberish. Every time he talks, the stain talks. The interviewer can't help notice and doesn't appear to hear a word the young man is saying.]

SUPER: **Silence the Stain. Tide-to-Go.**

Gold
Television :30/:25, *Single*

Art Director **Dan Lucey**
Writers **Nathan Frank, Peter Albores**
Agency Producer **Dani Stoller**
Production Company **DAB HAND Media**
Director **Calle Astrand**
Creative Directors **Tony Granger, Jan Jacobs, Leo Premutico, Audrey Huffenreuter**
Client **Procter & Gamble - Tide-to-Go**
Agency **Saatchi & Saatchi/New York**
Annual ID **08055T**

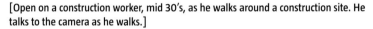

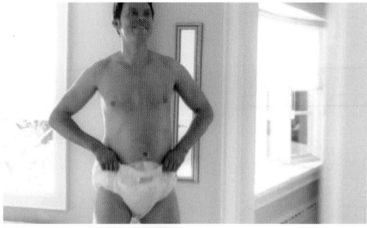

[Open on a construction worker, mid 30's, as he walks around a construction site. He talks to the camera as he walks.]

WORKER: A few weeks ago I was having problems staying regular. I felt sluggish. It even affected the way I worked.

[Behind him we see a group of construction workers pulling together to dislodge a long, horizontal iron beam from a concrete base.]

WORKER: Something had to give. So I tried the All-Bran 10 day challenge. And I'll tell you what . . .

[Behind him, the beam finally comes loose.]

WORKER: It worked.

[In the background, we see barrels tumbling from the back of a truck. His body is positioned in a way that makes it appear as though the barrels are tumbling out of him.]

WORKER: Once a day. Ten days. That's all it took. My energy came back, I felt invigorated.

[In the background, a large dump truck pulls into frame.]

WORKER: Tell you what—somebody offers you 10 days to a better you? You take it.

[We see the truck unload an enormous pile of bricks. In the foreground, he takes a bite of All Bran and smiles.]

LOGO: Kellogg's All-Bran 10-day challenge.

SUPER: Do it. Feel it.

MUSIC: Comfeze, they're for me, Comfeze I feel free.

[We see a man looking happy like a kid in a typical diaper commercial. Then we cut to another man in diapers walking down the hall as if he's two years old. And then a chubby guy comes down the stairs in slow motion wearing the diapers.]

VO: Introducing the best-fitting Comfeze yet. They're super absorbent and guaranteed to last all day long!

[Cut to the Comfeze pack shot. We see it on its own. Then we see it with a demo of blue liquid going in it from a jug in a side-by-side comparison.]

MUSIC: I can laugh and joke all the time

[Then we see a shot of one guy reaching for a remote on the top of a bookshelf. He gets on his tippy toes. Then we see the three sitting on a couch. One looks at the remote and then clicks it. On the TV we see a scary scene from a horror movie. The three men are watching and then one of the guys looks like he's had an accident in his diaper.]

MUSIC: Because of Comfeze, they're for me. Because of Comfeze, I'm worry-free. Because of Comfeze, I can Watch Scream TV.

SUPER: Get scared more often.

LOGO: Scream TV.

Silver
Television :30/:25, *Single*

Art Director Brian Shembeda
Writer Avery Gross
Agency Producer Scott Gould
Production Company Biscuit
Director Noam Murro
Creative Directors John Condon, Mark Oosthuizen, Dave Linne
Client Kellogg's
Agency Leo Burnett/Chicago
Annual ID 08056T

Silver
Television :30/:25, *Single*

Art Director Stephen Leps
Writer Aaron Starkman
Agency Producer Sharon Nelson
Production Company Radke Films
Director Craig Brownrigg
Creative Directors Stephen Leps, Aaron Starkman, Martin Beauvais
Client Corus Entertainment - SCREAM TV
Agency Zig/Toronto
Annual ID 08057T

[A baby is talking directly into a Webcam with an adult voice.]

BABY: A lot of people are like, "Aren't you too young to invest in markets?" And you know...

[He counts on his fingers.]

BABY: A - Don't worry about it, I just look young...you don't know how old I am.

And B - I use E*Trade, so...check it...click...

[He clicks the mouse to the left and then looks into the camera.]

BABY: I just bought stock...you just saw me buy stock. No big deal...I mean you know if I can do it, you can do it....

[He suddenly burps and spits up.]

BABY: Whoa!

VO: It's so easy there are a thousand new accounts a day at E*Trade.

LOGO: E*Trade

Bronze

Television :30/:25, *Single*

Art Director Steve Krauss
Writers Ari Halper, Randy Krallman
Agency Producers Bennett McCarroll, Alison Horn
Production Company Smuggler
Director Randy Krallman
Creative Directors Tor Myhren, Jonathan Cranin
Client E*Trade
Agency Grey/New York
Annual ID 08058T

[A man is sitting in a stable hooked up to a cow milking machine. A farmer walks in holding a bottle of milk.]

FARMER: Why does this milk taste sour?

MAN: Beats me.

FARMER: Maybe it's something you're eating.

[Man looks down at a bag of Sour Skittles he's eating. He then shuts down the machine.]

MAN: What are you driving at?

FARMER: Look, all I'm saying is, maybe if you ate less Sour Skittles, I'd have less sour milk.

MAN: Well that's a risk I'm willing to take.

SUPER: Sour the rainbow. Taste the rainbow.

Bronze

Television :30/:25, *Single*

Art Director Craig Allen
Writer Eric Kallman
Agency Producer Nathy Aviram
Creative Directors Gerry Graf, Ian Reichenthal, Scott Vitrone
Client Mars Snackfood - Skittles
Agency TBWA\Chiat\Day/New York
Annual ID 08059T

[The scene opens with an outside shot of a Burger King with the caption: [Las Vegas, NV – 10/30/07 – 3:30 PM]

VO: We swapped out the Whopper for a Wendy's burger to see what would happen.

CASHIER: **This is clearly a Wendy's burger.**

CUSTOMER: **Clearly.**

CASHIER: **OK, they have the square patty...**

CUSTOMER: **I hate Wendy's!**

COWORKER: **What's going on?**

CUSTOMER: **I eat Burger King, I don't eat Wendy's.**

COWORKER: **What can I do to resolve this?**

CUSTOMER: **All I want is a Whopper. Get me a Whopper!**

[Just then The King comes out with a Whopper on a platter and there's applause all around.]

VO: Whopper. Anything else is a freakin' disappointment.

SUPER: WhopperFreakout.com

Gold

Television :30/:25, *Campaign*

Art Directors Paul Caiozzo, Andy Minisman, Dan Treichel, Julia Hoffman
Writers Ryan Kutscher, Omid Farhang, Nathan Dills
Designers Lifelong Friendship Society, Michael Tseng
Agency Producers David Rolfe, Winston Binch, Chris Kyriakos, Harshal C. Sisodia, Aymi Beltramo, Bill Meadows, Jessica Locke
Production Companies Smuggler, Patrick Milling Smith, Brian Carmody, Lisa Rich, Allison Kunzman, Laura Thoel, Drew Santarsiero, Rock Paper Scissors, Adam Pertofsky, Chan Hatcher, Matt Murphy, Wyatt Jones, Crissy DeSimone, Tricia Sanzaro, Dan Aronin, Gabriel Britz, Neil Meiklejohn, Amber Music, RED Interactive, Dan Sormani, RIOT, Mark Dennison, Andy Davis, Stephanie Boggs, Shawna Drop
Directors Henry-Alex Rubin, Scott Prindle, Matthew Ray, Matthew Walsh
Creative Directors Rob Reilly, Bill Wright, Jeff Benjamin, Ryan Kutscher
Client Burger King
Agency Crispin Porter + Bogusky/Miami
Annual ID 08060T

[The Mac and PC guys are standing with a sunglass-wearing security guard-type in between them.]

MAC: **Hello, I'm a Mac...**

GUARD: Mac has issued a salutation, cancel or allow?

PC: **Allow. And I'm a PC.**

GUARD: You're returning Mac salutation, cancel or allow?

PC: **Allow.**

MAC: **OK, what gives?**

GUARD: Mac is asking a question, cancel or allow?

PC: **Allow. He's part of Vista, my new operating system. PCs have a lot of security problems so it asks me to authorize pretty much anything I do.**

GUARD: You're pointing out Vista's flaws, cancel or allow?

PC: **Allow. I could turn him off but then he wouldn't give me any warnings at all and that would defeat the purpose.**

GUARD: You are coming to a sad realization, cancel or allow?

PC: **Allow.**

LOGO: **Mac**

Gold
Television :30/:25, *Campaign*

Art Director Scott Trattner
Writers Jason Sperling, Barton Corley, Alicia Dotter
Agency Producers Mike Refuerzo, Anne Oburgh, Cheryl Childers, Hank Zakroff
Production Company Epoch Films
Director Phil Morrison
Creative Directors Lee Clow, Duncan Milner, Eric Grunbaum, Scott Trattner, Jason Sperling, Barton Corley
Client Apple
Agency TBWA\Media Arts Lab/Los Angeles
Annual ID 08061T

[The Mac guy is standing next to the PC guy and a cart filled with several people lying on it.]

MAC: Hello, I'm a Mac.

PC: And I'm a PC. Mac, I'm going to be going away for a while.

MAC: Where are you going?

PC: Well, over to IT. I've been getting these funky error messages that keep popping up...

MAC: Ah, that's annoying...

PC: WMP.DLL

MAC: What?

PC: I don't even know what that means, it just happens. Do you know what it means?

MAC: No, Mac's don't get those cryptic error messages. Are they sick too?

PC: Oh yeah, he's error 692, and then syntax error down the end, and down here, fatal error. Don't worry, you'll be up handling spreadsheets in no time. [Whispers] He's a goner!

LOGO: Mac

Silver
Television :30/:25, *Campaign*

Art Directors Scott Trattner, Chuck Monn
Writers Jason Sperling, Alicia Dotter
Agency Producers Cheryl Childers, Mike Refuerzo, Hank Zakroff
Production Companies Epoch Films, LAIKA/house
Directors Phil Morrison, Drew Lightfoot
Creative Directors Lee Clow, Duncan Milner, Eric Grunbaum, Scott Trattner, Jason Sperling, Chuck Monn
Client Apple
Agency TBWA\Media Arts Lab/Los Angeles
Annual ID 08062T

SUPER: **Coke vs. Coke Zero**

[Two representatives from Coke are sitting across from a lawyer in a meeting.]

MARKETER 1: **We represent the Coke brand and we would like to sue Coke Zero.**

MARKETER 2: **Would you say that we have a case?**

LAWYER: **For what?**

MARKETER 1: **For taste infringement.**

MARKETER 2: **We wanna just sue them back to the Stone Age to send them a message that they're tampering with the flagship of the company.**

LAWYER: **It's one company. It's like you suing yourself.**

MARKETER 2: **Yeah, but they're on a different part of our floor.**

SUPER: **Coca-Cola Taste. Zero Calories.**

Merit

Bronze

Television :30/:25, *Campaign*

Art Director Dayoung Ewart
Writer Erkki Izarra
Designer Jiwon Lee
Agency Producers Rupert Samuel, Matthew Anderson, Paul Gunnarson, Bill Meadows
Production Companies Villians, Richard Goldstein, Phil Rose, Leif Johnson, RIOT, Cosmo Street NY, Jason Macdonald, Beacon Street, Sound Lounge
Director Fred Goss
Creative Directors Dave Schiff, Alex Burnard
Client Coke Zero

Agency Crispin Porter + Bogusky/Miami
Annual ID 08063T

ALSO AWARDED
❋ Merit Television :30/:25, *Single*

[Two men are throwing a frisbee that a dog chases.]

MAN 1: Thank you for that, Spunk.

MAN 2: Noogie di Viagra.

MAN 1: Nocker tut.

MAN 2: Viagra dingo monkey quank? Viagra mufti chuck wabbo.

MAN 1: Whoa...payser ran tufty here..

SUPER: The international language of Viagra.

Bronze

Television :20 and under, *Single*

Art Director Jason Hill
Writer Michael Murray
Agency Producer Jennifer Mete
Production Companies Partizan LA , Radke Films
Director Eric Lynne
Creative Directors Zak Mroueh, Ron Smrczek
Client Pfizer Canada
Agency TAXI Canada/Toronto
Annual ID 08064T

[A blindfolded man sits at a table with two cups. One is labeled Buckley's while the other is labeled Cardio Workout Perspiration. He drinks the Cardio cup.]

MAN: It's the same as the first one.

SUPER: Buckley's Cough Mixture. It tastes awful. It works.

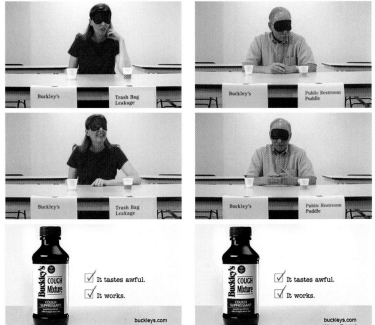

Gold
Television :20 and under, *Campaign*

Art Director Kristin Graham
Writer Aryan Aminzadeh
Agency Producers Diane Burton, Dennis Liu
Directors Jan Jacobs, Leo Permutico
Creative Directors Tony Granger, Jan Jacobs, Leo Premutico, Joseph Pompeo
Client Novartis - Buckley's Cough Syrup
Agency Saatchi & Saatchi/New York
Annual ID 08065T

[We see a guy having sex with a girl from her P.O.V. He's thrusting away, grunting with his eyes half closed.]

SUPER: **Lesbians. Who can blame them?**
The L Word. 9:30 Sunday on Prime.

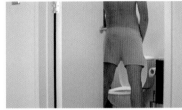

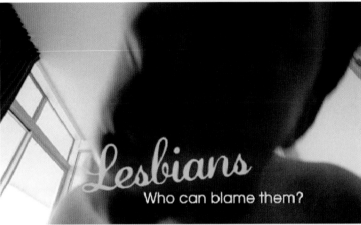

![Prime logo and The L Word]

Bronze

Television :20 and under, *Campaign*

Art Director Kelly Lovelock
Writer Matt Simpkins
Agency Producer Esther Watkins
Production Company Flying Fish
Director Luke Savage
Creative Director James Mok
Client Prime
Agency DraftFCB/Auckland
Annual ID 08067T

75

[A logo with 18 and SNVL appears.]

VO: **The following program contains sex, nudity, violence and strong language. Profanity, blasphemy, obscenity, racism, ageism, chauvinism, anti-semitism, anti-arabism, heterosexism, homosexism, monosexism, sexism, misogyny, heterophobia, homophobia, toilet humor, and an adult breastfeeding scene which we're just not certain which category it fits into.]**

SUPER: **Little Britain. You've been warned. MUSICA. Listen with your soul.**

Complete series now available.

You've been warned.

Silver

Television Under $50K Budget, *Single*

Art Director Gareth McPherson
Writer Dave Topham
Agency Producer Leila Haneker
Production Company Wicked Pixels
Director Andrew Shaw
Creative Director Darren MacKay
Client Musica
Agency The Jupiter Drawing Room SA/Cape Town
Annual ID 08068T

[A father is holding his hands over his daughter's eyes as the mother videotapes them. They walk out to the driveway.]

FATHER: **Here you go.**

[He lets her open her eyes and she starts screaming with excitement. We see a car with a large red ribbon on it. She runs over and hugs her father.]

SUPER: **Car rentals from $27 a day.**

LOGO: **Thrifty. Now that's Thrifty thinking.**

Bronze

Television Under $50K Budget, *Single*

Art Directors Adam Fine, Brendan Donnelly, John Lam
Writers Adam Fine, Brendan Donnelly, John Lam
Agency Producer Tania Templeton
Production Company Plaza Films
Director Dave Klaiber
Creative Directors Jay Benjamin, Andy DiLallo
Client Thrifty Car Rentals
Agency JWT/Sydney
Annual ID 08069T

ALSO AWARDED

✐ Merit Television :30/:25, *Single*

[Open inside a little kid's bedroom. His mother is talking to her husband on her cell phone.]

MOM: No he's still up, you want to say goodnight? [Whispering to boy] Here's Daddy.

[Mom gives the little boy the phone.]

BOY: Hi Daddy.

[Immediately Martin Scorsese walks into the room.]

MARTIN: No, no, no, no, no. Look, the plot of this phone call just isn't working for me. It's ordinary. It's pedestrian. I've seen it a million times. Okay?

MOM: Excuse me.

MARTIN: Excuse me. There's no edge. There's no edge to it. There's no edge to it. He's just got out of prison. Alright? He's just got out of prison.

MOM: Daddy's in Cleveland.

MARTIN: He just got out of prison. He's a very dark and mysterious figure in your life. Very dark and mysterious to you.

MOM: No he's not.

MARTIN: Yes he is. Dark and mysterious. You hardly know him. In fact, you don't even call him Daddy. To you, he's Frank. To you, he's Frank. That's how detached you are. That's how separate you are. He betrayed you. You want to kill him but you keep it locked up inside, in here. Okay? But one day, vengeance. Vengeance. Can you say vengeance?

BOY: Vengeance.

MARTIN: Vengeance. Excellent, he's doing fine. And you, you're trapped in a loveless marriage. Totally loveless, okay? And you should be drinking something out of a bottle. You have a bottle around?

MOM: Downstairs.

MARTIN: Get it please.

[Martin exits room.]

SUPER: We won't interrupt your phone calls.

Please don't interrupt our movies.

A message from Martin Scorsese and AT&T.

Gold

Cinema Advertising, *Single*

Art Director Rodney White
Writer Matthew Zaifert
Agency Producers Bob Emerson, Julie Andariese
Producer Ralph Laucella - O Positive
Production Company O Positive
Director Jim Jenkins
Creative Directors David Lubars, Bill Bruce, Susan Credle, Darren Wright, David Skinner
Client AT&T
Agency BBDO/New York
Annual ID 08070T

Recommendation

Do **not** move forward
with concept
without significant
changes.

[We open on an animated testing board of Apple's seminal "1984" spot. A narrator describes the spot in detail.]

NARRATOR: This commercial starts on a wide shot of a futuristic-looking industrial complex. We see a long line of drones marching single file down a glass-enclosed hallway. They are all shaved bald and wear drab, ill-fitting clothes. Some of them wear gas masks. We can see small television screens attached to the ceiling on which a speech is being broadcast.

LEADER: Today we celebrate the first glorious anniversary of the Information Purification Directives.

NARRATOR: We then cut quickly to a young blonde woman, running down a separate hallway carrying, what appears to be, a large sledgehammer. We see she is being chased by a team of Stormtroopers in full riot gear.

LEADER: We have created for the first time in all history a garden of pure ideology, where each worker may bloom, secure from the pests of any contradictory true thoughts.

Our Unification of Thoughts is more powerful a weapon than any fleet or army on earth.

We are one people, with one will, one resolve, one cause.

Our enemies shall talk themselves to death and we will bury them with their own confusion.

NARRATOR: Just then the young woman runs into the theater with the Storm troopers right behind her.

LEADER: We shall prevail!

NARRATOR: The young woman swings her sledgehammer in a wide circle, then lets it fly with a labored scream. We see the hammer fly through the air. The hammer hits the movie screen. The screen explodes, bathing the drones in white light. Just then we hear a voice over say, "On February 4th, Apple Computer will introduce the iCube and you'll see why 2008 won't be like '1984.'" We then cut to the Apple Computer logo.

[Just then we see the testing board is being viewed by actual focus groups. The focus groups proceed to tear apart the greatest spot ever produced.]

SUPER: Several weeks and thousands of dollars later.

VO: Qualitative testing suggests adopting the following optimizers to boost appeal with target audience—use real people. Preferably without gas masks. Make fewer references to Nazism. Bring up Apple logo sooner. Perhaps on characters' wardrobe or a superimposed "bug." Above all, every attempt should be made to make the commercial less depressing. A palate of bright colors could achieve this. For entertainment value, consider using a dog or a chimpanzee. Based on initial testing, we recommend you do not move forward with this communication without significant changes before Quant Tests.

[Just then we cut to the climatic clip of the iconic woman hurling her hammer into the giant monitor which explodes in burst of white.]

SUPER: Tonight we celebrate creativity. The 2007 Hatch Awards.

Gold
Non-Broadcast, *Single*

Writers Roger Baldacci, Lawson Clarke
Illustrator Charlie Hoar
Agency Producer Lucy Benini
Production Company Arnold Worldwide
Creative Directors Pete Favat, Roger Baldacci
Client The Ad Club
Agency Arnold Worldwide/Boston
Annual ID 08071T

[A young couple walks into a movie theater lobby. The man stops and puts a coin into a Coke vending machine. Inside we see the coin roll in and there is an animated world inside. One of the workers inside shuts down the machine as the man outside tries to push the button again and again. A drop falls from the giant Coke bottle in the sky and the worker runs to catch it in a small bottle. He hands it to a giant Polar Bear creature that appears to be their leader. He sends him on an adventure with the Coke bottle. He goes through strange worlds with creatures and then into an underwater world. Then he enters an arctic world and climbs up a mountain. He then enters a forest where he encounters a large tree that he climbs aboard. Through a portal, he winds up back in the machine and puts the Coke he saved in with the rest that goes into the big bottles. The bottle eventually rolls out of the vending machine and the young man races inside the movie theater.]

LOGO: **The Coke Side of Life**

Silver
Non-Broadcast, *Single*

Art Directors John Norman, Hunter Hindman
Writers Al Moseley, Rick Condors
Agency Producers Sandy Reay, Kimia Farshidzad, Tom Dunlap
Production Company Psyop
Directors Todd Mueller, Kylie Matulick
Creative Directors Al Moseley, John Norman
Client Coca-Cola
Agency Wieden+Kennedy/Amsterdam
Annual ID 08072T

[The scene opens inside the Museum of Humanity. We see two older veterans walking toward a display showing an alien gun.]

SUPER: Maj. Roland Huffman; UNSC (ret.) active duty 2548-2573

HUFFMAN: I was a sniper, used a standard high-powered sniper rifle. At 600 yards it would go through about 13 feet of flesh and bone.

INTERVIEWER: What about you?

NAVARRO: Well I used a shotgun.

SUPER: Sgt. Tomas Navarro; UNSC (ret.) active duty 2555-2567

INTERVIEWER: Could you tell us a bit about that one?

HUFFMAN: This one, sure. We saw a lot of these, this is an old covenant rifle. It's a spike rifle, we called it the Spiker.

INTERVIEWER: And who used it?

HUFFMAN: Well the brutes, mostly.

INTERVIEWER: Can you show us how it works.

HUFFMAN: Sure. They used it as a handgun. That's heavy. Holding an enemy weapon like this...feels...I don't like it. If you'd have told me a few years ago we would be here in this place talking about this, I would have said, "No way, it's not gonna happen." If there's one reason why we're here, um, I would say it's because of The Chief.

SUPER: Believe.

VO: Rated M for mature.

LOGO: Halo 3
XBOX 360 Live

SUPER: Jump in.

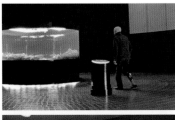

Gold

Non-Broadcast, *Campaign*

Art Director Ben Wolan
Writer Rick Herrera
Agency Producers Vince Genovese, Hannah Murray
Production Companies GO Film, MJZ
Directors Simon McQuoid, Rupert Sanders
Creative Directors Geoff Edwards, Scott Duchon, John Patroulis
Client Microsoft Xbox Halo 3
Agency McCann Worldgroup SF & T.A.G./San Francisco
Annual ID 08073T

[We see a medieval lord, a pilgrim, a greek, an island native and a Viking in a car.]

LORD: Hand me a Snickers, pilgrim, or I shall have you horse whipped.

PILGRIM: Sure you will.

LORD: Don't you take that tone with me you rascal or I shall have you horse whipped.

PILGRIM: Whatever.

LORD: You are so totally headed for an HW...

PILGRIM: What?

LORD: Horse whipping!

SUPER: Feast

Silver
Non-Broadcast, *Campaign*

Art Directors Jeff Anderson, Mark Schruntek
Writers Isaac Silverglate, Pierre Lipton
Agency Producer Jason Souter
Creative Directors Gerry Graf, Ian Reichenthal, Scott Vitrone
Client Mars Snackfood - Snickers
Agency TBWA\Chiat\Day/New York
Annual ID 08074T

SUPER: **New York City 2007**

[On a stage set we see a man being hoisted up on ropes. A full orchestra is playing on the stage while Martin Scorsese is directing actors and the production staff. An interviewer is talking to Scorsese about making the Key to Reserva, based on a three-and-a-half page, unfinished script for a movie that Alfred Hitchcock was going to make. His mission is to make it as if Hitchcock was making it.]

SUPER: Freixenet presents an RSA Films production. The Key to Reserva.

[We see a close-up of an orchestra. A man with a case comes out of the bathroom and hurries upstairs. He puts the case down in one of the balcony seats. A woman from below turns her head. The man searches around in the balcony for something. He then looks up at the light bulb and notices a key in it. He reaches for it and burns his hand. One of the violinists notices him and plucks a note that signals to a man in the audience. The man nods over to he violinist who walks off the stage. Meanwhile, the man in the balcony is trying to break the light bulb to get to the key. From behind he is strangled. A struggle ensues and the attacker is hit in the eye. He falls out of the balcony. The other man then unlocks the case with the key and takes out a bottle of Freixenet. He looks at the cork and it says "Top Secret." The movie ends with a inspector taking the cork and the man and a woman embracing.]

INTERVIEWER: **Do you feel that you've successfully preserved Hitchcock's vision with us?**

SCORSESE: Well sometimes, you know, I would hope so. Sometimes, even when I'm doing this, I kinda feel him looking over our shoulders, you know, or looking over my shoulder, anyway. I just hope he takes it in the right spirit. [Laughing] You know? I mean, that would be terrible if, you know...if it was like...I just hope he understood the fun of it, the spirit...

[The camera pans out and we see a giant flock of black crows gathering on the window sills of the building outside.]

Gold

Innovation in Advertising & Marketing, *Single*
Agency Producer Diana Belmonte
Production Company RSA Films
Director **Martin Scorsese**
Creative Directors **Alex Martínez, Rory Lambert, Carlos Puig**
Client Freixenet
Agency JWT/Barcelona
Annual ID 08451A

The Museum of Humanity

Gold

Innovation in Advertising & Marketing, *Single*

Art Director **Ben Wolan**
Writer **Rick Herrera**
Agency Producers **Vince Genovese, Hannah Murray**
Director **T.A.G.**
Creative Directors **Scott Duchon, Geoff Edwards, John Patroulis**
Client **Microsoft XBOX Halo 3**
Agency **McCann Worldgroup SF & T.A.G./San Francisco**
Annual ID **08075A**

Bronze
Innovation in Advertising & Marketing, *Single*

Art Director Mike Hughes
Writer Lyle Yetman
Information Architect Matt Butner
Creative Directors John Butler, Mike Shine
Client MINI
Agency Butler, Shine, Stern & Partners/Sausalito
Annual ID 08077A

Merit

Merit   Merit   Merit

Gold

Innovation in Advertising & Marketing, *Campaign*

Art Directors James Clunie, Chuck Tso
Illustrators Kustaa Saksi, McFaul
Agency Producers JD Michaels, Bronwen Gilbert
Creative Directors David Lubars, Bill Bruce, James Clunie
Client Havaianas
Agency BBDO/New York
Annual ID 08078A

ALSO AWARDED
- Bronze Outdoor, *Campaign*
- Merit Outdoor, *Single*
- Merit Outdoor, *Single*
- Merit Outdoor, *Single*
- Merit Outdoor, *Single*

Silver

Innovation in Advertising & Marketing, *Campaign*

Writers Jess Willis, Amelia Charlton
Designers David Taylor, Lida Baday, Kerri Galvin, Leo Tsalkos
Agency Producers Jacinte De Luca, Kevin Saffer, Tracy Haapamaki
Creative Directors Paul Lavoie, Steve Mykolyn
Client TAXI
Agency TAXI Canada/Toronto
Annual ID 08079A

Bronze

Innovation in Advertising & Marketing, *Campaign*

Writer Douglas Coupland
Director Gary Thomas
Creative Director Stefan Woronko
Client Random House
Agency Crush/Toronto
Annual ID 08080A

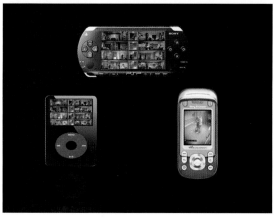

Gold

Innovation in Advertising & Marketing, *Campaign*

Art Director David Carter
Writers Greg Hahn, Mike Smith, David Carter
Digital Artist/Multimedia Big Spaceship
Agency Producers Brian DiLorenzo, Jiffy Iuen
Production Company RSA Films
Director Jake Scott
Creative Directors David Lubars, Bill Bruce, Greg Hahn, Mike Smith, David Carter
Client HBO/Voyeur
Agency BBDO/New York
Annual ID 08081A

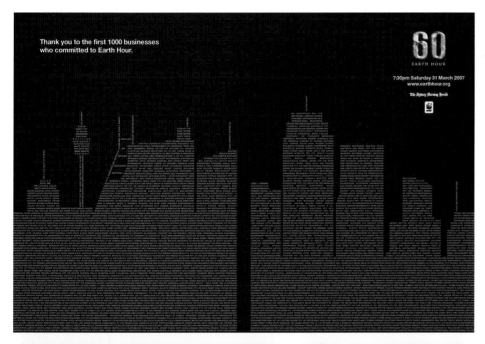

Thank you to the first 1000 businesses who committed to Earth Hour.

60
EARTH HOUR

7:30pm Saturday 31 March 2007
www.earthhour.org

The Sydney Morning Herald

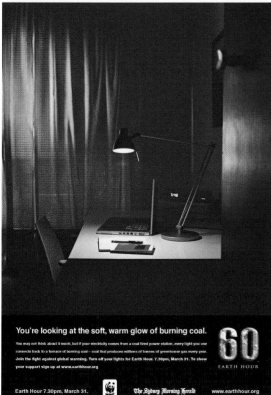

You're looking at the soft, warm glow of burning coal.

You may not think about it much, but if your electricity comes from a coal-fired power station, every light you use connects back to a furnace of burning coal – coal that produces millions of tonnes of greenhouse gas every year. Join the fight against global warming. Turn off your lights for Earth Hour. 7.30pm, March 31. To show your support sign up at www.earthhour.org

Earth Hour 7.30pm, March 31.   WWF   The Sydney Morning Herald   www.earthhour.org

60
EARTH HOUR

60
EARTH HOUR

ONLY USE LIGHTS WHEN YOU NEED THEM

Switch off for Earth Hour
7.30pm, March 31.

60
EARTH HOUR

Bronze

Innovation in Advertising & Marketing, *Campaign*

Art Director Michael Spirkovski
Writer Grant McAloon
Digital Artist/Multimedia Kieran Ots
Creative Director Mark Collis
Content Strategist Mark Pollard
Client World Wildlife Fund
Agency Leo Burnett/Sydney
Annual ID 08082A

Gold

Integrated Branding, *Campaign*

Art Director David Carter
Writers Greg Hahn, Mike Smith, David Carter
Digital Artist/Multimedia Big Spaceship
Agency Producers Brian DiLorenzo, Jiffy Iuen
Production Company RSA Films
Director Jake Scott
Creative Directors David Lubars, Bill Bruce, Greg Hahn, Mike Smith, David Carter
Client HBO/Voyeur
Agency BBDO/New York
Annual ID 08083G

ALSO AWARDED
◗ Merit Outdoor, *Single*

[LAS VEGAS, NV - 11/02/07]

[ACTUAL CUSTOMERS ON HIDDEN CAMERA]

[ACTUAL CUSTOMERS]

[ACTUAL CUSTOMERS ON HIDDEN CAMERA]

[ACTUAL CUSTOMERS ON HIDDEN CAMERA]

[ACTUAL CUSTOMERS ON HIDDEN CAMERA]

[ACTUAL CUSTOMERS ON HIDDEN CAMERA]

WHOPPERFREAKOUT.COM

Gold

Integrated Branding, *Campaign*

Art Directors Paul Caiozzo, Andy Minisman
Writers Ryan Kutscher, Omid Farhang, Nathan Dills
Designers Thomas Rodgers, Lifelong Friendship Society, Michael Tseng
Photographer Learan Kahanov
Agency Producers Dave Rolfe, Winston Binch, Chris Kyriakos, Aymi Beltramo, Harshal C. Sisodia, Bill Meadows, Jessica Locke
Production Companies Smuggler, Patrick Milling Smith, Brian Carmody, Lisa Rich, Allison Kunzman, Laura Thoel, Drew Santarsiero, Rock Paper Scissors, Adam Pertofsky, Chan Hatcher, Matt Murphy, Wyatt Jones, Crissy DeSemone, Tricia Sanzaro, Dan Aronin, Gabriel Britz, Neil Melkejohn, Amber Music, Eugen Cho, Dan Sormani, RIOT, Mark

Dennison, Andy Davis, Stephanie Boggs, Shawna Drop, Lime Studios, Dave Wagg, Rohan Young, Loren Silber, Mark Meyuhas
Information Architect RED Interactive
Directors Henry-Alex Rubin, Scott Prindle, Matthew Ray, Matthew Walsh
Creative Directors Rob Reilly, Bill Wright, Jeff Benjamin, Ryan Kutscher
Content Strategists Stewart Warner, James Luckensow
Client Burger King
Agency Crispin Porter + Bogusky/Miami
Annual ID 08084G

ALSO AWARDED
Silver Television :20 and Under - Campaign

Gold

Integrated Branding, *Campaign*

Art Directors Nate Able, Tim Steir, Ben Wolan, Kevin Hsieh, Erin Wendel, Elliot Harris
Writers Mat Bunnell, Rick Herrera, Joel Kaplan, Keith Hostert, Lauren McCrindle, Cameron Mitchell
Agency Producers Hannah Murray, Vince Genovese, Nancy Cardillo, Larry Ewing, David White
Production Companies MJZ, GO Film, T.A.G.
Directors Rupert Sanders, Simon McQuoid
Creative Directors Scott Duchon, Geoff Edwards, John Patroulis, Rei Inamoto, John Jakubowski
Client Microsoft XBOX Halo 3
Agency McCann Worldgoup SF & T.A.G./AKQA/San Francisco
Annual ID 08085G

Silver

Integrated Branding, *Campaign*

Art Director **Dean Maryon**
Writer **Sean Thompson**
Designers **Julian Wade, Alan von Lutzau**
Photographer **David Turnley**
Digital Artist/Multimedia **Dan Sumich**
Agency Producers **Tony Stearns, Kate Morrison**
Production Company **Passion Pictures**
Directors **Sean Thompson, Dean Maryon**
Client **adidas**

Agency **180 Amsterdam (180\TBWA)**
Annual ID **08086G**

ALSO AWARDED

✎ Merit **Television Over :30 - Campaign**

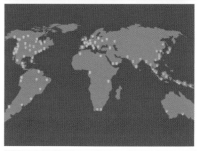

"This single idea will literally save millions of children's lives."

STEVAN MILLER
UNICEF

Silver

Integrated Branding, *Campaign*

Art Director Ji Lee
Writer David Droga
Agency Producer Maggie Meade
Creative Directors Ted Royer, David Droga, Duncan Marshall
Content Strategist Andrew Essex
Client Unicef/Tap Project
Agency Droga5/New York
Annual ID 08087G

NEW **Diamond Shreddies** Cereal

OLD (Boring)

NEW (Exciting!)

Same 100% Whole Grain Wheat
DiamondShreddies.com

NEW **Diamond Shreddies** Cereal

Mmmm... Diamond-ier!

What makes Diamond Shreddies Cereal so hip, so now? They're diamond-ier. They're angular-ier. They're 45 more degrees of good times. Some say they can't taste the difference, and that's because there isn't any! But we're willing to bet that somehow, Diamond Shreddies Cereal will add just that much more sparkle to your mornings.

NEW **Diamond Shreddies** Cereal
www.diamondshreddies.com

OLD (Boring)

New (Exciting)

Bronze

Integrated Branding, *Campaign*

Art Directors Tim Piper, Ivan Pols, Liz Kis, Ron Gligic, Flavio Viana
Writers Jane Murray, Hunter Somerville, Tim Piper, Jen Durning
Photographer Robyn Vickers
Agency Producers Shenny Jaffer, Chris Rozak
Production Company OPC
Director Michael Downing
Creative Directors Janet Kestin, Nancy Vonk, Carlos Garavito
Client Kraft Canada - Shreddies
Agency Ogilvy & Mather/Toronto
Annual ID 08088G

Gold
Branded Content, *Single*

Agency Producer Diana Belmonte
Production Company RSA Films
Director Martin Scorsese
Creative Directors Carlos Puig, Rory Lambert, Alex Martinez
Client Freixenet
Agency JWT/Barcelona
Annual ID 08089T

Gold

Branded Content, *Campaign*

Art Director David Carter
Writers Greg Hahn, Mike Smith, David Carter
Agency Producers Brian DiLorenzo, Jiffy Iuen
Production Companies RSA Films, Big Spaceship
Director Jake Scott
Creative Directors David Lubars, Bill Bruce, Greg Hahn, Mike Smith, David Carter
Client HBO/Voyeur
Agency BBDO/New York
Annual ID 08091T

Silver

Branded Content, *Campaign*

Art Director Jon Randazzo
Writers Jon Randazzo, Aaron Bergeron, Gideon Evans, Tom Johnson, Julian Katz, Jordan Kramer, Justin Wilkes, William Gelner, Amir Farhang
Agency Producer Julian Katz
Production Company @radical.media
Directors Dave Hamilton, Luke McCoubrey, Peter McCoubrey
Creative Director Kevin Roddy
Client Unilever - Axe
Agency BBH/New York
Annual ID 08092T

Radio Pencil Winners

Gold
Radio, *Single*

Writer David Eastman
Agency Producer Sheri Cartwright
Production Company Post-Op
Creative Director Chris Smith
Client Motel 6
Agency The Richards Group/Dallas
Annual ID 08040R

Gold
Radio, *Campaign*

Art Director Jeff Anderson
Writer Isaac Silverglate
Agency Producer Laura Rosenshine
Creative Directors Gerry Graf, Ian Reichenthal, Scott Vitrone
Client Mars Snackfood - Combos
Agency TBWA\Chiat\Day/New York
Annual ID 08043R

ALSO AWARDED

Silver Radio, *Single*: "Prison Guard"
Merit Radio, *Single*: "Lullaby"
Merit Radio, *Single*: "Broken Heart"

Bronze
Radio, *Single*

Writer Markus Ruf
Production Company Renzo Selmi
Creative Directors Markus Ruf, Danielle Lanz
Client Sport Factory Outlet
Agency Ruf Lanz/Zurich
Annual ID 08042R

Silver
Radio, *Campaign*

Writers Brian Ahern, Icaro Doria, Menno Kluin
Creative Director Tony Granger
Client Smith Micro Software/StuffIt Deluxe
Agency Saatchi & Saatchi/New York
Annual ID 08044R

Gold on Gold

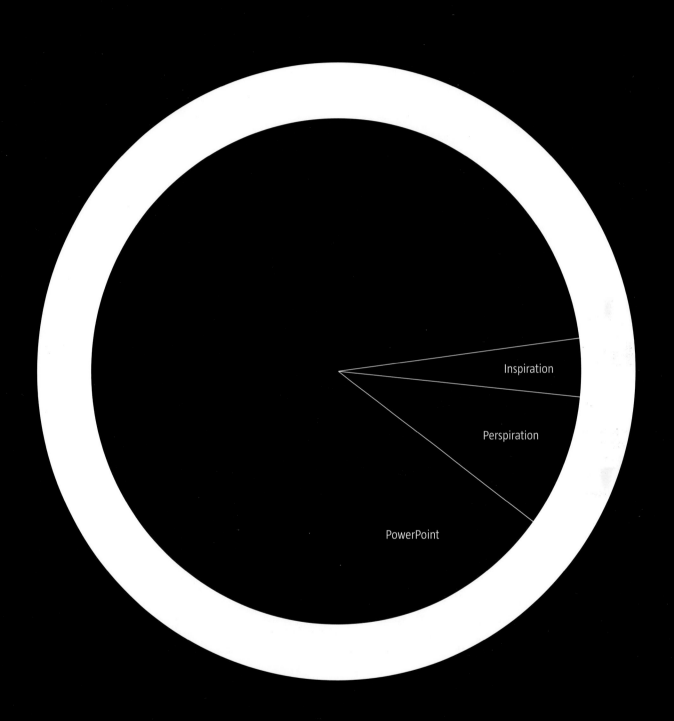

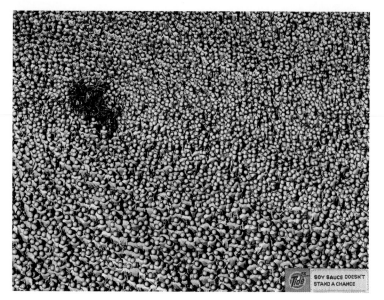

08004A

Jake Benjamin, Mark Voehriger
Saatchi & Saatchi/New York

CASTING SPECS: Male or female. 18-45. Average build. Any background or ethnicity. Needs to be comfortable in large crowds. Capable of standing for long periods of time. Strong bladder control a must.

08012A

Yooshin Lee
Cheil Worldwide/Seoul

The aim of the HomePlus outdoor campaign was to evoke a vision of illusion as well as urge passers-by to go shopping. The subway pillars were transformed to look like supermarket stands. Upon entering the station, one wonders, "Wait a second... Did I just enter HomePlus supermarket?"

Opening a store in the Chamsil area where the rival chain stores are strong, HomePlus needed a solution to grab people's attention.

This outdoor campaign did just that.

The expected sales profit for the opening day was exceeded by 550%. Just like the slogan for this campaign, it also gave a One Show Gold plus to my team.

08007A

Grant Parker
DDB/London

If you choose to wear sensible shoes, you will lead a sensible life. If you wear the latest Harvey Nichols "must haves" your life will be full of adventure, wild parties, sexy women, palm-fringed beaches and lovely award ceremonies.

08022A

Tom Hauser
Jung von Matt/Hamburg

The IKEA 3-D Cover was an essential part of the annual IKEA campaign 2008 in Germany with the motto "Fashion for your most beautiful home in the world." We are very proud about winning a One Show Gold Pencil for this work. First of all I would like to thank our client IKEA Germany for believing in this idea. I also would like to thank Act Agency Hamburg and Stein Promotions for the implementation of the 3-D Cover. And last but not least, my thanks goes to the whole agency team that was involved. Great job! Mycket, mycket bra.

08026A

Wisit Lumsiricharoenchoke, Nopadol Srikieatikajohn, Gumpon Laksanajinda
Ogilvy & Mather/Bangkok

The many advantages of having trees:
- Reduces global warming
- Allows wild animals to inhabit them
- Provides a source for rivers
- Changes carbon dioxide into oxygen
- Gives beautiful furniture to decorate our homes
- Allows tree cutters to eat and relax underneath the shade
- Helps Ogilvy Thailand receive a Gold in the One Show

08032A

Nami Hoshino, Yoshiyuki Mikami
HAKUHODO Architect/Tokyo

Wildlife endangerment is a widely known fact. But what is not known is how serious the situation is. So we used the current population of the endangered species as pixels, to graphically show how few of them are left, real time. Less the population, more vague the picture becomes. Calling immediate action.

The idea worked perfectly.

08036T

Matthew Branning
Nordpol+ Hamburg

The idea to personify the wind is one thing. Finding an actor who can pull it off is another. When Guillaume walked into the casting session (the very last person, on the very last day) we knew immediately that he was the one. This unforgettable actor makes the film's message more memorable as well.

08052T

Kevin Brady
Droga5/New York

We really wanted to do this live action. Whatever.

08061T

Eric Grunbaum, Jason Sperling
TBWA\Media Arts Lab/Los Angeles

In 2006, the "Get a Mac" campaign began a humorous debate between two characters, "Mac" and "PC", that illustrated their many differences and the myriad reasons Macs were a better choice. But the campaign took on a whole new direction in 2007 when a bold new shade of white paint was selected for the set's background.

OK, that's not true. We used the exact same shade of white. What kept the sopho-more season of the campaign as fresh and relevant as ever were a bevy of new topics (thank you, Microsoft) and the ever-evolving relationship between the two characters.

08055T
Nathan Frank, Dan Lucey
Saatchi & Saatchi/New York

It was fun to dramatize the subject but in reality a stain is nothing to laugh at. When people go to job interviews with stains on their shirts they oftentimes miss out on really great opportunities. We are glad we could address this problem and maybe inspire people to take better care of themselves.

08070T
Rodney White, Matthew Zaifert
BBDO/New York

The first day we got the brief, our concepting went as follows...
The Departed was awesome.
I hope we don't screw this up.
Maybe he'll sign my *Goodfellas* DVD.
You think his eyebrows look like that in person?
Oh man, we better not screw this up.
I should add *Cape Fear* to my queue.
Can we call him Marty?
Maybe we should just get him to write it.
What do you mean he won't write it?
We're definitely gonna screw this up.

08065T
Aryan Aminzadeh, Kristin Graham
Saatchi & Saatchi/New York

We tried so hard to get asparagus-fed donkey urine in there.

08071T
Roger Baldacci, Lawson Clarke
Arnold Worldwide/Boston

Well, I guess you could say this has been a true labor of hate. I know we're preaching to the choir here, but concept testing, by and large, is simply ruining our industry. We are in the telling business, not the asking business. Some of the most successful brands don't test because they are lead by visionaries—not nervous, risk-adverse middle managers. So for us, testing an anemic animatic of Apple's legendary "1984" Super Bowl spot seemed to be the best way to illustrate this—put the biggest, most iconic spot in front of the smallest minds. Comedy gold.

08451A

JWT Spain Team
JWT/Barcelona

- Hello... good evening. Could I speak to Mr. Martin Scorsese?
- You talkin' to me?
- Em..yes...Hi, Martin, I'm calling from JWT Spain.
- You talkin' to me?
- Yes. We'd like to propose a project to you, for Freixenet. (Sparkling wine called Cava here, you know...).
- You talkin' to me?
- Yes I am. Would you be interested? Maybe... I haven't made myself clear.
- You talkin' to me?
- (...)
- You talkin' to me?

08084G

Ryan Kutscher, Paul Caiozzo
Crispin Porter + Bogusky/Miami

What would happen if one day America's favorite burger just went away? What happened was the Whopper Freakout.

It was a social experiment in which hidden cameras were installed in a BK franchise. They filmed the candid reactions of customers who were told that the Whopper was discontinued. The resulting content was released in a variety of integrated media, including TV, radio, and the Web, and an eight-minute documentary which was screened at whopperfreakout.com.

In the wake of Whopper Freakout, sales of the Whopper increased by 29%. Whopper Freakout became the most-recalled campaign in IAG history. The site received 4 million views by mid-March, simultaneously becoming a pop-culture and marketing success.

08083G

David Carter, Greg Hahn, Mike Smith, Brian DiLorenzo
BBDO/New York

Thank you One Show for this award and legitimizing our perversions.

08085G

Scott Duchon, John Patroulis
T.A.G. + McCann Worldgroup/San Francisco

We believed a 7-foot-2-inch golden-armored video game character could be seen as a hero for humanity.

And then did everything we could to help the rest of the world believe it, too.

08040R

David Eastman
The Richards Group/Dallas

What I was going for in this spot was a sense of childlike innocence with a subtext of man's eternal struggle against ennui and stuff. I think I got it.

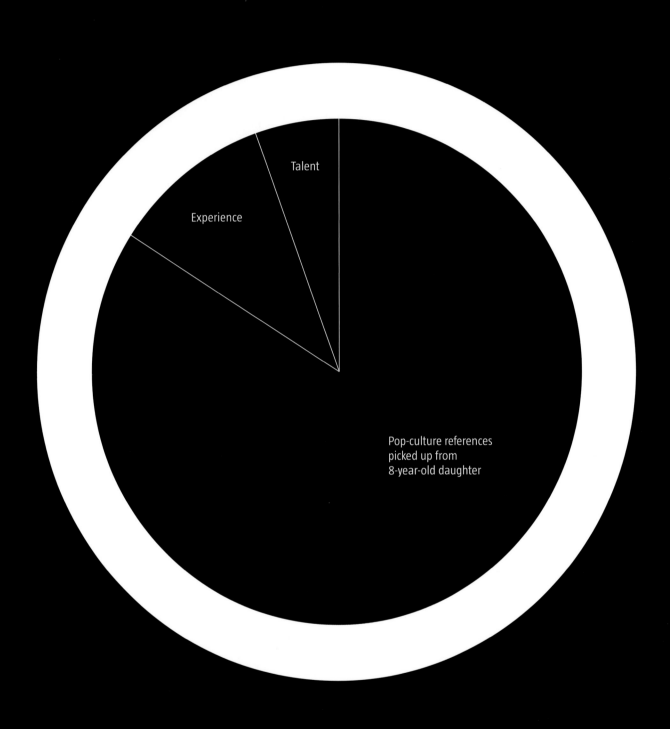

Talent

Experience

Pop-culture references
picked up from
8-year-old daughter

08029A
Toronto Humane Society
Paul Belford
This is Real Art/London

How can a humble piece of low-budget print compete with today's multi-million dollar, global, interactive Web 2.0, fully-integrated multimedia, branded entertainment extravaganzas?

By being wonderfully art directed, written, illustrated and designed. That's how. Congratulations to the team.

08036T
Epuron/German Ministry for the Environment
Norman Tan
Bates/Shanghai

It's hard to select a single favorite work out of so many great works in the show. But when I walked out of the judging room, this one stayed with me for the longest time: "Power of Wind" for Epuron/German Ministry for the Environment.

I was very involved with the storytelling.
I was curious.
The humor made me smile, and at the same time I was touched by it.
The casting, execution and the hint is brilliant.
The copywriting is insightful and emotional.
I watched the story with full attention.
The most important thing was, I was very convinced with the message.

It was surprising and honest, and it worked for me.

That's why I love it.

08050T
Cadbury
Nick Spahr
Goodby, Silverstein and Partners/San Francisco

There are a few things floating around at the top of my favorite pile, but the one that I keep wanting to watch again and again is the Cadbury "Gorilla" spot. It is mesmerizing. Some people may complain that it's too indulgent or that it doesn't make sense, and maybe that's part of why I do like it. I mean, what do you really need to know about chocolate? It's brown. And it's delicious. Just like gorillas.

08083G
HBO

Filip Nilsson
Forsman & Bodenfors/Stockholm

The "Top Ten List" made me very happy. At least six or seven of those pieces were big, bold and truly innovative ideas and I had to think twice before the discussion about Best of Show took off.

Now, thinking back, one campaign pops up before the others. And that is HBO Voyeur.

Everybody talks about integration today. Very few people know what it really means. We are drowning in media stunts. Fake news. Fake road movies. Fake companies. Fake everything.

HBO Voyeur is the opposite of that. It's for real. A brand that creates an interesting, beautiful and totally relevant happening in the middle of New York and then manages to take that experience one step further on the Web —what do you say? Congratulations.

08085G
Xbox

Adriana Cury
McCann Erickson/Brazil

There has never been a multi-disciplinary campaign that was so in accordance with its theme: BELIEVE.

I confess that, while analyzing the work entirely, sometimes I wondered if the battle between humanity and the alien civilization did not in fact exist.

They created such a powerful environment around the game, it's hard not to feel touched by the messages.

They set up a museum with a war-like background. There are testimonies of supposed former veterans that are old already, recalling battles, the artillery they used, the most memorable scenes told in detail. A black-and-white photo exhibit illustrates the battle.

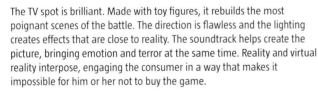

The TV spot is brilliant. Made with toy figures, it rebuilds the most poignant scenes of the battle. The direction is flawless and the lighting creates effects that are close to reality. The soundtrack helps create the picture, bringing emotion and terror at the same time. Reality and virtual reality interpose, engaging the consumer in a way that makes it impossible for him or her not to buy the game.

Joe De Souza
Fallon/London

For me, the most compelling piece of work at the One Show was the *Halo 3* "Believe" campaign. It's a huge, multi-layered idea—future/fictional war veterans —one that transcends conventional video game communications (and most other advertising messages) to create a believable narrative, populated by convincing characters and imbued with real emotions. Perhaps I like the work because of the beautiful and meticulous execution. Or maybe I like it because it echoes events going on in the world around us right now. Either way, it's an inspirational campaign that raises the bar for agencies and clients alike.

Ian Reichenthal
Y&R/New York

Every year in the *One Show* annual, there's that one judge in the Judges Choice section who uncovers a great ad that the rest of the jury somehow overlooked. A small space newspaper ad or something that's simple and brilliant but somehow went unrecognized. The judges who find those ads always seem so smart and unique. I wanted to be that judge this year, I really did. But instead, here I am on the same page with everyone else who loved Xbox 360 *Halo 3* "Believe." The moment I saw it, I thought it was the best thing of the year, and nothing that I saw the rest of the year, or while judging the show, made me feel otherwise. It's so different for the category. It told me everything I needed to know about the game without one screenshot. Every one of the hundreds of miniature models was a painstaking work of art in itself. The music was perfect. And on top of all of that, it really made me want to play *Halo 3*. The nomination process for Best of Show was less of a debate and more of a gigantic, unanimous, and well-deserved love festival for this campaign.

Ted Royer
Droga5/New York

I watched the *Halo 3* "Believe" spot 20 times. Not as a judge, but because I wanted to. I saw something new each time. And, you know what? It's actually funny! To be that serious, morbid and moving about a video game filled with aliens is ultimately hilarious. A level to the work no one's even mentioned yet. Clearly my favorite piece this year.

08084G
Burger King

Chris Adams
TBWA\Chiat\Day/Los Angeles

"Whopper Freakout" was it for me. A brave idea, for a big brand, flawlessly executed, that took a low-interest product and made it somehow incredibly relevant. And it's a fantastic use of media to boot. I can imagine hundreds of reasons why most clients would kill this campaign, and thousands of ways that the agency could have fumbled the production. "Freakout" does the two things I think a great campaign should do: it rewards the client for taking a chance, and it makes me want to do my job better. Congrats to the King.

James McGrath
Clemenger BBDO/Melbourne

This was the year of the greatest, most generous acts by clients.

A year where they allowed not just the creative idea to create an extraordinary vulnerability, but allowed their product to be dangerously involved as well.

There were a number of these campaigns, but the finest was "Whopper Freakout." They took away something really important to prove its true value.

Kai Roeffen
TBWA\Duesseldorf

It is a new and innovative way of thinking and of advertising. Brilliantly executed in a professional candid camera kind of way. They did not put the hero-product on a platform like advertising usually does—they did the opposite. They made the hero-product unavailable.

That is such a great and strong idea. The customers' statements and reactions are the best advertising Burger King could get. It is authentic and because of that, believable. It is cheeky, provoking, bold, funny—simply genial.

08087G
UNICEF Tap Project

Glenn Cole
72andSunny/El Segundo

Favorite work from this year's show: The Tap Project. It shows the way forward. It is actionable, scalable, comprehensive, smart, fun, cool, beautiful, inspiring, simple...the list goes on. The only failure would be allowing it to remain a once-a-year NYC thing. It deserves and requires ubiquity.

Elspeth Lynn
Zig/Toronto

Ideas that I loved:
- 15 below coat for the homeless
- HBO Voyeur integrated campaign
- Careerbuilder.com "Larry" TV
- London Ink installations
- Burger King "Whopper Freakout" integrated campaign
- League of Evil Net10 campaign
- IKEA personalized catalogue covers
- Sony "Play-Doh" TV
- The idea I loved the most: The Tap Project. Brilliant. An idea that the world can admire, and participate in.

Beth Ryan
BBH/New York

The Tap Project changed the way I look at and think about advertising. Hands down, it was the best idea I saw this year.

Rob Strasberg
Doner/Southfield

The Tap Project. It's an idea that should outlive us all.

Nancy Vonk
Ogilvy/Toronto

The Tap Project is my top choice this year. The simplicity and intelligence of this inspired idea, and its dramatic demonstration of creative problem solving should redefine the role of ad agency. It created awareness of the clean water crisis while presenting a meaningful solution, setting it apart from most well-intended social marketing. And there's hope in the world when a Droga5 idea is implemented globally by competing agencies that park their egos and apply their brain cells to helping the planet.

08088G
Kraft - Diamond Shreddies
Paul Hirsch
Hirsch/Denberg/Chicago

There was a lot to like at the show this year: *Halo 3*, HBO Voyeur, "Whopper Freakout," Tap Project, Levi's, and WK-12's book. But I wanted to laugh and since no spot had anyone getting kicked in the nuts (Buckley's was close), my favorite piece was O&M Toronto's "Diamond Shreddies." One of the best things to come out of Canada since Loverboy.

I like it because it's sly and subversive, yet rewards those who think. I like it because it extends a big middle finger to testing as non-thinking gospel (see the Hatch Awards' "1984" for more goodness). And I love it because the client actually had the balls to run this campaign instead of some of the mind-numbing work that is done by their counterparts in the States. It's pretty genius. Congrats to everyone who worked on this campaign.

Paul Keister
Goodness Mfg/Venice

Diamond Shreddies is freakin' genius. The moment I saw this, jealousy and rage entered my body. They took a pretty mundane category and an even more mundane segment of that category and created a compelling symbol of re-evaluation. Simply by starting with the product and turning it 45 degrees, their big idea was able to stretch into every conceivable form of media, including packaging. Then on top of that, they invite consumers to be a part of this technological feat of cereal engineering. Such a strategically smart idea that even has me rethinking whole-wheat cereal again.

Steve Mapp
Butler, Shine, Stern and Partners/Sausalito

The level of craft and detail that went into the *Halo 3* campaign was truly impressive, and the Burger King "Whopper Freakout" campaign was stupid smart, but the Diamond Shreddies work impressed me the most. It was a great idea that required involvement from both the agency and the client to pull off. It is creative to do television spots about a square cereal accidentally being turned 45 degrees and calling it diamond-shaped. Convincing a packaged-goods client to be brave enough to go along with you and repackage their product, however...that deserves two Pencils!

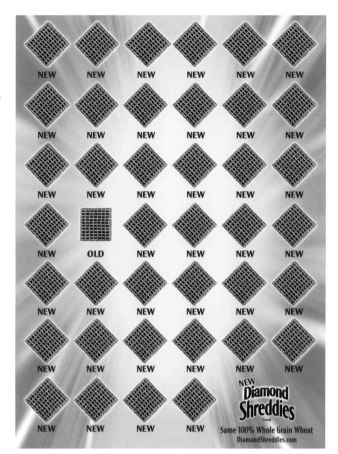

08055T
Procter & Gamble
Masako Okamura
Dentsu/Tokyo

Although we live in the age of 360-degree advertising, I cannot help but pick this 30-second TV spot. Because I always have sesame seeds stuck between my teeth or something like that, clients are sometimes more fascinated with that than listening to me. Nice idea with keen human insight. It had me smiling the whole time. "Silence the Stain" works well. Just decided to point this copy out as a brilliant example to my students at the university! The art of the TVC is alive!

Judge's Choice **111**

08089T

Freixenet

Andy Azula
The Martin Agency/Richmond

Yes, "The Key to Reserva" is incredibly long. But it's also incredibly brilliant. The beginning is like any typical Christopher Guest mockumentary. But it's the follow through and attention to detail that really sells it. Of course, it helps that Scorsese directed it (it was a good year for him, as he acted in another Gold Pencil-winning spot this year). Anyway, any "film" that actually gets me to go online and look up an extremely hard-to-spell champagne gets my vote.

Marty Cooke
SS+K/New York

Martin Scorsese is wearing surgical gloves. He's gingerly handling three-and-a-half pages of a recently discovered Alfred Hitchcock screenplay that was never shot. In the ultimate act of film preservation, he's going to preserve a film that never existed. And Scorsese being Scorsese, he does it flawlessly. Period styling. That wonderful old saturated Technicolor look. And a man falling off a balcony that's straight out of *Vertigo*. All for a cheap Spanish sparkling wine called Freixenet. This is branded entertainment of the first order.

Andy Greenaway
Saatchi & Saatchi/Singapore

I thought this was a remarkable piece of communication which signals a strong shift to what I believe to be an emerging trend in the world of communication: the closer collaboration between the advertising industry and Hollywood—and possibly a true convergence in years to come. The concept was original, the screenwriting was masterly, the production values impeccable and the acting top notch (Scorsese is as a good a thespian as he is a director). It is one of those pieces you can watch again and again.

Arno Lindemann
Lukas Lindemann Rosinski/Hamburg

The film fan Martin Scorsese, a brilliant actor and director, shot a wonderfully executed Alfred Hitchcock stylish short film, which had a great idea and a nice and discreet twist to Freixenet at the end.

Eric Silver
BBDO/New York

In the TV category, Burger King's "Whopper Freakout" is simple and smart. I absolutely love Coke's "It's Mine" spot, where the floats at the parade compete for the bottle. But, if I have to pick one, it's a commercial called "Key to Reserva" for Freixenet. Martin Scorsese shoots 3-and-a-half pages of a mysterious lost Hitchcock script. It's just over 9 minutes long. Go find it on YouTube. It is brilliant.

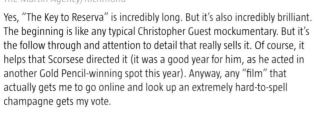

08373T
Monster.com
Bob Barrie
Barrie D'Rozario Murphy/Minneapolis

OK, two surprises: I chose a TV commercial, not an interactive viral content-driven new media game-changer. And, I chose an entry that didn't even make it into the One Show as a single entry, although it apparently squeaked through as part of a campaign.

The story, elegantly told: We see a stork carrying a newborn baby through a long gauntlet of great distance, oppressive weather, rough terrain, threats from predators, raging oceans, you get the idea. He delivers his package to a thrilled young couple. Cut ahead to thirty years in the future. The baby, now a grown man, is wasting away at a menial desk job late at night. His delivery stork appears at the office window. They exchange a long, poignant stare. The stork looks disappointed, bows its head, and flies off into the night. Supers at end: "Are you reaching your potential? Monster. Your calling is calling." (Monster.com, for those of you from other lands, is a job recruitment resource.)

This spot still sticks with me, months later. It actually made jaded, old me stop and consider whether I was fully living up to my abilities. I even wondered whether the kind souls who saw me through my early years would be proud of what I've become. I imagine thousands of others did the same. And that's one hell of a lot to ask from a TV commercial. Or even an interactive viral content-driven new media game-changer.

7227
Scott Towels
Yang Yeo
JWT/Shanghai

As we focus our attention on innovative/integrated/non-traditional mediums, I'd like to devert your attention to a traditional print campaign for Scotts kitchen towel — "Oil," "Wine," and "Coffee."

Although I'm a huge fan of the Xbox's *Halo 3* and HBO's Voyeur campaigns, quietly in my heart lurks the Scotts print ads I remembered judging and loved. The idea is simple, yet very clever. No frills executions, yet they feel fresh. And the best part, the product benefit is crystal clear and I'm left absolutely convinced. Ads at their best.

As the industry is quickly running out of great print ideas (as reflected in the judging and this annual), it's refreshing to see the Scotts campaign, which is truly original.

Print Merit

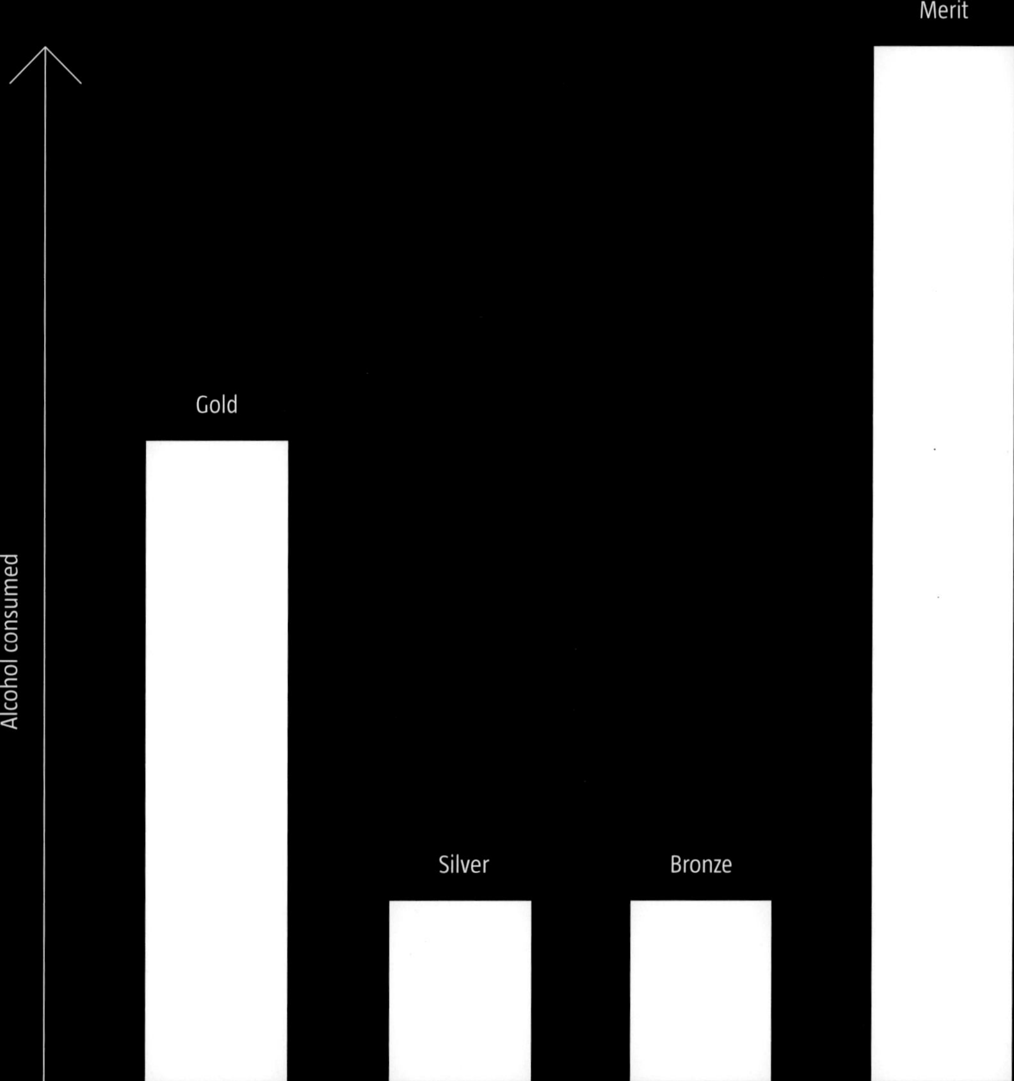

Alcohol consumed

Merit

Gold

Silver

Bronze

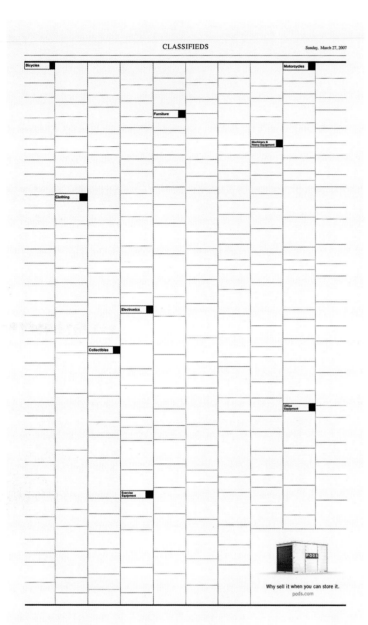

Merit

Newspaper Full Page or Spread, *Single*

Art Director Dámaso Crespo
Writer Dámaso Crespo
Photographer Studio Fuster
Creative Director Antonio López
Client Procter & Gamble - Tide
Agency Conill Saatchi & Saatchi/New York
Annual ID 08100A

Merit

Newspaper Full Page or Spread, *Single*

Art Director Dámaso Crespo
Writer Dámaso Crespo
Photographer Studio Fuster
Creative Director Antonio López
Client Procter & Gamble - Tide
Agency Conill Saatchi & Saatchi/New York
Annual ID 08101A

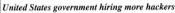
Merit

Newspaper Full Page or Spread, *Single*

Art Director Tim Green
Writer Tim Cairns
Photographer George Scott
Creative Director Matt Eastwood
Client Hasbro
Agency DDB/Sydney
Annual ID 08102A

Merit

Newspaper Full Page or Spread, *Single*

Art Directors Jay Marsen, Alexei Beltrone
Writers Alexei Beltrone, Jay Marsen
Creative Director Sal DeVito
Client Legal Sea Foods
Agency DeVito/Verdi/New York
Annual ID 08103A

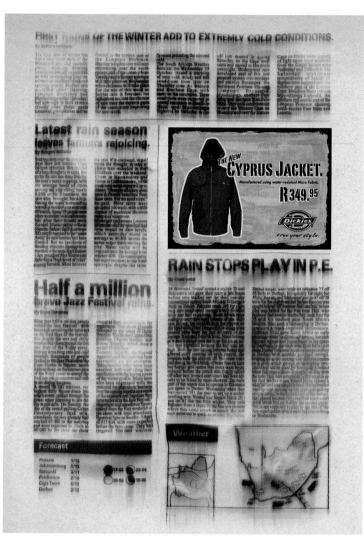

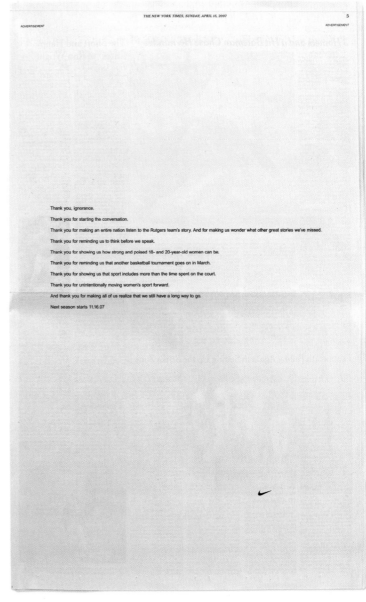

Merit

Newspaper Full Page or Spread, *Single*

Art Directors Ashidiq Ghazali, Adrian Chan, Eric Yeo, Andrew Goh
Writers Troy Lim, Serene Loong
Photographer Jimmy Fok
Creative Director Todd McCracken
Client FHM
Agency Ogilvy/Singapore
Annual ID 08107A

Merit

Newspaper Full Page or Spread, *Single*

Writer Sheena Brady
Creative Directors Jeff Williams, Alberto Ponte
Client Nike
Agency Wieden+Kennedy/Portland
Annual ID 08108A

YOU CAN'T KNOW EVERYTHING ABOUT EVERYTHING

The Economist

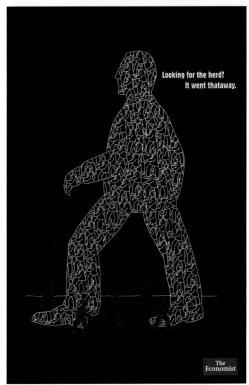

Looking for the herd?
It went thataway.

The Economist

Merit

Merit

Newspaper Full Page or Spread, *Campaign*

Art Director Paul Cohen
Writer Mark Fairbanks
Illustrators Non-Format, Mick Marston, Seymour Chwast
Creative Director Paul Brazier
Client The Economist
Agency Abbott Mead Vickers BBDO/London
Annual ID 08109A

ALSO AWARDED
✎ Merit Magazine Full Page or Spread, *Single*
✎ Merit Magazine Full Page or Spread, *Campaign*

VII

You're **selective** about which **books** you **read**, shouldn't you be as **discerning** about which **words**?

So MANY BOOKS, SO LITTLE TIME. Last year, there were over 360 **thousand books** published. (And those are just the ones printed in English.) I wonder how many little orphan novels are gathering dust on your bookshelves right now. With an **average reading speed** of 210wpm, it would take you roughly 12 hours to read a 300 page novel. But here's an idea, what if those books had only 150 pages each. You'd be able to read them twice as fast right. Truth is, those eyes of yours can see a lot more than you think. *It's all a matter of selective reading.* By just identifying key words as you go, you not only pick up the big picture ideas, but also dramatically improve your reading speed. So while you are breezing over the pages, your eyes are hunting for key words and your brain automatically fills in the rest.

Admittedly, it's not the best way to read a book, but the information is enough for you to get the idea.

The next big step is training your eyes to move over the page at a faster pace. And while this takes a little practice, you can learn to skim over words, sentences, and later full paragraphs. Scanning through a page like this takes a little getting used to of course. But it's easy once you get the hang of it. Taking a few minutes to flip through the book beforehand can make all the difference. It's the same reason why racecar drivers like to walk the track before the race. To see what's coming before they get to it. The idea is to map out the road ahead so you will know just what to pay attention to, and what to ignore. Every author structures their writing differently. But writers are usually good enough to give us little clues along the way. Like words in bold for instance. What more could you ask for? It's also a good practice to make sure you pay close attention to the first and last sentence of every paragraph. Think of them as literary bookends.

If you're an avid reader, you'll notice that the more words you know, the less time you'll need to spend on them. And that's where you make up the most time. After a while, your autopilot kicks in and it becomes second nature. It is rumoured that advanced students can take in a whole page at a time. With that kind of speed, you can plow through your private library in no time at all. But let's first start with a few sentences and take it from there. Sadly, most people haven't improved their vocabulary or their reading speed since they were old enough to drive. An average reader can read between 100-210wpm. Advanced readers can read over 800wpm. Doubling your current reading speed is easier than it sounds. If you're ready to make that first bold step to reading faster, try logging into our *website** below and see just how fast you are. If you're keen on improving your reading speed from there, just meet us half way and enroll in one of our upcoming seminars to help get you on your way. It's a lot easier than it looks. And with just a little practice, you can clear that bookshelf in no time at all.

96

[*] To check your current reading speed just log on to www.readbetterfaster.com or call us at [65] 9046 3952

III

You don't have to right order the read in to get the message whole.

XI

The voice in your head can only read at 210wpm. Time to silence the middleman.

XV

Double your reading speed by reading half as much.

Merit

Newspaper Full Page or Spread, *Campaign*

Art Director Chris Tan
Writer Robert Gaxiola
Creative Directors Robert Gaxiola, Paul Soady
Client Read Better Faster
Agency Batey/Singapore
Annual ID 08110A

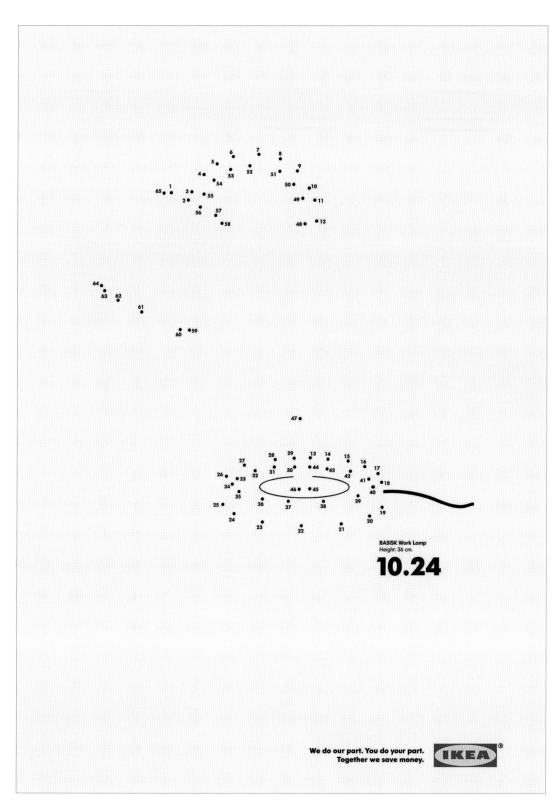

BASISK Work Lamp
Height: 36 cm.

10.24

We do our part. You do your part.
Together we save money. **IKEA**®

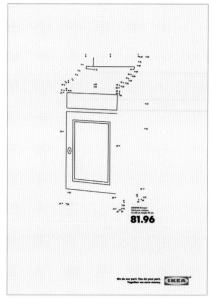

81.96

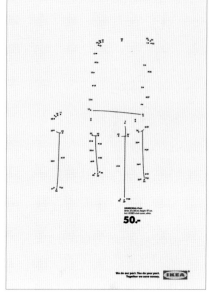

50.-

Merit

Newspaper Full Page or Spread, *Campaign*

Art Directors Djik Ouchiian, Tobias Haack
Writers Martin Grass, Ole Lisberg
Illustrator Tobias Haack
Creative Directors Ralf Heuel, Dirk Siebenhaar
Client IKEA Deutschland
Agency Grabarz & Partner/Hamburg
Annual ID 08111A

Merit

Newspaper Full Page or Spread, *Campaign*

Art Director Oliver Zboralski
Writer Constantin Sossidi
Illustrator Sugar Power c/o Margarethe Hubauer
Creative Directors Ralf Heuel, Ralf Nolting, Patricia Pätzold
Client Volkswagen
Agency Grabarz & Partner/Hamburg
Annual ID 08112A

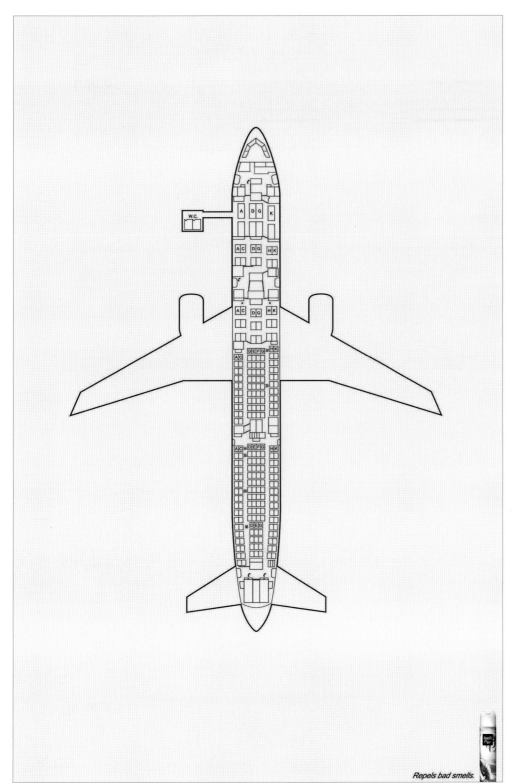

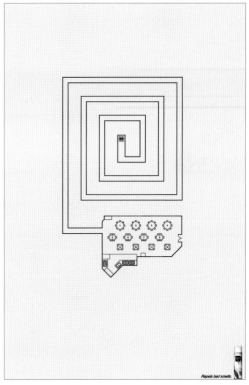

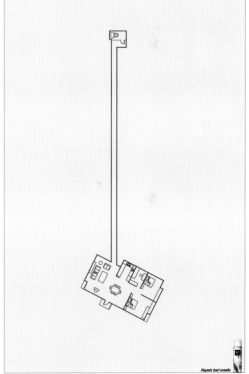

Merit

Newspaper Full Page or Spread, *Campaign*

Art Director Ming Chan
Writers Timothy Chan, Paul Chan
Illustrator Raymond Kong
Creative Directors Keith Ho, Timothy Chan, Ming Chan
Client Sara Lee Hong Kong
Agency Grey/Hong Kong
Annual ID 08113A

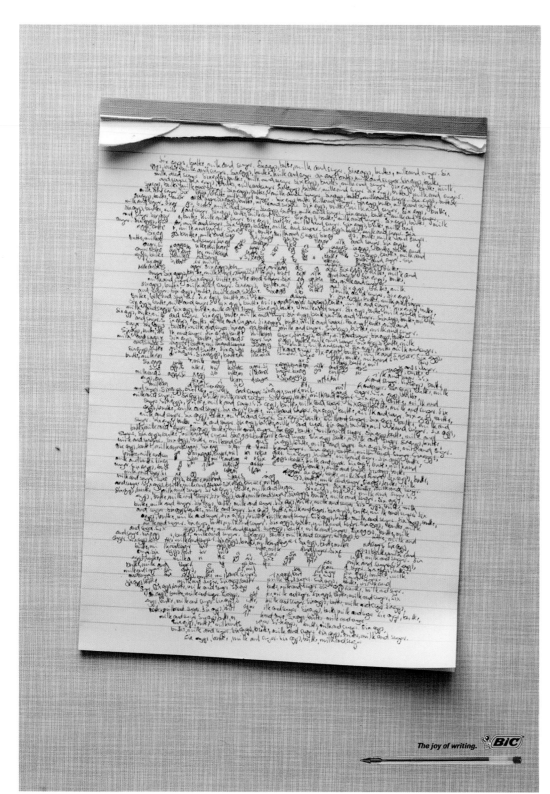
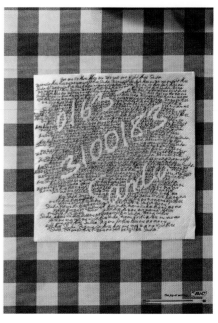
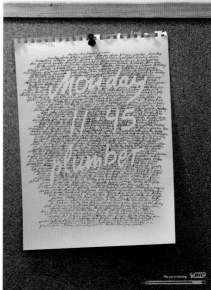

Merit

Newspaper Full Page or Spread, *Campaign*

Writer Nicolas Linde
Photographer Dan Zoubek
Illustrator Duc Nguyen
Creative Directors Wolfgang Schneider, Mathias Stiller, David Mously, Jan Harbeck
Client BIC Deutschland
Agency Jung von Matt/Berlin
Annual ID 08114A

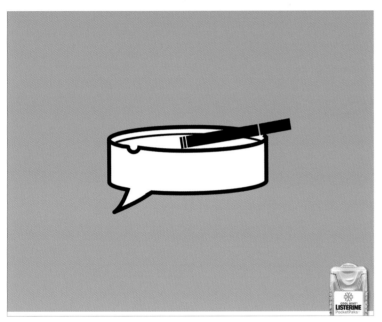
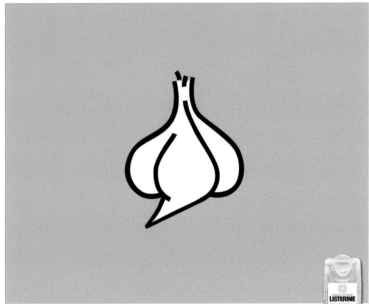

Merit

Newspaper Full Page or Spread, *Campaign*

Art Director Johanna Santiago
Writer Miguel Fernández
Creative Director Jaime Rosado
Client Johnson & Johnson - Listerine Pocket Paks
Agency JWT/San Juan
Annual ID 08115A

Merit

Newspaper Full Page or Spread, *Campaign*

Art Director Simon Morris
Writer Patrick McClelland
Designers Dave Towers, Sebastien Delahaye
Illustrator David Lawrence
Creative Director Ed Morris
Client InBev
Agency Lowe/London
Annual ID 08116A

ALSO AWARDED

✐ Merit Magazine Full Page or Spread, *Campaign*

Merit

Newspaper Full Page or Spread, *Campaign*

Art Directors Porakit Tanwattana, Rotrob Ramakomut, Supon Khaotong, Peerapat Peeraman
Writers Wesley Hsu, Kittinan Sawasdee, Piya Churarakpong
Photographers Anuchai Secharunputong, Nok Pipattungkul
Creative Directors Supon Khaotong, Kittinan Sawasdee, Piya Churarakpong, Peerapat Peeraman
Client Ogawa Electric
Agency Lowe/Bangkok
Annual ID 08117A

ALSO AWARDED

✎ Merit Magazine Full Page or Spread, *Campaign*
✎ Merit Collateral Posters, *Campaign*

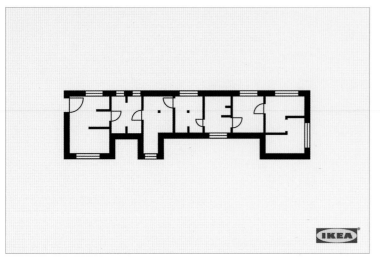

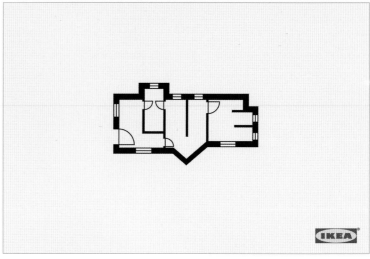

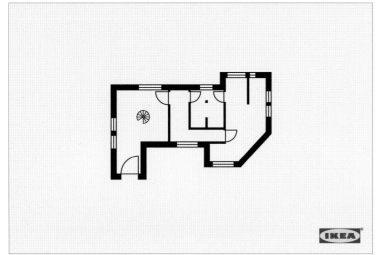

Merit
Newspaper Full Page or Spread, *Campaign*

Art Directors Szymon Rose, Markus Kremer
Writer Thomas Heyen
Creative Directors Arno Lindemann, Bernhard Lukas, Tom Hauser
Client IKEA Deutschland
Agency Lukas Lindemann Rosinski/Hamburg
Annual ID 08118A

ALSO AWARDED
✎ Merit Outdoor, *Campaign*

Merit

Newspaper Full Page or Spread, *Campaign*

Art Director Wong Shu Kor
Writers Ted Lim, Grenville Francis
Photographer Jesse Choo
Creative Director Ted Lim
Client PST Travel Services
Agency Naga DDB/Petaling Jaya
Annual ID 08119A

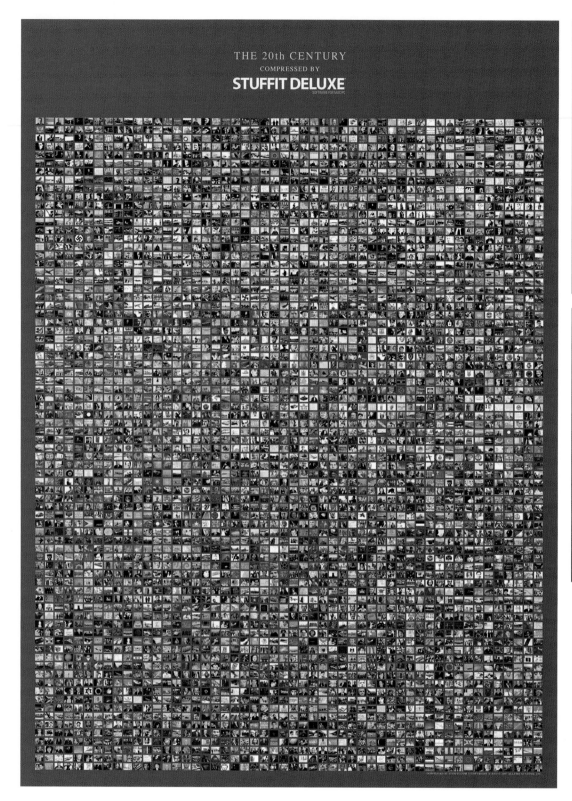

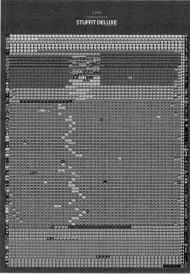

Merit

Newspaper Full Page or Spread, *Campaign*

Art Director **Menno Kluin**
Writer **Icaro Doria**
Creative Directors **Tony Granger, Jan Jacobs, Leo Premutico**
Client **Smith Micro Software**
Agency **Saatchi & Saatchi/New York**
Annual ID **08120A**

Merit

Newspaper Full Page or Spread, *Campaign*

Art Directors Amani Qian, Susie Sun, Lang Nie, Zheng Xia, Elvis Chau
Writers Michelle Wu, Nicky Zhang, Sarawut Hengsawad, Lesley Zhou
Photographer Mark Zibert
Illustrator Ming Lu
Creative Directors Lesley Zhou, Sarawut Hengsawad, Elvis Chau, John Merrifield, Yang Yeo
Client adidas
Agency TBWA\China/Shanghai (180\TBWA)
Annual ID 08121A

WHAT PARIS WOULD HAVE TO DO TO GET INTO THE MAIL & GUARDIAN.

100 MILLION PEOPLE REPORTED TO HAVE DOWNLOADED VIDEO CLIP OF PARIS FLASHING HER "KITTY BASKET".

IN WORLD EXCLUSIVE, CARTER BROTHER SAYS HE IS SHOCKED SHE'S A BRUNETTE. "IT WAS BLONDE WHEN I SAW IT."

"IT LOOKS TO ME LIKE SHE'S HAD VAGINOPLASTY," SAYS PLASTIC SURGEON TO THE STARS IN TELL-ALL INTERVIEW.

CELEBRITY PR SVENGALI CLAIMS PARIS "CAN GET A LOT OF MILEAGE OUT OF EXPOSING HER HOO-HOO TO THE WORLD".

PARIS "TOO TRAUMATISED TO GET OUT OF BED" ACCORDING TO SOURCE CLOSE TO A "FRIEND".

PARIS FLASHES HER VA-JAY-JAY GETTING OUT OF A LIMO.

BOTTLES OF HER NEW FRAGRANCE, "AIR-RESS", ARE "FLYING OFF SHELVES," SAYS HER PUBLICIST.

MOM DEFENDS PARIS ON TALK SHOW, SAYS EVERYONE IS "JEALOUS".

PARIS-ENDORSED RANGE OF CROTCHLESS PANTIES HITS NATION'S SHELVES.

M&G DECLINES STORY

"WE DRANK CHAMPAGNE & MADE LOVE IN A PORT-A-LOO," SAYS PORN STAR.

"BULIMIC PARIS" RUMOURS APPEAR ON GOSSIP BLOGS AND WOMEN'S GLOSSIES.

"I DON'T DRINK OR DO DRUGS, LIKE, EVER," CLAIMS PARIS ON LATE-NIGHT CHAT SHOW.

PARIS VOMITS IN A NIGHTCLUB.

PUBLICIST CLAIMS SHE "JUST HAD A REALLY BAD REACTION TO HER NEW ASTHMA MEDICATION".

"SHE WAS SO DRUNK SHE SOILED THE BACKSEAT OF MY TAXI CAB," CLAIMS TAXI DRIVER IN $10-MILLION LAWSUIT.

PARIS AND NICOLE NO LONGER FRIENDS AFTER NICOLE SENDS PARIS A BILL FOR "CLEANING VOMIT OFF MY JIMMY CHOOS".

PAPARAZZI GET SHOT OF MYSTERY GREEK HEIR PUNCHING AN ONLOOKER AND HELPING A LEGLESS PARIS INTO A TAXI.

ACCORDING TO A FRIEND, PARIS "WANTS TO BE TAKEN SERIOUSLY LIKE THE PRESIDENT OF AFRICA, MANDELA".

M&G PUBLISHES AN ARTICLE ABOUT THE ALLEGED CORRUPTION AT THE NELSON MANDELA CHILDREN'S FUND.

Mail & Guardian — REAL NEWS

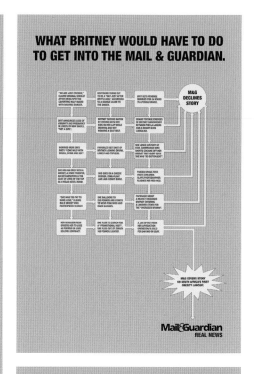

WHAT BRITNEY WOULD HAVE TO DO TO GET INTO THE MAIL & GUARDIAN.

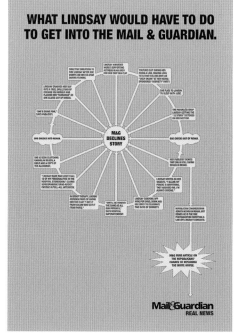

WHAT LINDSAY WOULD HAVE TO DO TO GET INTO THE MAIL & GUARDIAN.

Merit

Newspaper Full Page or Spread, *Campaign*

Art Director Nadja Lossgott
Writers Nicholas Hulley, Deon Wiggett
Creative Directors Nicholas Hulley, Damon Stapleton
Client Mail & Guardian
Agency TBWA\Hunt\Lascaris - Johannesburg/Sandton
Annual ID 08122A

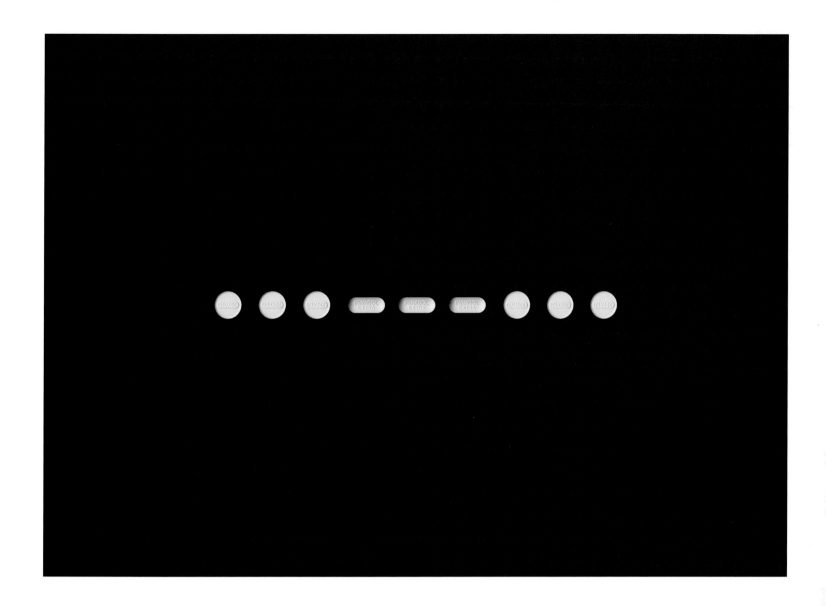

Merit

Magazine Black and White, Full Page or Spread, *Single*

Art Director Mo Chong
Writer Suchitra Gahlot
Photographer Bob Anderson
Creative Director Paul Anderson
Client GlaxoSmithKline
Agency Ogilvy/Singapore
Annual ID 08123A

On the left: Marie Curie, first woman awarded with a Nobel prize. MTV MUSIC TELEVISION

On the left: Alexander Graham Bell, inventor of the telephone. MTV

Merit

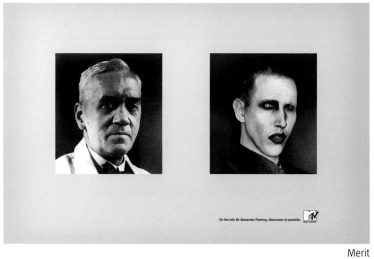

On the left: Sir Alexander Fleming, discoverer of penicillin. MTV

Merit

Merit
Magazine Black and White, Full Page or Spread, *Campaign*

Art Director Alejandro Sibilla
Writer Rodrigo Ruiz
Designer Daniel Romanos
Photographers Latinstock Argentina, Fernando Costanza
Creative Directors Guillermo Vega, Juan Frontini
Client MTV Latinoamerica
Agency Young & Rubicam/Buenos Aires
Annual ID 08126A

ALSO AWARDED
✎ Merit Magazine Black and White, Full Page or Spread, *Single*
✎ Merit Magazine Black and White, Full Page or Spread, *Single*

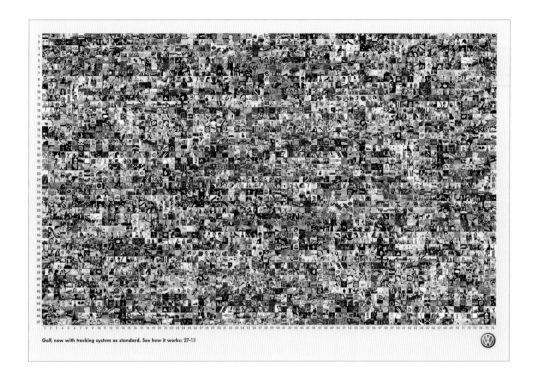

Merit

Magazine Color, Full Page or Spread, *Single*

Art Director **Gustavo Victorino**
Writer **Cesar Herszkowicz**
Creative Directors **Rodrigo Almeida, Tales Bahu**
Client **Volkswagen**
Agency **AlmapBBDO/São Paulo**
Annual ID **08129A**

ALSO AWARDED

✐ Merit Collateral P.O.P. and In-Store, *Single*

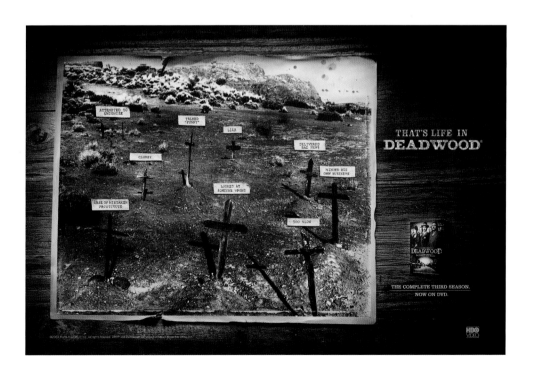

Merit

Magazine Color, Full Page or Spread, *Single*

Art Director **Crystal English**
Writer **Paul Johnson**
Creative Directors **Greg Bell, Paul Venables**
Client **HBO Video**
Agency **Venables Bell and Partners/San Francisco**
Annual ID **08130A**

Merit

Magazine Color, Full Page or Spread, *Single*

Art Director **Crystal English**
Writer **Paul Johnson**
Creative Directors **Greg Bell, Paul Venables**
Client **HBO Video**
Agency **Venables Bell and Partners/San Francisco**
Annual ID **08131A**

Merit

Magazine Color, Full Page or Spread, *Single*

Art Director **John Terry**
Writer **James Ansley**
Photographer **Philip Rostron**
Creative Directors **Ian MacKellar, Jack Neary**
Client **Chrysler Canada**
Agency **BBDO/Toronto**
Annual ID **08132A**

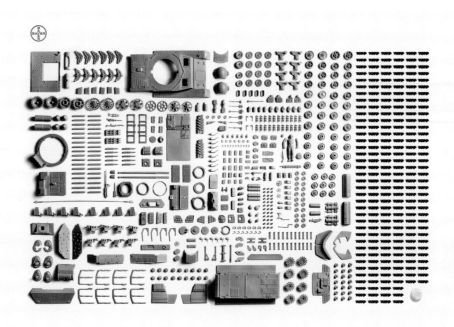

Merit

Magazine Color, Full Page or Spread, *Single*

Art Director Arief Budiman
Writer Awaluddin Rusdiansyah
Designer Agus Santoso
Photographer Mike Ting
Creative Director Didit Indra
Client PT Bayer Indonesia
Agency BBDO Indonesia/Jakarta
Annual ID 08133A

Merit

Magazine Color, Full Page or Spread, *Single*

Art Directors John Figone, Simon Tuplin, Adam Nelson
Writers Jim Dipiazza, Ben Purcell, Jenn Hertzig
Creative Directors David Angelo, Colin Jeffery
Client Cazadores
Agency davidandgoliath/El Segundo
Annual ID 08134A

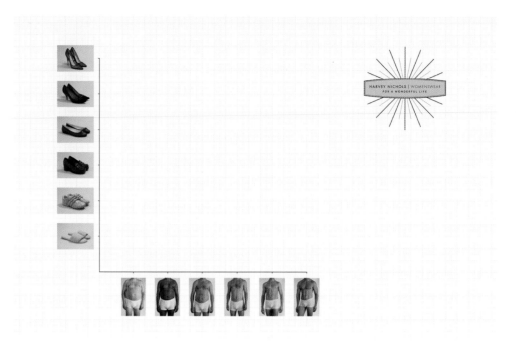

Merit

Magazine Color, Full Page or Spread, *Single*

Art Directors Grant Parker, Joanna Wenley
Writers Joanna Wenley, Grant Parker
Photographers Beate Sonnenberg, Wayne Parker
Client Harvey Nichols
Agency DDB/London
Annual ID 08135A

Merit

Magazine Color, Full Page or Spread, *Single*

Art Director Noah Davis
Writer Henry Mathieu
Creative Directors Christoph Becker, Rodd Chant, Terri Meyer, Sandy Greenberg
Client Kraft
Agency DraftFCB/New York
Annual ID 08136A

Merit

Magazine Color, Full Page or Spread, *Single*

Art Director Brandon Henderson
Writer Karl Lieberman
Creative Director Jeff Kling
Client Dos Equis
Agency Euro RSCG Worldwide/New York
Annual ID 08137A

Merit

Magazine Color, Full Page or Spread, *Single*

Art Director Kathrin Seupel
Photographers Annika Rose, Andreas Mock
Creative Directors Timm Hanebeck, Sascha Hanke, Wolf Heumann
Client Robert Bosch
Agency Jung von Matt/Hamburg
Annual ID 08139A

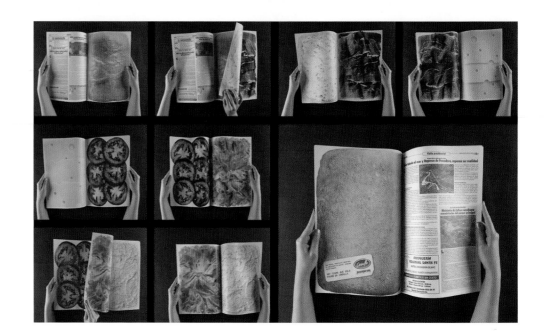

Merit

Magazine Color, Full Page or Spread, *Single*

Art Directors Fernando Reyes, Marcela Fonrodona
Writers Ciro Sarmiento, Andres Lamprea
Creative Directors Juan Posada, John Forero
Client Carulla
Agency Ogilvy & Mather/Bogota
Annual ID 08140A

Merit

Magazine Color, Full Page or Spread, *Single*

Art Directors Daniel Leitão, Guilherme Jahara
Writer Antonio Nogueira
Creative Director Guilherme Jahara
Client Puma
Agency Publicis/São Paulo
Annual ID 08141A

Merit

Magazine Color, Full Page or Spread, *Single*

Art Directors Edmund Choe, Wai Khuen Yee, Gigi Lee
Writers Adrian Miller, Chia Seang Quah
Illustrator Jeann Chew
Creative Directors Edmund Choe, Adrian Miller
Client ACP Magazine
Agency Saatchi & Saatchi/Petaling Jaya
Annual ID 08142A

ALSO AWARDED

✒ Merit Outdoor, *Single*

Merit

Magazine Color, Full Page or Spread, *Single*

Art Directors Sifiso Tshabalala, Liam Wielopolski
Writer Eric Wittstock
Photographer Michael Meyersfeld
Creative Directors Michael Blore, Liam Wielopolski
Client Procter & Gamble - Olay
Agency Saatchi & Saatchi/Johannesburg
Annual ID 08143A

It's the hat.

Merit

Magazine Color, Full Page or Spread, *Single*

Art Director Jonathan Schupp
Writer Francisca Maass
Photographer Jo van de Loo
Creative Directors Alexander Schill, Axel Thomsen
Client Hut Weber
Agency Serviceplan/Munich
Annual ID 08144A

Merit

Magazine Color, Full Page or Spread, *Single*

Art Director Philippe Taroux
Writer Benoit Leroux
Designer Thomas Mangold
Creative Director Erik Vervroegen
Client Sony
Agency TBWA\Paris/Boulogne-Billancourt
Annual ID 08146A

Big Bed   Wide   Turds   Raid

Bug   Buddy   Beat   Nezeril

Available in 0.5 mg/ml, 0.25 mg/ml and 0.1 mg/ml. AstraZeneca Sweden, SE-151 85 Södertälje, www.egenvard.nu Oxymetazoline hydrochloride is a constituent of Nezeril which is a decongestant for treating nasal congestion. Nezeril should be used for a maximum of ten consecutive days.

Merit

Magazine Color, Full Page or Spread, *Single*

Art Directors Lars Holthe, Johan Baettig, Fredrik Joséfsson
Client AstraZeneca/Nezeril
Agency Akestam Holst/Stockholm
Annual ID 08127A

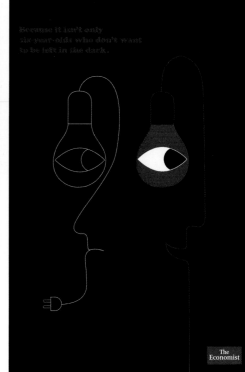

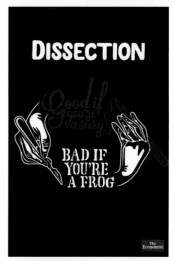

Merit (2)

Merit

Magazine Color, Full Page or Spread, *Campaign*

Art Director Paul Cohen
Writer Mark Fairbanks
Illustrators Geoff McFetridge, Mick Marston, Non-Format, Matthew Green
Creative Director Paul Brazier
Client The Economist
Agency Abbott Mead Vickers BBDO/London
Annual ID 08148A

ALSO AWARDED
✦ Merit Magazine Full Page or Spread, *Single*
✦ Merit Newspaper Full Page or Spread, *Single*

1 2 3 **9** 4 5 6 7 8

With Gollog, it gets there earlier. **Gollog** express
Logistics Management www.gollog.com.br

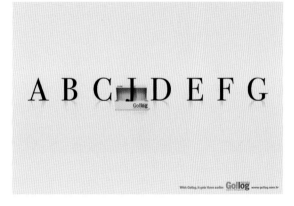

A B C J D E F G

With Gollog, it gets there earlier. Gollog www.gollog.com.br

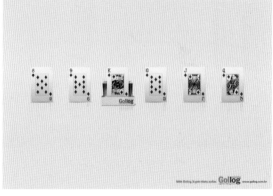

Merit

Magazine Color, Full Page or Spread, *Campaign*

Art Director **Marcos Medeiros**
Writer **Wilson Mateos**
Photographer **Hugo Treu**
Creative Director **Luiz Sanches**
Client **Gol Linhas Areas**
Agency **AlmapBBDO/São Paulo**
Annual ID **08149A**

Merit

Magazine Color, Full Page or Spread, *Campaign*

Art Directors David Seah, Norman Tan
Writers Mike Ludwig, Tinus Strydom, Craig Howie
Photographers Sam Tan, Edwin Ho
Illustrators Nelson Yu, KC Mirage
Creative Directors Norman Tan, Raymond Chan, David Seah
Client Zeal Automobile
Agency BatesAsia/Shanghai
Annual ID 08150A

150

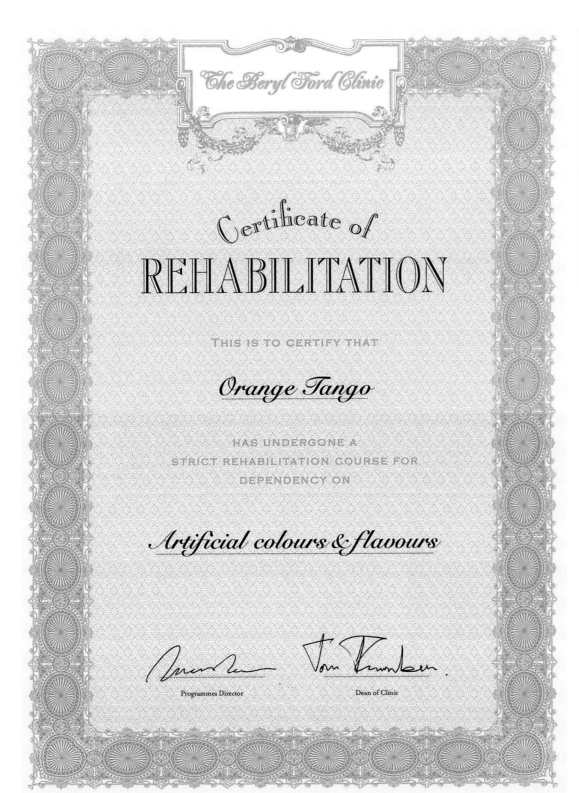

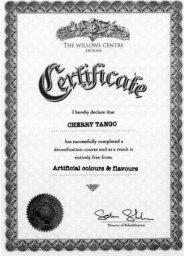

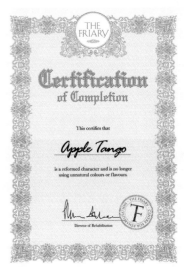

Merit

Magazine Color, Full Page or Spread, *Campaign*

Art Director **Dave Masterman**
Writer **Ed Edwards**
Designer **Kylie McLean**
Creative Director **Ewan Paterson**
Client **Tango**
Agency **CHI & Partners/London**
Annual ID **08151A**

Merit

Magazine Color, Full Page or Spread, *Campaign*

Art Director **José Mª Cornejo**
Writer **Fernando Galindo**
Creative Director **Antonio Montero, José Mª Cornejo, Fernando Galindo**
Client **Smart Fortwo**
Agency **Contrapunto/Madrid**
Annual ID **08152A**

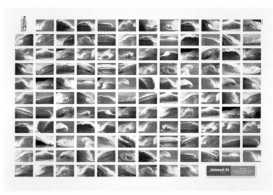

Merit

Magazine Color, Full Page or Spread, *Campaign*

Art Directors Carlos Di Celio, Eric Ribeiro
Writers Rafael Genu, Pedro Prado, Fred Moreira
Photographers Aderi Costa, Fernando Alan
Creative Directors Carlos Di Celio, Fabio Fernandes
Client Unimed
Agency F/Nazca Saatchi & Saatchi/São Paulo
Annual ID 08153A

Merit

Magazine Color, Full Page or Spread, *Campaign*

Art Director Andrew Whitehouse
Writer Justin Gomes
Photographer Andrew Whitehouse
Illustrators Andrew Whitehouse, Clive Kirk, Dave Whitehouse - Nine Degrees
Creative Directors Justin Gomes, Andrew Whitehouse, Noel Cottrell
Client National Geographic Kids Magazine
Agency FoxP2/Cape Town
Annual ID 08154A

Merit

Magazine Color, Full Page or Spread, *Campaign*

Art Directors Javier Suarez Argueta, Till Monshausen, Jens Paul Pfau, Julia Ziegler
Writers Bjoern Ingenleuf, Jo Marie Farwick, Jan-Florian Ege, Tobias Grimm
Illustrator Johan Kleinjan
Creative Directors Goetz Ulmer, Oliver Voss, Fabian Frese
Client CinemaxX
Agency Jung von Matt/Hamburg
Annual ID 08155A

Being the only one who wants to play Monopoly and follow all the rules. Continuing the game alone. Rock concert at school, but you have to work at the kiosk. Learning to swim with the sharks before you can swim. Actually knowing how to use $\sum$, ∂ and Δ on a calculator. Reaching column VQ in Excel. Forgetting to save. Futures, options, derivatives, margins. Explaining several times that Dow Jones is not a singer. Coming in to the office at 6 am. Half an hour late. Getting slightly excited watching "curves" on Bloomberg TV. Nasdaq, Dax, FTSE, CAC-40, M&A, MFS, A&A. Counting the millions that aren't yours. Sitting next to the alarm button during a robbery. Having to foreclose on your friend's house. Having that friend live in your house. Celebrating New Year's Eve 1999 one day later. Your favorite newspaper has more numbers than words. You catch yourself saying "synergy" and "value proposition." Waking up at 1:00 am to check the Tokyo markets. And again at 5:00 am to check the Frankfurt markets. "Sent from my BlackBerry Wireless Handheld." Black Monday. Having to think "outside the box" while working in one. The only sunset you've seen in years is on your screensaver. Black Thursday. You have a €72,000 kitchen and nothing but instant soup in the cupboard. Great news! Your client just got permission to clearcut a Brazilian rainforest! Red Bull actually lowers your blood pressure. Not getting a reservation at Dorsia. Membership at the squash club (if only you could play). Getting called ancient before you're even 40. Being the one who recommended Enron shares. Quoting Sun Tzu's Art of War in a wedding toast. Pronouncing Seychelles properly. Watching your best friend make it to the top — only to jump out the window. An autographed photo of Alan Greenspan on your desk. In front of your wife's. Your second wife. Practicing your Gordon Gecko impression in front of the mirror. "Greed is Good." Buy! Sell! Sell! Buy! You have to go through hell to reach heaven.

Mercedes-Benz

Wanting to become an artist but only over your father's dead body. Starting an "ego wall" with your kindergarten diploma. Civil code volumes I-II-III-IV-V-VI-VII-VIII-IX-X-XI-XII plus errata. Little white lies. Practical training with grandmothers who fell into holes in the street. Having your graduation party in a club that only allows men. Being the most hated profession on earth (according to Time Magazine issue No. 372). A bigger lie here, another one there. Winning the trial and sending an innocent man to jail instead. Invoking dementia. Sending the defendant to the electric chair, along with your principles. Lying to yourself. Managing the tuition of someone's kids. Losing the tuition of your own kids. "What is truth?" Asking your client to wear an orthopedic neck brace to court. Needing a back brace after carrying books and files around. Feeling guilty when your client is found innocent. Taking an already lost case and losing it again. "Why did the lawyer cross the road?" Legally Blond. Where others see cute huts and palm trees you see liability. Speaking in euphemisms. Nobody in your family likes to talk to you because you win every argument. So used to libraries that you even whisper at football matches. Working at a firm that's 12 names long. Your secretary buys the wrong present for your daughter's birthday. Your son says "Pool party!" and you think "Waivers!" The killer you convicted 10 years ago just got out. Plea bargaining a mass murder down to spitting on the sidewalk. Everyone at the jailhouse knows you by your first name. Your first client paid in cigarettes. Having to act nice when you want to be an asshole. Having to act like an asshole when you want to be nice. Starring in your own infomercial. Finding a way to bill hours during your wedding. Getting divorced because you work too much. Contract page 78 §6, contradicts with page 14 §3 Marg. Note 104. Objection! Overruled! Objection! Objection! Sustained! You have to go through hell to reach heaven.

Mercedes-Benz

Spending all your paper route money on a chemistry set. Learning that O_2+Na+S_3 = scorched eyebrows. Hundreds of innocent frogs that died under your scalpel without the proper dose of anesthesia. Your first loan for medical school is big enough to buy a house. Memorizing 206 bone names in Latin (and in English). Spending your birthday at the morgue. Microwave lasagna, instant soup, frozen burritos (and knowing what they do to your body). You don't get headaches, you get cephalgia. Knowing how many germs are in a kiss. Making love to your girlfriend via voicemail. Kissing the chief surgeon's ass. Developing terrible handwriting. Always having to wear white. Too late to switch to interior design studies, you're already €200,000 in debt. PS - your 20s are over. Missing your best friend's wedding. On call at your own wedding. 36-hour shifts every day. That "clean" smell that permeates your clothes. Falling asleep while standing at the operating table. Quitting smoking. Resetting bones. Pumping stomachs. Stitching chins. Liposuctions. Loving it. Getting sued for malpractice by the guy whose life you've just saved. Starting smoking again. Emergency call at 1:00 am. Phone calls that begin with "Surely you remember what happened with patient 56895." Delivering "the bad news." People always asking if the urban legend about the light bulb is true. Emergency call at 3:00 am. Lots of "He was sick and couldn't make it to work" notes for friends. Having a hypochondriac in the family. Pharmaceutical salesmen on lines 3, 5 and 7. Emergency call at 4:59 am. Free advice for your family, friends of the family, family of friends, and friends of the family of friends. "Well, I want a second opinion." Writing a 5-page summary on an ingrown nail. Constantly being asked your opinion about E.R. "Is there a doctor on the plane?" People at parties asking you to look at their blisters. Gold diggers. Fundraisers. Flatliners. "Clear!" You have to go through hell to reach heaven.

Mercedes-Benz

Merit

Magazine Color, Full Page or Spread, *Campaign*

Art Directors **Sebastian Groebner, Ricardo Distefano**
Writers **Dylan Berg, Maximiliano Lüders, Daniel Pieracci**
Creative Directors **Jan Rexhausen, Dörte Spengler-Ahrens**
Client **Daimler**
Agency **Jung von Matt/Hamburg**
Annual ID **08156A**

Merit

Magazine Color, Full Page or Spread, *Campaign*

Art Directors Tim Belser, Simon Jasper Philipp
Photographer Karsten Wegener
Illustrator Mathias Lamken
Creative Director Mathias Lamken
Client Comedy
Agency Kempertrautmann/Hamburg
Annual ID 08157A

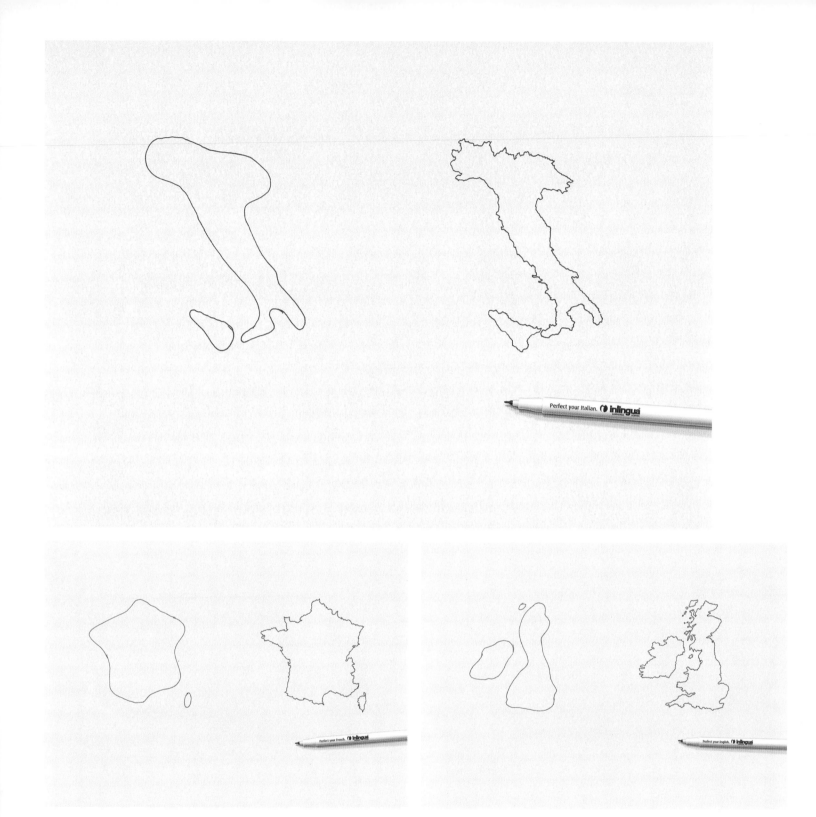

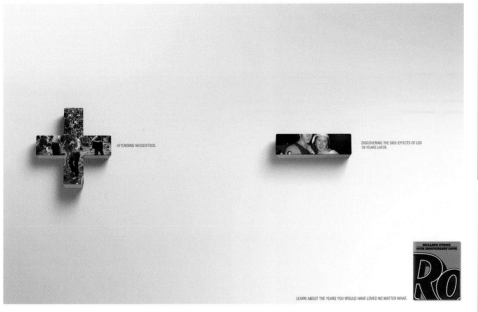

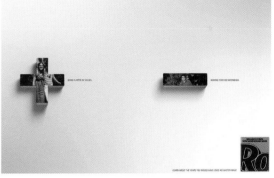

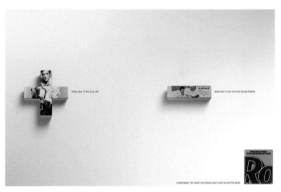

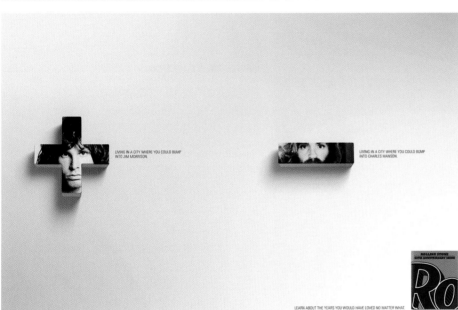

Merit

Magazine Color, Full Page or Spread, *Campaign*

Art Directors Fernando Sosa, John Kubik
Writers Ramiro Raposo, Francisco Bledel, Stuart Dearnley
Creative Directors José Mollá, Joaquin Mollá
Client Publirevistas/Rolling Stone
Agency la comunidad/Miami Beach
Annual ID O8159A

Merit

Magazine Color, Full Page or Spread, *Campaign*

Art Director Michael Anderson
Writers James Mikus, Brooks Jackson
Photographer Andrew Yates
Creative Directors Cameron Day, James Mikus
Client Spoetzl Brewery
Agency McGarrah/Jessee/Austin
Annual ID 08162A

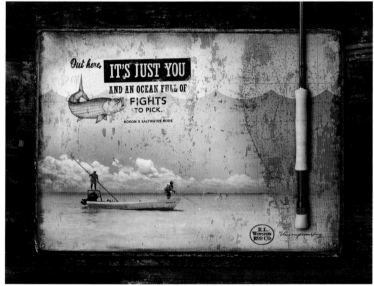

Merit

Magazine Color, Full Page or Spread, *Campaign*

Art Director Michael Shaughnessy
Writer Bryan Karr
Photographers David Ondaatje, Michael Faye, John Konkal
Illustrators Alice Blue, Mike Shaughnessy
Creative Director Jim Hagar
Client Winston Rods
Agency Mullen/Wenham
Annual ID 08163A

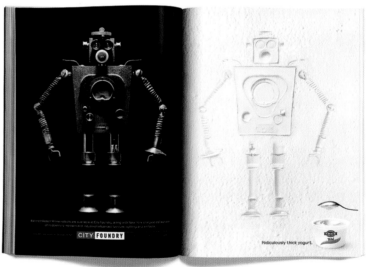

Merit

Magazine Color, Full Page or Spread, *Campaign*

Art Director Arturo Gigante
Writer Debbie Kasher
Photographers Giblin and James, Martin Wonnacott
Creative Directors David Apicella, Joe Johnson
Client Fage
Agency Ogilvy & Mather/New York
Annual ID 08164A

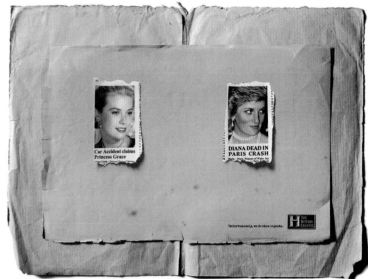

Merit

Magazine Color, Full Page or Spread, *Campaign*

Art Directors Ian Broekhuizen, Mike Martin
Writers Jonathan Beggs, David Fraser
Photographer Michael Doran
Creative Directors Jonathan Beggs, Gerry Human
Client DStv
Agency Ogilvy/Johannesburg
Annual ID 08165A

ALSO AWARDED

✎ Merit Collateral Posters, *Campaign*

LIKE MOST THINGS AROUND HERE THE PELORUS JUMPER CAN GO A LONG TIME BETWEEN WASHES

We don't want to cast aspersions on our customers, but we'd like to admit they don't always take the best care of themselves. In fact, a habit of getting dirty and sweaty tends to be accompanied by a proportional contempt for the niceties of personal grooming.

Part of the reason the metrosexual trend has yet to reach the further outposts of Swanndri country is the ability of our garments to take up some of the slack. Fine merino wool is a remarkable commodity, evolved over millions of years to cope with adverse conditions from the inside as well as the outside.

As well as being able to neutralise your bodily odours, Swanndri's Pelorus jumper is naturally resistant to dirt. What's more, its composition of 100% merino means the ultra-fine fibres lock together to provide natural wind-resistance. And the elasticity of wool allows you to get on with your job unimpeded while the softness of merino feels perfect next to your bare bits. But of course all these tricks are just sideshows to the main event. By releasing moisture, the Pelorus pullover keeps you cool when things heat up. And by trapping a layer of air next to your body, it keeps you warm when conditions start to deteriorate.

While we're not saying you're averse to a nice hot shower, sometimes we know it's just not an option. And when those times come around, it's good to know your Pelorus jumper will put up with the punishment without complaint.

www.swanndri.co.nz

WE HAVE TO MAKE A GOOD GARMENT

MOST OF OUR CUSTOMERS HAVE GUNS

SOMETIMES IT GETS SO COLD IN HERE YOU HAVE TO PUT ON A JERSEY.

Merit

Magazine Color, Full Page or Spread, *Campaign*

Art Director John Fisher
Writers Nick Worthington, Ken Double
Photographer John MacDermott
Creative Director Nick Worthington
Client Swanndri
Agency Publicis Mojo/Auckland
Annual ID 08166A

164

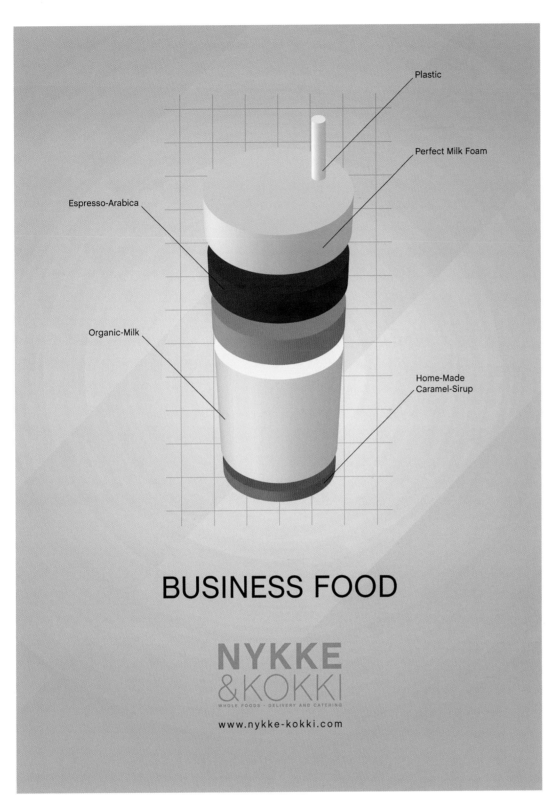

Plastic

Perfect Milk Foam

Espresso-Arabica

Organic-Milk

Home-Made
Caramel-Sirup

BUSINESS FOOD

**NYKKE
&KOKKI**
WHOLE FOODS · DELIVERY AND CATERING

www.nykke-kokki.com

BUSINESS FOOD

**NYKKE
&KOKKI**

www.nykke-kokki.com

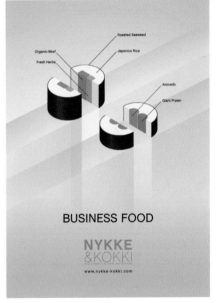

BUSINESS FOOD

**NYKKE
&KOKKI**

www.nykke-kokki.com

Merit

Magazine Color, Full Page or Spread, *Campaign*

Art Director Sascha Mauson
Writer Lena Krumkamp
Creative Directors Heiko Schmidt, Gunnar Loeser, Stefan Setzkorn, Matthias Schmidt
Client Nykke & Kokki
Agency Scholz & Friends/Hamburg
Annual ID 08167A

suggested retail: $5,335.00

Introducing the 2007 Titus Oseo. For a dealer near you visit titusti.com.

suggested retail: $6,585.00

Introducing the 2007 Titus Ligero. For a dealer near you visit titusti.com.

suggested retail: $7,750.00

Introducing the 2007 Titus Solero. For a dealer near you visit titusti.com.

Merit

Magazine Color, Full Page or Spread, *Campaign*

Art Directors Alex Rice, Thomas Dooley
Writer Jonathan Schoenberg
Photographer Brooks Freehill
Creative Director Jonathan Schoenberg
Client Titus Bicycles
Agency TDA Advertising & Design/Boulder
Annual ID 08168A

Merit

Magazine Color, Full Page or Spread, *Campaign*

Art Director Mark Slack
Writer Gemma Phillips
Creative Director Justin Tindall
Client Heineken
Agency The Red Brick Road/London
Annual ID 08169A

JUST A T-SHIRT

THE WAY LT'S 31 TOUCHDOWNS ARE JUST A RECORD.

Introducing the Nike**Sports**Tee. It feels like cotton but helps keep you dry.
BUILT TO BE THE WORLD'S GREATEST SPORTS TEE.

JUST A T-SHIRT

THE WAY MARIA IS JUST A TENNIS PLAYER.

JUST A T-SHIRT

THE WAY TOM BRADY'S RINGS ARE JUST LIKE EVERYBODY ELSE'S.

Merit

Magazine Color, Full Page or Spread, *Campaign*

Art Director Shannon McGlothin
Writers Burks Spencer, Dylan Lee
Designer Matthew Carroll
Photographer Terry Richardson
Creative Directors Steve Luker, Michael Folino
Client Nike
Agency Wieden+Kennedy/Portland
Annual ID 08170A

Merit

Small Space Print Black and White or Color, *Single*

Art Director Amanda Casabella
Writer Sue Batterton
Creative Director John Jaeger
Client Gus's Fried Chicken
Agency archer>malmo/Memphis
Annual ID 08171A

Merit

Small Space Print Black and White or Color, *Single*

Art Director Vijay Solanki
Writer Vijay Solanki
Photographers Avadhut Hembade, Photo Library
Illustrator Deepak Jadhav
Creative Directors Agnello Dias, Nandita Chalam
Client GM Pens International
Agency JWT/Mumbai
Annual ID 08172A

Merit

Small Space Print Black and White or Color, *Single*

Art Director Menno Kluin
Writer Icaro Doria
Photographer Jenny Van Sommers
Creative Directors Tony Granger, Jan Jacobs, Leo Premutico
Client Procter & Gamble - Glide Dental Floss
Agency Saatchi & Saatchi/New York
Annual ID 08173A

SNIGLETS - N. WORDS THAT DON'T APPEAR IN THE DICTIONARY, BUT SHOULD. E.G. SNIGLETS.

ad hock – adv. *Committee set up to pawn the property of an ailing company.*

bank draught – n. *The beer they never serve you in a bank while you wait at the queue.*

bonsigh – v. *Short, happy sigh as one emitted when you sign a hard won contract.*

coinus interruptus – n. *The universal tradition of delaying annual increments to employees.*

dementor – n. *A teacher who guides you, trains you and drives you nuts.*

eek – n. *A geek who knows what a wiki is but doesn't know what a deo or soap is.*

exxx worker – n. *Someone who has lost his job because of constantly surfing adult sites at work.*

incognito in the wheel – n. *Unknown, inconsequential employee.*

jetsettison – n. *Boss' son who is constantly flown around everywhere so he doesn't make trouble anywhere.*

nest omelette – n. *Retirement funds just about to be devoured.*

pittense – adj. *Dark, unstable mood in office that follows immediately after salaries are paid.*

subtletea – n. *The kind of weak, insipid tea usually served in office canteens.*

xero – n. *An IT manager who's one step away from being a zero. He talks endlessly about how an IBM Bladecenter server can improve reliability and save money, but never does anything about it.*

NB: Sniglets were invented and popularized by the American comedian Rich Hall in the 1980s.

IT'S NOT CONCLUDED TILL THE ROTUND LADY **VOCALISES MUSICALLY.**

It's not over till the fat lady sings would have sufficed above. But then, no one calls a spade a spade anymore. Today, euphemisms are in and with it, prefentiousness. A little guide to help you get through this man-made maze of hype and words follows.

Administrative aides - Secretaries (For a while they were upgraded to personal assistants.)

Brand services executive - Usually the genius behind a brand's falling market share.

Career upgrade relocation - An opportunity to spend a few years in cities you've never heard of before.

Company stock option beneficiary - The chance to pick up complimentary shares of your sinking company.

Complimentary Continental breakfast - One unchewable doughnut, one undrinkable coffee, one uncrackable boiled egg.

Conceptualizing - A quick nap.

Global warming initiative - Goodbye office AC.

In-house gourmet dining experience - Food as served by all the rats and roaches in your office building.

Italian cuisine mobile service associate - Pizza delivery boy.

Loss-prevention managers - Security guards.

Not-for-profit organization - We didn't work. We survive on donations.

Mid-market actualization president - The boss needed to get his son into that company.

Random services attendant - Peon.

Top-of-the-line, power-saving server - Top of what line? And it saves power only because it's on the blink most of the time. If you want credible words go ahead and buy it. But if you want a server that's truly hard working and power-saving, try the IBM Bladecenter.

IBM

FROM THE DEPARTMENT OF **REDUNDANCY** DEPARTMENT

An early, anticipative forewarning in advance to all corporate companies involved in business: a seriously critical crisis may possibly, in all likelihood, perhaps occur if the servers you use are inefficient. And ergo, therefore, as a result, not efficient. This unproductive lack of efficiency can alone, by itself, result in colossally huge losses of monumental proportions. The honest truth is, this tragic, misfortunate tragedy can be erased, eliminated and deleted by one single, solitary IBM Bladecenter. The server that actually works and makes others seem superfluous, unnecessary, inessential, totally dispensable and, like this copy, redundant.

IBM

Merit

Small Space Print Black and White or Color, *Campaign*

Art Director Anand Menon
Creative Directors Malvika Mehra, Amit Akali, Peter Jacobsen, Nicholas Turner, Deepak Joshi
Client IBM
Agency Ogilvy & Mather/Bangalore
Annual ID O8174A

Grand Coupe Sedan 1978. Low Rider Hybrid Vehicle: Rallye-getestet, V12-Motor, 80.000 km, Hybrid-Diesel, dunkles Samt-Interieur, verstärktes Heck, verstärkte Frontstoßleiste. Schwarzes gepolstertes XL-Vinyl-Lenkrad. Inklusive 4-fach „Aus dem Weg, ihr Affen"-Dachscheinwerfer. Preis: € 61,95 Weitere Infos unter www.motorstorm.com

Atom RLY Modell 1150, Bj. 2002. Race Quad Bike: nitrogeladen, 4 brandneue Rallye-Reifen, erweiterter Schlamm- und Feuerschutz. Inklusive Schlammkatapult und Lötlampe. Original Büffelleder-Sitz. Bisher acht Besitzer, 3 noch lebend. Preis: € 61,95. Weitere Infos unter www.motorstorm.com

M48 Russisches Off-Road-Vehikel. 3,5 Tonnen Rallye Truck: Doppelbereifung vorne und hinten, elektrische Turbine (1500 Megawatt) wurde zu einem Verbrennungsmotor konvertiert. Inkl. GPS-Navigationssystem, 150 db Hupe. 3 Vorbesitzer. Auf Wunsch mit 120 kg Beifahrerin (31 Vorbesitzer). Preis: € 61,95. Weitere Infos unter www.motorstorm.com

Nikita 850cc, Bj. 1995, japanischer Prototyp. Getunte 121 PS Crossmaschine, rotgrün, 150.000 km, Titanspike-Reifen, Kohlefaser-Chassis, Doppel-Kevlar-Federung, benötigt hochoktaniges Ethanolgemisch, leichte Kratzer, keine Rückspiegel. Preis: € 61,95. Weitere Infos unter www.motorstorm.com

Merit

Small Space Print Black and White or Color, *Campaign*

Art Director Jaime Mandelbaum
Writer Emiliano Trierveiler
Creative Directors Dirk Henkelmann, Philip Borchardt
Client Sony Playstation3
Agency TBWA\Germany/Berlin
Annual ID 08175A

Merit

Outdoor, *Single*

Art Director James Clunie
Creative Directors David Lubars, Bill Bruce, James Clunie
Client Havaianas
Agency BBDO/New York
Annual ID 08176A

Merit

Outdoor, *Single*

Art Directors Vince Cook, Gary Fox-Robertson, Avery Gross, Brian Shembeda
Creative Directors Mark Tutssel, John Condon, John Montgomery
Client McDonald's
Agency Leo Burnett/Chicago
Annual ID 08182A

ALSO AWARDED

✏ Merit Innovative Advertising, *Single*

Merit

Outdoor, *Single*

Art Director Dominic Stallard
Writer Clinton Manson
Photographer Clive Stewart
Creative Directors Dominic Stallard, Clinton Manson
Client Axe Shower Gel
Agency Lowe MENA/Dubai
Annual ID 08183A

Merit

Outdoor, *Single*

Art Directors Laurence Thomson, Johan Holmgren
Writers Erik Enberg, Erik Bergqvist
Designer Mark Ward
Illustrator Louis Malloy
Creative Directors Robert Saville, Mark Waites
Client Discovery Real Time
Agency Mother/London
Annual ID 08184A

Merit

Outdoor, *Single*

Art Director **John Koay**
Writer **Veronica Copestake**
Photographer **Nick Smith**
Creative Director **Mike O'Sullivan**
Client **Sanyo**
Agency **Saatchi & Saatchi/Auckland**
Annual ID **08186A**

Merit

Outdoor, *Single*

Art Directors Eve Roussou, Viken Guzel
Writer Veronique Sels
Designer Baptiste Masse
Creative Director Erik Vervroegen
Client Nissan
Agency TBWA\Paris/Boulogne-Billancourt
Annual ID 08188A

Merit

Outdoor, *Single*

Art Director Judd Oberly
Writer Michael Page
Photographer Andy Mahr
Creative Directors Leigh Sander, Bob Brihn, Jim Walker
Client Nationwide Insurance
Agency TM Advertising/Dallas
Annual ID 08189A

SHOES SAY A LOT ABOUT A PERSON.
BUT IT'S SANDALS THAT REVEAL THE INTIMACIES.   havaianas

IN YOUR BODY'S SOUTHERN HEMISPHERE,
IT'S SPRINGTIME ALL YEAR LONG.   havaianas

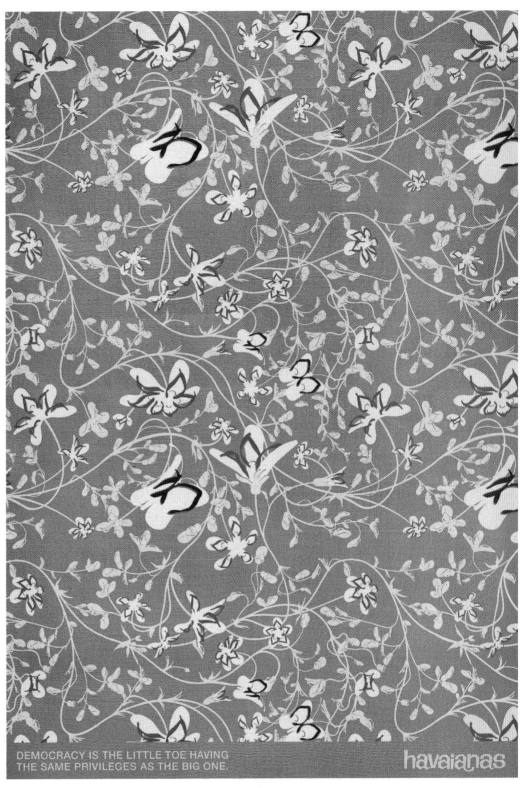

DEMOCRACY IS THE LITTLE TOE HAVING
THE SAME PRIVILEGES AS THE BIG ONE.   havaianas

Merit

Outdoor, *Campaign*

Art Directors Danilo Boer, Marcos Kotlhar, Marcus Sulzbacher
Writer Sophie Schoenburg
Illustrators Danilo Boer, Marcos Kotlhar
Creative Directors Marcello Serpa, Marcus Sulzbacher
Client São Paulo Alpargatas
Agency AlmapBBDO/São Paulo
Annual ID 08190A

Merit

Outdoor, *Campaign*

Art Director Chuck Tso
Writer Adam Kanzer
Creative Directors David Lubars, Bill Bruce, Eric Silver
Client FedEx Kinko's
Agency BBDO/New York
Annual ID 08191A

MOCHA LATTE $4.23   6-PK HIGH LIFE $4.04

NATIONAL SUPERMARKET 12 WEEK AVG. HIGH LIFE PRICE ACCORDING TO AC NIELSEN.   LIVE RESPONSIBLY *Miller*

PROOF THE WORLD HASN'T GONE COMPLETELY CRAZY

DESIGNER PUGGLE $1480   12-PK HIGH LIFE $6.78

PROOF THE WORLD HASN'T GONE COMPLETELY CRAZY

GALLON OF GAS $2.69   6-PK HIGH LIFE $4.04

PROOF THE WORLD HASN'T GONE COMPLETELY CRAZY

MOVIE & SNACKS $18.50   12-PK HIGH LIFE $6.78

PROOF THE WORLD HASN'T GONE COMPLETELY CRAZY

6-PK WATER $5.99   6-PK HIGH LIFE $4.04

NATIONAL SUPERMARKET 12 WEEK AVG. HIGH LIFE PRICE ACCORDING TO AC NIELSEN.   LIVE RESPONSIBLY

PROOF THE WORLD HASN'T GONE COMPLETELY CRAZY

Merit
Outdoor, *Campaign*

Art Director Vivienne Wan
Writer Paul Johnson
Photographer Sebastian Gray
Creative Directors Paul Keister, Paul Johnson
Client Miller High Life
Agency Crispin Porter + Bogusky/Miami
Annual ID 08192A

Merit

Outdoor, *Campaign*

Art Director James Tucker
Writer Simon Vicars
Creative Director Toby Talbot
Client SKY Television
Agency DDB/Auckland
Annual ID 08193A

Merit

Outdoor, *Campaign*

Art Director Marcin Zaborski
Writer Natalia Dudek
Creative Directors Marcin Mroszczak, Jakub Korolczuk, Ryszard Sroka
Client Kompania Piwowarska -Tyskie Beer
Agency DDB/Warsaw
Annual ID 08194A

Merit

Outdoor, *Campaign*

Art Directors Gen Sadakane, Tim Stübane
Writer Jan Hendrik Ott
Photographer David Cuenca
Creative Directors Bert Peulecke, Stefan Schulte
Client Volkswagen
Agency DDB/Berlin
Annual ID 08195A

Merit

Outdoor, *Campaign*

Art Director Francesco Epifani
Writer Davide Rossi
Photographer Francesco Epifani
Creative Directors Sergio Rodriguez, Enrico Dorizza
Client Nintendo
Agency Leo Burnett/Milan
Annual ID 08197A

183

Merit

Outdoor, *Campaign*

Art Directors David Fischer, Tabea Rauscher
Writers Daniel Boedeker, Axel Tischer
Photographer Hans Starck
Creative Directors Matthias Spaetgens, Oliver Handlos
Client jobsintown.de
Agency Scholz & Friends/Berlin
Annual ID 08200A

ALSO AWARDED
✏ Merit Innovative Advertising, *Campaign*

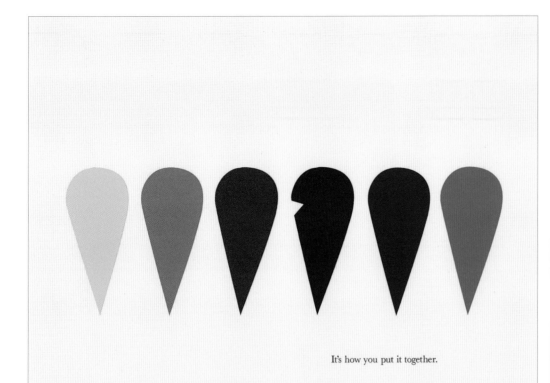

It's how you put it together.

MINNEAPOLIS COLLEGE OF ART AND DESIGN OFFERING 14 VISUALIZATION MAJORS INCLUDING ADVERTISING, ILLUSTRATION AND PHOTOGRAPHY. CHALLENGING EYES AND MINDS SINCE 1886. **APPLY TODAY AT MCAD.EDU**

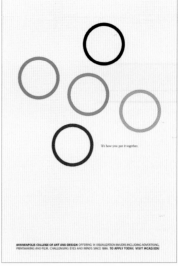

Merit

Outdoor, *Campaign*

Art Director Daniela Montanez
Writer Matthew Bottkol
Creative Director Joe Alexander
Client Minneapolis College of Art & Design
Agency The Martin Agency/Richmond
Annual ID 08302A

185

Merit

Outdoor, *Campaign*

Art Directors Isabelle Hauser, Christian Bobst
Writer Johannes Raggio
Creative Directors Urs Schrepfer, Christian Bobst
Client Leica
Agency Young & Rubicam/Gockhausen
Annual ID 08201A

Merit

Trade Full Page or Spread, *Single*

Art Director **Vincent Lee**
Writer **Joji Jacob**
Creative Directors **Neil Johnson, Terrence Tan**
Client **DDB**
Agency **DDB/Singapore**
Annual ID **08202A**

Merit

Trade Full Page or Spread, *Single*

Art Director **Dean Hanson**
Writer **Dean Buckhorn**
Creative Director **Todd Riddle**
Client **St. Paul Travelers**
Agency **Fallon/Minneapolis**
Annual ID **08203A**

Merit

Trade Full Page or Spread, *Campaign*

Art Director Doug Pedersen
Writer Heath Pochucha
Creative Director Jim Nelson
Client Schutt
Agency Carmichael Lynch/Minneapolis
Annual ID 08204A

We plan for every eventuality:
Mechanical failure. Human error.
Inquisitive giraffe.

Risk is no stranger to the oil and gas industry. To keep your well running like a well-oiled machine, you need an insurance company that knows drilling inside out. At Travelers, you can tap into the services of our globally recognized risk-control experts, who help identify and minimize hazards, from the initial seismic survey to the ongoing operation of your well. And should risk ever rear its ugly head, we're only a direct call away. To discover what it's like to work with a company that's in-synch with yours, talk to an independent agent today.

TRAVELERS
Insurance. In-synch.
travelers.com

In farming, conditions change.
Sometimes even overnight.

TRAVELERS
Insurance. In-synch.

Labeling your risks and managing them
are two different things.

TRAVELERS
Insurance. In-synch.

Merit

Trade Full Page or Spread, *Campaign*

Art Directors Emily McDowell, Bobby Appleby
Writers Dean Buckhorn, Tom Sebanc, Jen Stocksmith, Simon Roseblade
Creative Director Todd Riddle
Client St. Paul Travelers
Agency Fallon/Minneapolis
Annual ID 08205A

Merit

Collateral P.O.P. and In-Store, *Single*

Art Director Paul Pateman
Writer Mike Nicholson
Creative Director Paul Brazier
Client Museum Of Childhood
Agency Abbott Mead Vickers BBDO/London
Annual ID 08206A

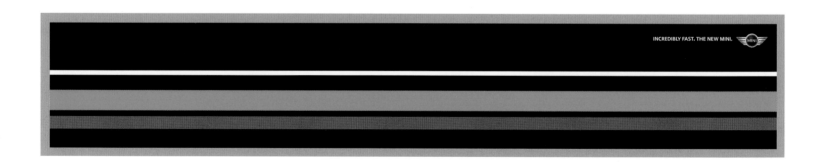

Merit

Collateral P.O.P. and In-Store, *Single*

Art Directors Mun, Kelvin Leong, Eric Hor, Pebble Goh
Writers Ronald Ng, Mun
Creative Directors Ronald Ng, Mun
Client BMW Malaysia
Agency BBDO/Proximity Malaysia/Kuala Lumpur
Annual ID 08208A

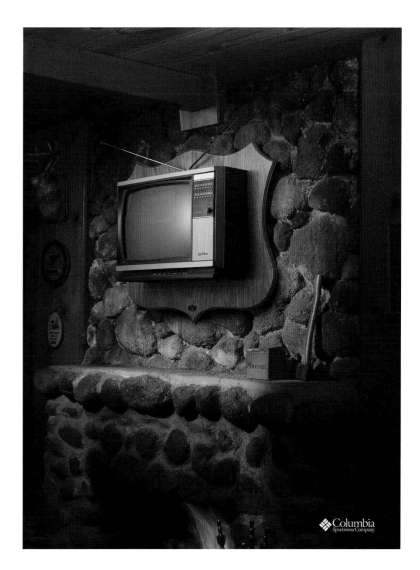

Merit

Collateral P.O.P. and In-Store, *Single*

Art Director Jeremy Boland
Writer Eric Terchila
Photographer David Emmite
Creative Director Terry Schneider
Client Columbia Sportswear
Agency Borders Perrin Norrander/Portland
Annual ID 08209A

Merit

Collateral P.O.P. and In-Store, *Single*

Art Director Jay Lorenzini
Writer Robyn Gunn
Creative Directors John Butler, Mike Shine
Client MINI
Agency Butler, Shine, Stern & Partners/Sausalito
Annual ID 08210A

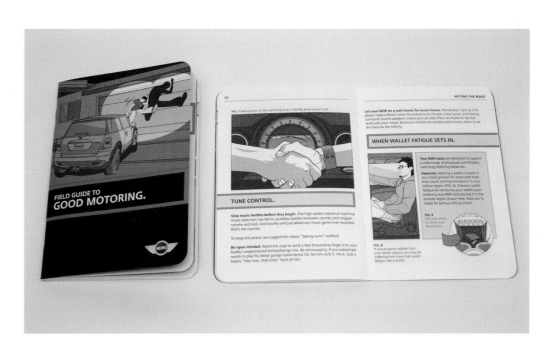

Merit

Collateral P.O.P. and In-Store, *Single*

Art Directors James Tucker, Emmanuel Bougneres
Writers Simon Vicars, Mike Felix
Photographer Mat Baker
Creative Director Toby Talbot
Client SSL - Durex
Agency DDB/Auckland
Annual ID 08211A

Merit

Collateral P.O.P. and In-Store, *Single*

Art Director Ben Tollett
Writer Emer Stamp
Photographer Dimitri Daniloff
Creative Director Adam Tucker
Client Harvey Nichols
Agency DDB/London
Annual ID 08212A

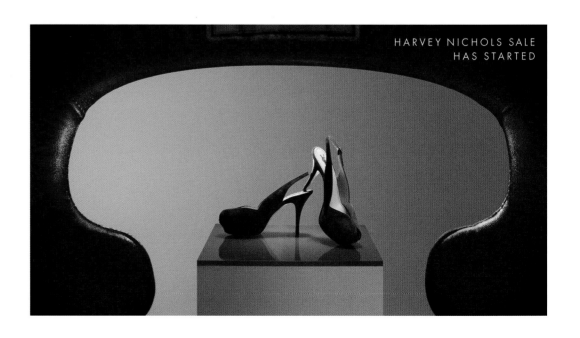

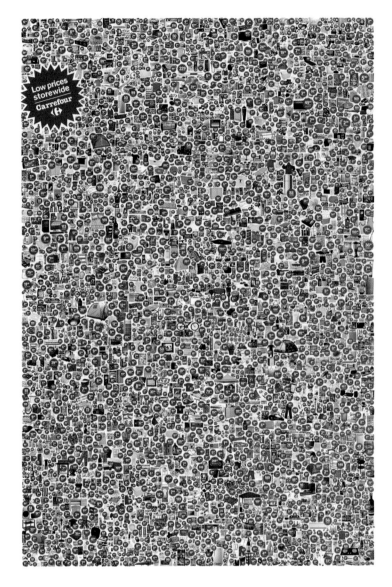

Merit

Collateral P.O.P. and In-Store, *Single*

Art Directors Ben Tollett, Emer Stamp
Writers Emer Stamp, Ben Tollett
Creative Director Neil Dawson
Client Philips
Agency DDB/London
Annual ID 08213A

Merit

Collateral P.O.P. and In-Store, *Single*

Art Directors Tan Chee Keong , Jarrod Reginald
Writer Donevan Chew
Designers Jarrod Reginald, Tan Chee Keong
Creative Directors Daniel Comar, Brian Capel
Client Carrefour Malaysia
Agency Ogilvy Malaysia/Kuala Lumpur
Annual ID 08216A

Merit

Collateral P.O.P. and In-Store, *Single*

Art Director **David Joubert**
Writer **Lauren Shewitz**
Photographer **Clive Stewart**
Creative Directors **Adam Weber, Damon Stapleton**
Client **Nissan Interstar**
Agency **TBWA\Hunt\Lascaris – Johannesburg/Sandton**
Annual ID **08217A**

ALSO AWARDED

✎ Merit Innovative Advertising, *Single*

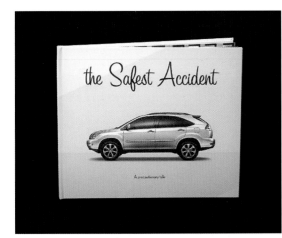

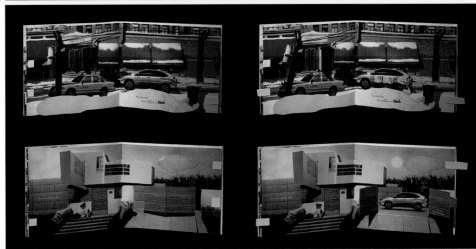

Merit

Collateral P.O.P. and In-Store, *Single*

Art Director Kevin R. Smith
Writer Dave Horton
Creative Directors Chris Graves, Jon Pearce, Gavin Lester
Client Lexus
Agency Team One/El Segundo
Annual ID 08218A

Merit

Collateral P.O.P. and In-Store, *Single*

Creative Director Manolo Moreno
Client Miramax/Buenavista España
Agency Zapping/M&C Saatchi/Madrid
Annual ID 08219A

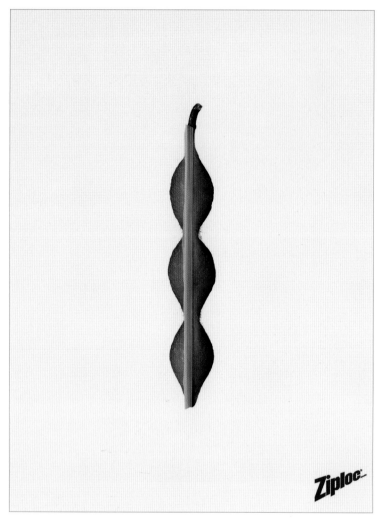

Merit

Collateral P.O.P. and In-Store, *Campaign*

Art Directors Suthisak Sucharittanonta, Nirun Sommalardpun
Writers Taewit Jariyanukulpun, Arnicknard Krobnoparat
Photographer Chub Nokkaew
Illustrator Chubcheevit
Creative Directors Suthisak Sucharittanonta, Vasan Wangpaitoon, Weerachon Weeraworawit
Client Ziploc
Agency BBDO/Bangkok
Annual ID 08220A

You pick it. We'll match it. ⊛ Dulux

You pick it. We'll match it. ⊛ Dulux

You pick it. We'll match it. ⊛ Dulux

Merit

Collateral P.O.P. and In-Store, *Campaign*

Art Directors Sin Eng Lee, Lee Lilian
Writer Farrokh Madon
Photographer Corbis
Illustrator Ng Invy
Creative Director Farrokh Madon
Client ICI Dulux
Agency BBDO/Singapore
Annual ID 08221A

197

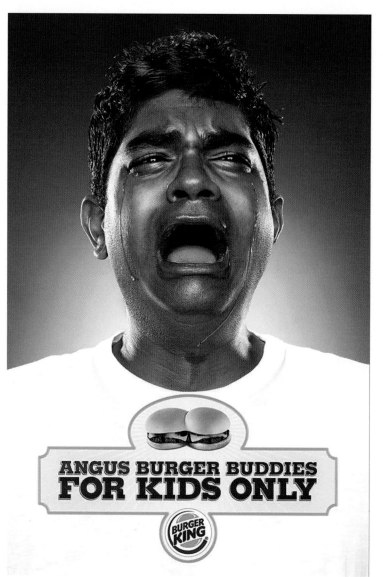
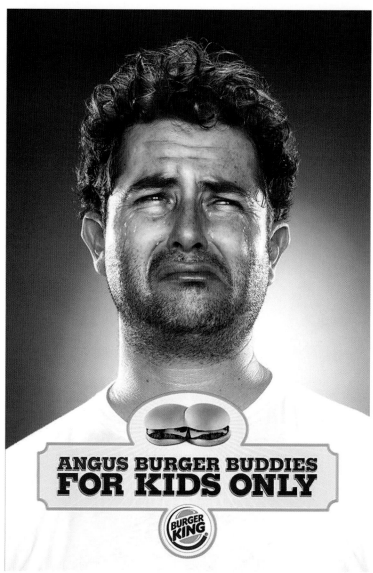

Merit

Collateral P.O.P. and In-Store, *Campaign*

Art Director Patrick Horn
Writers Yutaka Tsujino, Jeremy Seibold
Designers Jody McClean, Eduardo Santiesteban
Photographer Jill Greenberg
Creative Directors Rob Reilly, Bill Wright, James Dawson-Hollis
Client Burger King
Agency Crispin Porter + Bogusky/Miami
Annual ID 08222A

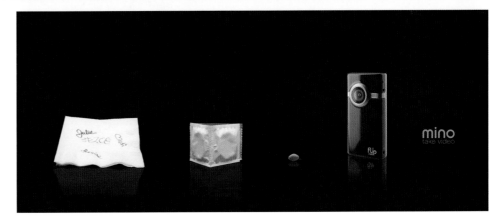

Merit

Collateral P.O.P. and In-Store, *Campaign*

Art Director Greg Smith
Writer Aimee Lehto
Designer John Gordon
Creative Directors Lisa Bennett, Mike Andrews
Client Pure Digital
Agency DDB/San Francisco
Annual ID O8223A

Merit

Collateral P.O.P. and In-Store, *Campaign*

Art Director Keka Morelle
Writer André Faria
Creative Directors Eduardo Lima, Fabio Fernandes
Client Plastik
Agency F/Nazca Saatchi & Saatchi/São Paulo
Annual ID 08224A

Merit

Merit

Collateral P.O.P. and In-Store, *Campaign*

Art Directors Sompat Trisadikun, Pipat Uraporn
Writer Noranit Yasopa
Photographer Chub Nokkaew
Creative Directors Keeratie Chaimoungkalo, Sompat Trisadikun
Client Clima Bicycle Lock
Agency Leo Burnett/Bangkok
Annual ID 08225A

ALSO AWARDED

🖋 Merit P.O.P. and In-Store, *Single*

Merit

Collateral P.O.P. and In-Store, *Campaign*

Art Directors Martin Tong, Leo Yeung
Writer Alfred Wong
Photographer Kai Wing Kwan
Creative Directors Connie Lo, Brian Ma
Client Zoo Records
Agency Leo Burnett/Hong Kong
Annual ID 08226A

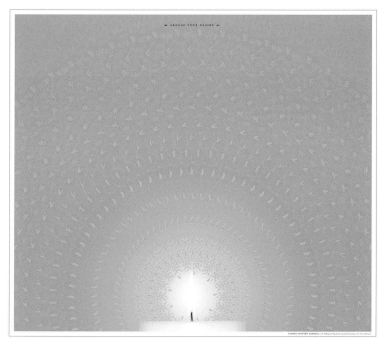
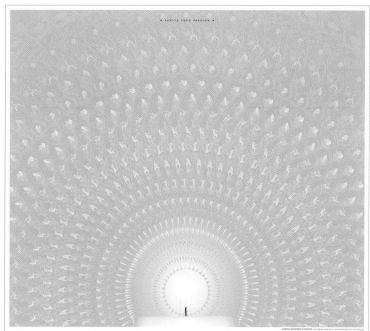
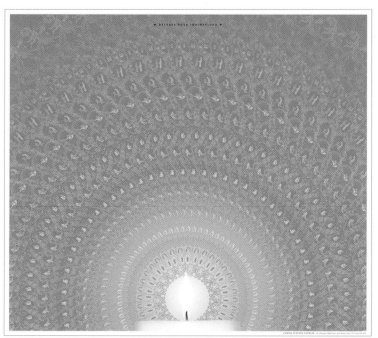
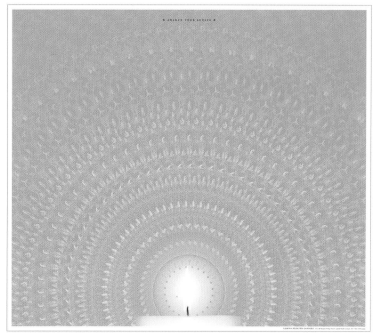

Merit

Collateral P.O.P. and In-Store, *Campaign*

Art Directors Nazly, Gigi Lee
Writers Adrian Miller, Audrey Lean
Designers Siow Foon Ng, Nazly, Davina Tan
Photographer Edmund Leong
Illustrators Siow Foon Ng, Nazly, Davina Tan
Creative Directors Edmund Choe, Adrian Miller
Client Lumina
Agency Saatchi & Saatchi/Petaling Jaya
Annual ID O8227A

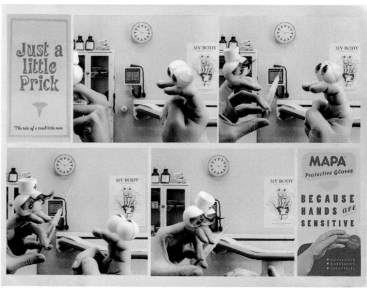

Merit

Collateral P.O.P. and In-Store, *Campaign*

Art Directors Jonathan Santana, Bjoern Ruehmann, Joakim Reveman
Writer Xander Smith
Photographer Sven Glage
Creative Director Erik Vervroegen
Client Mapa Spontex
Agency TBWA\Paris/Boulogne-Billancourt
Annual ID 08228A

POLICE MEGAPHONE

SOFT FOOTSTEPS

LOUD PARTY MUSIC

Use the power of sound for your TV advert or film: www.njp.ch

njp

THE SOUND MAKES THE FILM. NJP TONSTUDIO

Merit

Collateral P.O.P. and In-Store, *Campaign*

Art Directors Isabelle Hauser, Christian Bobst
Writer Johannes Raggio
Photographer Serge Hoeltschi
Creative Directors Christian Bobst, Urs Schrepfer
Client NJP Tonstudio
Agency Young & Rubicam/Gockhausen
Annual ID 08229A

Merit

Collateral Posters, *Single*

Creative Directors Alex Martínez, Oscar Alcaraz, Napi Rivera, Joan Garrigosa
Client Century Travel
Agency JWT Spain/Barcelona
Annual ID 08230A

Merit

Collateral Posters, *Single*

Art Director Santosh Padhi
Writer Russell Barrett
Illustrator Kunal Mhabadi
Creative Directors K.V. Sridhar, Santosh Padhi
Client Luxor
Agency Leo Burnett/Mumbai
Annual ID 08231A

Merit

Collateral Posters, *Single*

Art Director Daniel Upputuru
Writer Abhinav Pratiman
Designer Daniel Upputuru
Illustrator Daniel Upputuru
Creative Directors Daniel Upputuru, Abhinav Pratiman,
Sagar Mahabaleshwarkar, Ramanuj Shastry
Client Amway India
Agency Rediffusion DYR/Gurgaon
Annual ID 08237A

If he praises your eyes, he's thinking about your breasts. If he praises your smile, he's thinking about your breasts.

If he praises your Havaianas, either the guy has a foot fetish or he's thinking about your breasts.

Merit

Collateral Posters, *Campaign*

Art Director Bruno Prosperi
Writer Renato Simões
Photographer Fernando Nalon
Illustrators Daniel Moreno, José Cortizo Jr.
Creative Director Marcello Serpa
Client São Paulo Alpargatas
Agency AlmapBBDO/São Paulo
Annual ID 08238A

Merit

Collateral Posters, *Campaign*

Art Directors Marcelo Serpa, Marcos Kotlhar
Photographer Fernando Nalon
Illustrator Rodrigo Gelmi
Creative Director Marcelo Serpa
Client São Paulo Alpargatas
Agency AlmapBBDO/São Paulo
Annual ID 08239A

EXERCISE E.
WRONG SIDE STRETCH

MUSCLES WORKED:

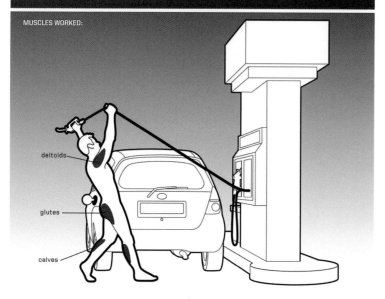

deltoids

glutes

calves

EXERCISE M.
GERMOPHOBIC COMMUTING

MUSCLES WORKED:

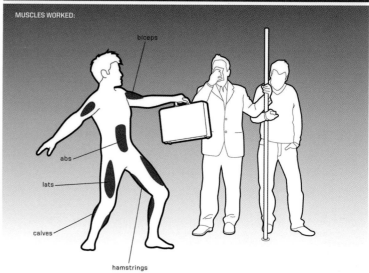

biceps

abs

lats

calves

hamstrings

LIFE IS EXERCISE. SNICKERS MARATHON® IS ENERGY.

Try a great-tasting, nutritious, long-lasting SNICKERS MARATHON® for all the demands of your day. Grab one in the energy bar aisle.

LIFE IS EXERCISE. SNICKERS MARATHON® IS ENERGY.

Try a great-tasting, nutritious, long-lasting SNICKERS MARATHON® for all the demands of your day. Grab one in the energy bar aisle.

EXERCISE H.
SAMPLE SALE

MUSCLES WORKED:

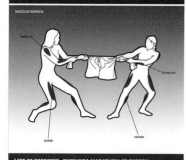

LIFE IS EXERCISE. SNICKERS MARATHON® IS ENERGY.

Try a great-tasting, nutritious, long-lasting SNICKERS MARATHON® for all the demands of your day. Grab one in the energy bar aisle.

EXERCISE L.
BACKSEAT PILATES

MUSCLES WORKED:

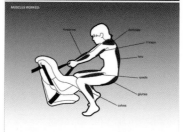

LIFE IS EXERCISE. SNICKERS MARATHON® IS ENERGY.

Try a great-tasting, nutritious, long-lasting SNICKERS MARATHON® for all the demands of your day. Grab one in the energy bar aisle.

EXERCISE G.
KENNEL PULL

MUSCLES WORKED:

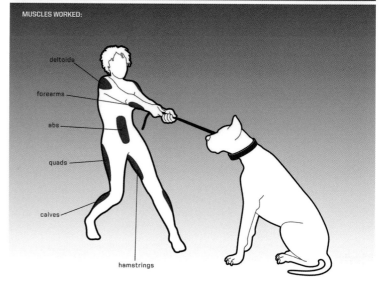

deltoids

forearms

abs

quads

calves

hamstrings

LIFE IS EXERCISE. SNICKERS MARATHON® IS ENERGY.

Try a great-tasting, nutritious, long-lasting SNICKERS MARATHON® for all the demands of your day. Grab one in the energy bar aisle.

Merit

Collateral Posters, *Campaign*

Art Director Gianfranco Arena
Writer Peter Kain
Designer Melinda Ward
Creative Directors David Lubars, Bill Bruce
Client Mars Snackfood - Snickers
Agency BBDO/New York
Annual ID 08240A

210

Merit

Collateral Posters, *Campaign*

Art Director Kele Dobrinski
Writer Noah Phillips
Creative Directors Travis Britton, Chuck McBride
Client Ray Ban
Agency Cutwater/San Francisco
Annual ID 08241A

Merit

Collateral Posters, *Campaign*

Art Director Hiroshi Miyakawa
Client Barber AZUSA
Agency E.Co./Tokyo
Annual ID 08242A

Merit

Collateral Posters, *Campaign*

Art Director Luciano Lincoln
Writer Eduardo Lima
Creative Directors Eduardo Lima, Fabio Fernandes
Client ANJ - National Newspaper Association
Agency F/Nazca Saatchi & Saatchi/São Paulo
Annual ID 08243A

Merit

Collateral Posters, *Campaign*

Art Directors Makarand Patil, Fadi Yaish
Writer Kartik Aiyar
Photographer Allen Dong Wizard Photography
Creative Director Fadi Yaish
Client Bayer
Agency FP7/Doha
Annual ID 08244A

Merit

Collateral Posters, *Campaign*

Art Director Kalpesh Patankar
Writer Kalpesh Patankar
Photographer Jeremy Wong - Nemesis Pictures
Illustrators Mirage Works, Magic Cube
Creative Director Fadi Yaish
Client SONY Playstation - Medal of Honor
Agency FP7/Doha
Annual ID 08245A

GATHERING THREAT
AXIS OF EVIL
WEAPONS OF MASS DESTRUCTION
SLAM DUNK
SHOCK AND AWE
MISSION ACCOMPLISHED
FIGHT 'EM THERE NOT HERE
BRING 'EM ON
STAY THE COURSE
LAST THROES
HECK OF A JOB BROWNIE
GLOBAL WAR ON TERROR
I AM THE DECIDER
STUFF HAPPENS

haven't we had enough? democrats 08

GEORGE W. BUSH
DICK CHENEY
KARL ROVE
ALBERTO GONZALES
SCOOTER LIBBY
JACK ABRAMOFF
CONDOLEEZZA RICE
RUMSFELD
PAUL WOLFOWITZ
HARRIET MIERS
PAUL BREMER GEORGE TENET
JOHN ASHCROFT MIKE BROWN
JOHN BOLTON

haven't we had enough? democrats 08

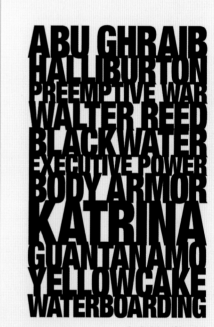

ABU GHRAIB
HALLIBURTON
PREEMPTIVE WAR
WALTER REED
BLACKWATER
EXECUTIVE POWER
BODY ARMOR
KATRINA
GUANTANAMO
YELLOWCAKE
WATERBOARDING

haven't we had enough? democrats 08

Merit

Collateral Posters, *Campaign*

Designers Rich Silverstein, Mark Rurka
Creative Director Rich Silverstein
Client Huffington Post
Agency Goodby, Silverstein & Partners/San Francisco
Annual ID 08246A

FHM
**2008
HOTTEST
BABES
CALENDAR**
FREE with the Jan issue

Merit

2008
HOTTEST
BABES
CALENDAR

Merit

2008
HOTTEST
BABES
CALENDAR

Merit

Merit

Collateral Posters, *Campaign*

Art Director Run Run Teng
Writer Gayle Lim
Designers Run Run Teng, Jenne Hew
Photographer Stock
Creative Director Farrokh Madon
Client Mediacorp Publishing
Agency McCann Worldgroup/Singapore
Annual ID 08248A

ALSO AWARDED

✎ Merit Collateral Posters, *Single*
✎ Merit Collateral Posters, *Single*

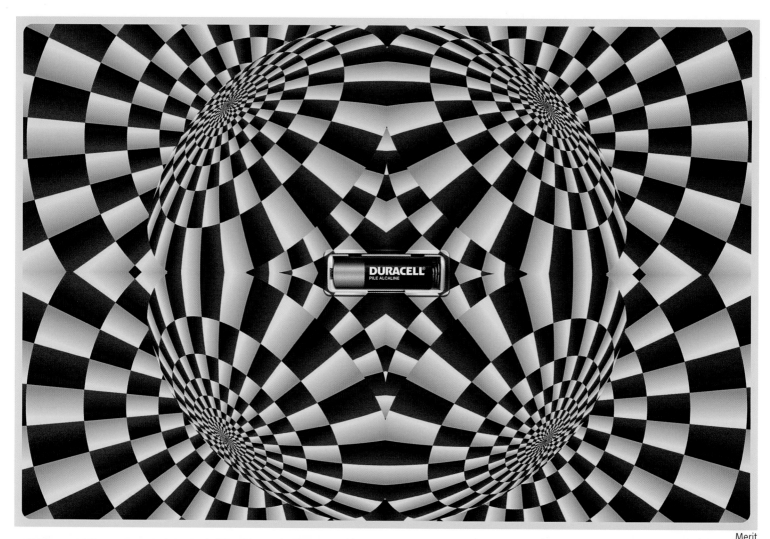

Merit

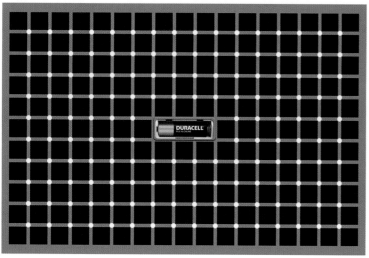
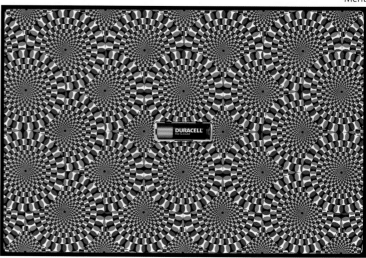

Merit

Collateral Posters, *Campaign*

Art Director Mario Salgado
Illustrator Mario Salgado
Creative Directors Miguel Angel Ruiz, Abraham Quintana
Client Duracell
Agency Ogilvy & Mather/Mexico City
Annual ID 08250A

ALSO AWARDED

✎ Merit Collateral Posters, *Single*

Volvo XC90 now with soundproof windows.

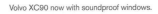

Volvo XC90 now with soundproof windows.

Volvo XC90 now with soundproof windows.

Merit

Merit

Collateral Posters, *Campaign*

Art Directors Ivan Carrasco, Francisco Hernandez
Writer Rafael Martinez
Photographer Flavio Bizzarri
Creative Directors Miguel Angel Ruiz, Luis Elizalde, Carlos Oxte
Client Ford Motor Company - Volvo
Agency Ogilvy & Mather/Mexico City
Annual ID 08249A

ALSO AWARDED
✎ Merit Collateral Posters, *Single*

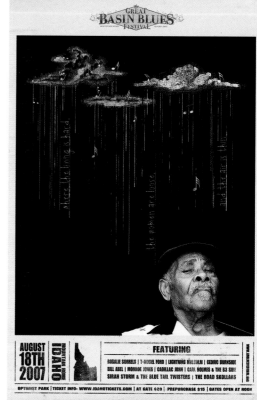

Merit

Collateral Posters, *Campaign*

Art Director Kellyn McGarity
Writer Mike Bales
Photographer Andy Anderson
Creative Director Jimmy Bonner
Client The Great Basin Blues Festival
Agency The Richards Group/Dallas
Annual ID 08252A

Merit

Collateral Promotion

Art Directors Julia Stoffer, Matthias Grundner
Writer Tom Hauser
Designer Melanie Raphael
Creative Directors Tom Hauser, Arno Lindemann, Bernhard Lukas
Client IKEA Deutschland
Agency Jung von Matt/Hamburg
Annual ID 08253A

Merit

Collateral Promotion

Art Directors Markus Kremer, Ole Kleinhans
Writers Markus Kremer, Ole Kleinhans
Creative Directors Arno Lindemann, Bernhard Lukas
Client TW1 - Astra Digital
Agency Jung von Matt/Hamburg
Annual ID 08254A

Merit

Collateral Self-Promotion

Art Directors Scott Kaplan, Chuck Tso
Writer Tom Kraemer
Creative Directors David Lubars, Bill Bruce, Greg Hahn
Client Positive Thinking
Agency BBDO/New York
Annual ID 08255A

Merit

Collateral Self-Promotion

Art Directors Scott Kaplan, Chuck Tso
Writer Tom Kraemer
Photographer Billy Siegrist
Creative Directors David Lubars, Bill Bruce, Greg Hahn
Client Positive Thinking
Agency BBDO/New York
Annual ID 08256A

THIS AD NEVER RAN.

But

that didn't stop us from entering it in The One Show.

Every year, hundreds of fake ads are submitted to advertising competitions.

We're sure that you've seen some of them already today. Ads for barber shops, condoms and Hot Wheels. A lot of them are awesome concepts. And some of them may have actually run. In places like a Singapore penny-saver, where an audience of two (the copywriter and the art director) actually saw the ad.

Well, the audience for this fake ad is almost 15 times that size. Yes, this ad directly targets 29 people. We can even name names. Chris Adams. Andy Azula. Robert Baird. Bob Barrie. Paul Belford. Mike Byrne. Glenn Cole. Marty Cooke. Adriana Cury. Joe DeSouza. Andy Greenaway. Paul Hirsch. Matt Ian. Paul Keister. Arno Lindemann. Steve Mapp. Filip Nilsson. Masako Okamura. Ian Reichenthal. Kai Roeffen. Ted Royer. Beth Ryan. Eric Silver. Rob Strasberg. Norman Tan. Monica Taylor. Nancy Vonk. Todd Waterbury. And Yang Yeo.

In case you guys are a bit hung over or just a little slow, we're talking to you, the 2008 One Show judges.

Of course, one of you might have had to cancel at the last-minute and in that case we're sure Mary Warlick found a last-minute substitute. (Side note to the last-minute substitute: You are the best judge The One Show has ever seen and the creators of this ad think you should have been on the original judge invitation list).

Hey, we're not above a little ass-kissing if it helps us reach our goal.

Our goal is to get this ad printed in the 2008 One Show Annual. Let's just call a spade a spade.

Why are we doing this, you ask? Maybe it's because as kids we were never given any positive feedback from our parents and are starved for attention.

Or it could be because having an ad (even if it's fake) in The One Show Annual is an amazing recruiting tool. It means that over 70,000 ad professionals will see it and think that we do cool work. And it might help convince graduates of prestigious ad schools like VCU Brandcenter to come work with us.

Of course, we might be doing it just to give you judges a little levity in a day when you look at over 16,000 ads. Ahh... ok... the real reason is the same reason every one else does fake ads. Because our real clients won't let us do any good work. Scratch that. Without our wonderful clients, we wouldn't have the resources to do cool fake ads like this one.

At least we're honest about it. And if you're honest with yourself, you've probably entered an ad or two in an award show that wasn't totally legit.

But this one is different.

It might not be the first fake ad to get into an award show. But it would be the first that was up front and truthful about it.

Truth in advertising. What a novel concept.

fig. 1 Abe The Honest Bunny

BOONEOAKLEY

We made our logo really big because this ad will only be about 4 inches tall when it's printed in The One Show Annual.

Merit

Collateral Self-Promotion

Art Directors Brian Fink, Eric Roch von Rochsburg
Writer David Oakley
Illustrator Brian Fink
Creative Directors David Oakley, John Boone
Client BooneOakley
Agency BooneOakley/Charlotte
Annual ID 08257A

Merit

Collateral Self-Promotion

Art Director King James
Writer King James
Designer King James
Photographer King James
Illustrator King James
Creative Directors Alistair King, Mark Stead
Client King James
Agency King James/Cape Town
Annual ID 08258A

Public Service / Political Merit

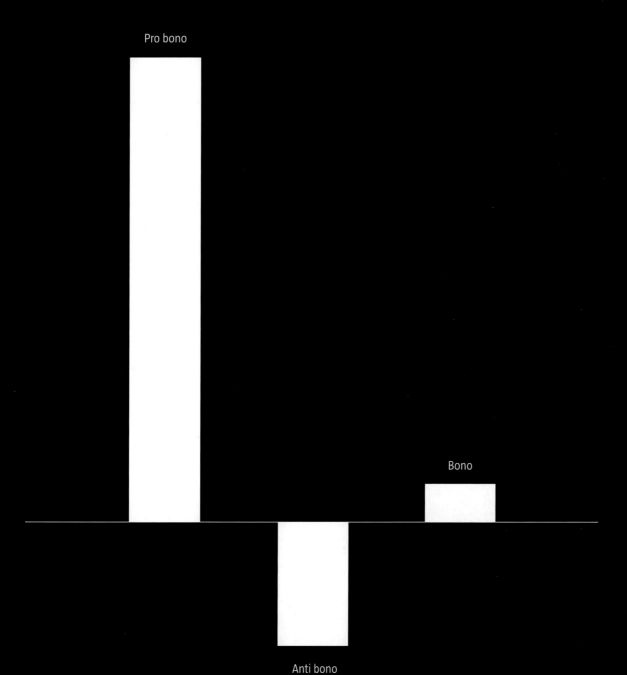

Merit

Public Service/Political Newspaper or Magazine, *Single*

Art Director **Paul Pateman**
Writer **Mike Nicholson**
Illustrator **Paul Pateman**
Creative Director **Paul Brazier**
Client **Museum Of Childhood**
Agency **Abbott Mead Vickers BBDO/London**
Annual ID **08259A**

Merit

Public Service/Political Newspaper or Magazine, *Single*

Art Director **Paul Wallace**
Writer **David Ross**
Creative Director **Andrew Simon**
Client **Canadian Blood Services**
Agency **DDB/Toronto**
Annual ID **08261A**

Merit

Public Service/Political Newspaper or Magazine, *Single*

Art Director Paul Wallace
Writer David Ross
Creative Director Andrew Simon
Client Canadian Blood Services
Agency DDB/Toronto
Annual ID 08262A

Merit

Public Service/Political Newspaper or Magazine, *Single*

Art Directors Esteban Sacco, Manuel Techera
Writers Ignacio Zuccarino, Enrique Codesido, Gabriel Bello
Creative Directors Manuel Techera, Esteban Sacco, Ignacio Zuccarino, Enrique Codesido
Client Cruz Roja Mexicana
Agency JWT/Mexico City
Annual ID 08263A

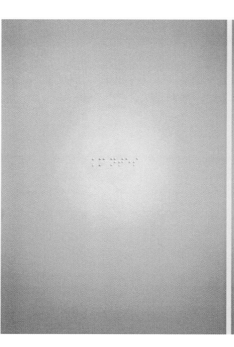

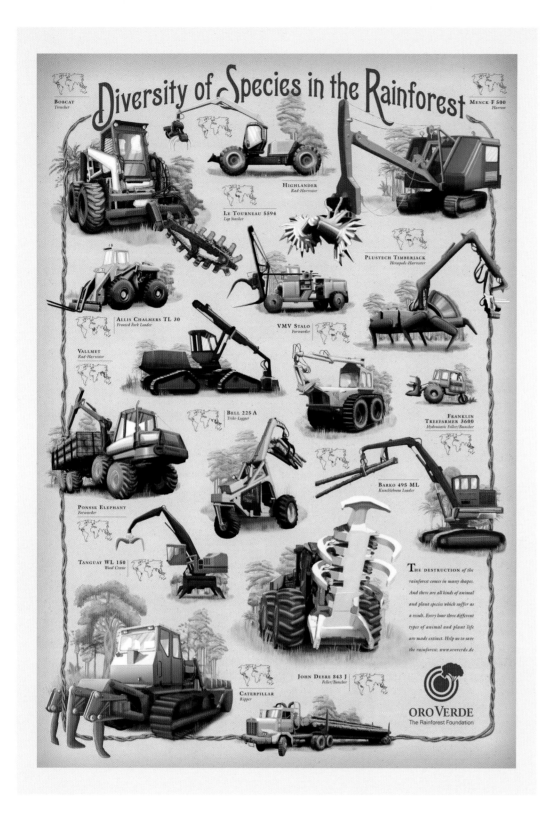

Merit

Public Service/Political Newspaper or Magazine, *Single*

Art Directors Christian Mommertz, Stefan Lenz
Writer Stefan Lenz
Designer Sonja Fritsch
Illustrator Anke Vera Zink
Creative Directors Christian Mommertz, Dr. Stephan Vogel
Client Oro Verde Rainforest Foundation
Agency Ogilvy/Frankfurt
Annual ID 08265A

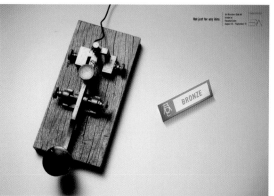

Merit

Public Service/Political Newspaper or Magazine, *Campaign*

Art Director Max Geraldo
Writer José Luiz Martins
Photographer Hugo Treu
Creative Directors Luiz Sanches, Rodrigo Almeida, Tales Bahu
Client Escola Panamericana de Arte
Agency AlmapBBDO/São Paulo
Annual ID 08267A

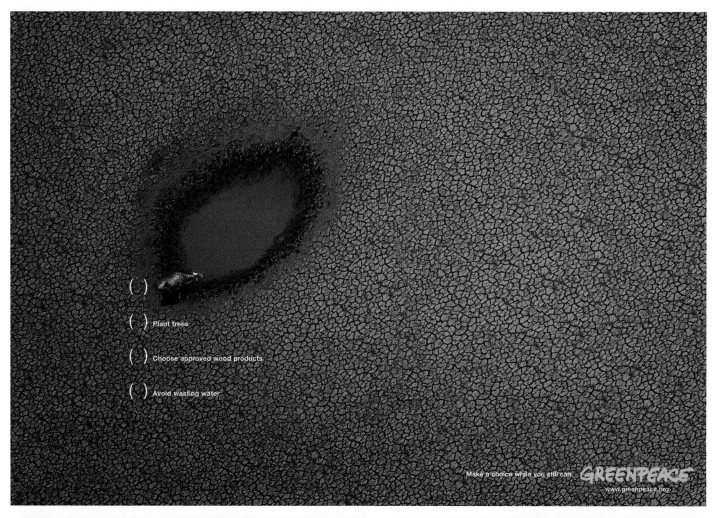

Merit

Public Service/Political Newspaper or Magazine, *Campaign*

Art Directors Bruno Prosperi, Marcos Medeiros
Writers Renato Simões, Wilson Mateos
Creative Directors Marcello Serpa, Luiz Sanches, Roberto Pereira
Client Greenpeace
Agency AlmapBBDO/São Paulo
Annual ID 08266A

Merit

Merit

Public Service/Political Newspaper or Magazine, *Campaign*

Art Directors Pamela Coatti, Rob Kottkamp, John Parker
Writers Marc Einhorn, John Kearse, Matt Ledoux, Will Chambliss, Evan Frye
Designer Ryan Habbyshaw
Photographer Greg Miller
Illustrator Eelus
Creative Directors Pete Favat, John Kearse, Alex Bogusky, Tom Adams
Client American Legacy Foundation
Agency Arnold Worldwide/Boston and Crispin Porter + Bogusky/Miami
Annual ID 08268A

ALSO AWARDED
✎ Merit Public Service/Political Newspaper or Magazine, *Single*

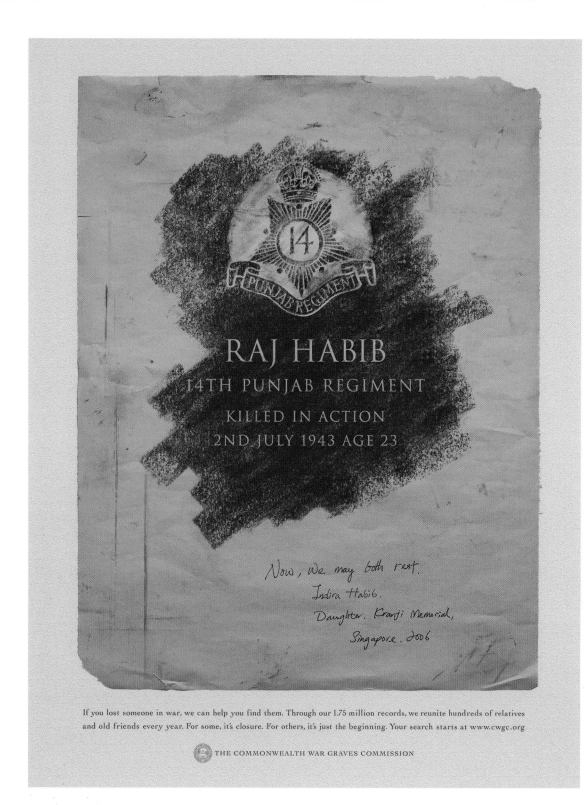

Merit

Public Service/Political Newspaper or Magazine, *Campaign*

Art Director Mark Bamfield
Writer Jason Hodges
Photographer Derrick Lim
Illustrator Procolor
Creative Director Mark Bamfield
Client Commonwealth War Graves Commission
Agency BBDO/Singapore
Annual ID 08269A

Merit

Public Service/Political Newspaper or Magazine, *Campaign*

Art Director Márcio Ribas
Writer Isabella Paulelli
Creative Director Alexandre Gama
Client ADESF
Agency Neogama/BBH/São Paulo
Annual ID 08270A

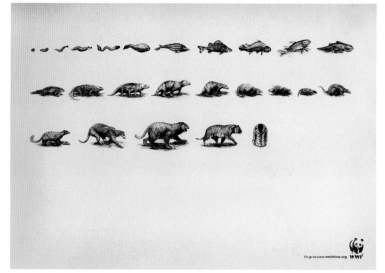

Merit

Public Service/Political Newspaper or Magazine, *Campaign*

Art Directors Rain Yu, Nils Andersson
Writers Doug Schiff, Nils Andersson
Illustrators Xiaoming Liu, Rain Yu
Creative Directors Nils Andersson, Doug Schiff
Client WWF
Agency Ogilvy/Beijing
Annual ID 08271A

Merit

Public Service/Political Newspaper or Magazine, *Campaign*

Art Director Yew Pong Hor
Writers Primus Nair, Audrey Lean
Photographer Wei Joo Gan
Illustrator Simon Ong
Creative Directors Edmund Choe, Adrian Miller
Client SPCA Malaysia
Agency Saatchi & Saatchi/Petaling Jaya
Annual ID 08272A

Merit

Public Service/Political Newspaper or Magazine, *Campaign*

Art Directors Richard Copping, Ronojoy Ghosh
Writer Jagdish Ramakrishnan
Photographer Jeremy Wong
Illustrators Richard Copping, Ronojoy Ghosh, Niharika Hukku
Creative Director Andy Greenaway
Client Thai SPCA
Agency Saatchi & Saatchi/Singapore
Annual ID 08273A

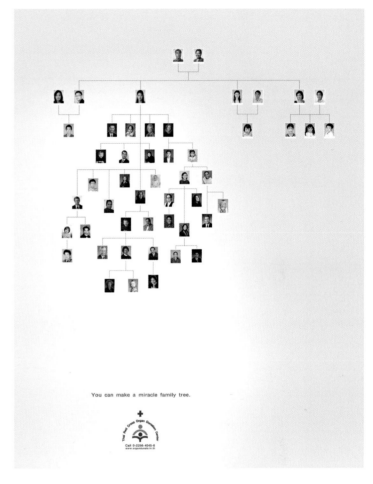

Merit

Public Service/Political Outdoor, *Single*

Art Director **Paul Pateman**
Writer **Mike Nicholson**
Illustrator **Paul Pateman**
Creative Director **Paul Brazier**
Client **Museum Of Childhood**
Agency **Abbott Mead Vickers BBDO/London**
Annual ID **08274A**

Merit

Public Service/Political Outdoor, *Single*

Art Director **Nopparat Siangsirisak**
Writers **Suthisak Sucharittanonta, Walita Jamonchureekul**
Creative Directors **Suthisak Sucharittanonta, Nikrom Kulkosa, Vasan Wangpaitoon, Juntiga Nasunee**
Client **Thai Red Cross Organ Donation Center**
Agency **BBDO/Bangkok**
Annual ID **08275A**

  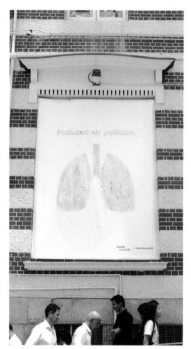 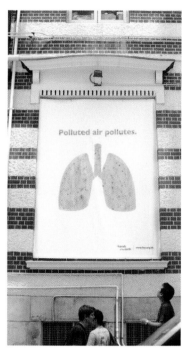

Merit

Public Service/Political Outdoor, *Single*

Art Directors Fei Leung, Arthur Tse, Chi Kit Kwong
Writers Yee Mui Cheung, Steven Lee, Jesse Wong
Creative Directors Steven Lee, Chi Kit Kwong
Client Friends of the Earth
Agency JWT/Hong Kong
Annual ID 08281A

Merit

Public Service/Political Outdoor, *Single*

Art Director Jay Gundzik
Writer Craig Ghiglione
Photographer Lindsey Wade
Creative Director Martin Dix
Client J. Paul Getty Trust/Getty Museum
Agency M&C Saatchi/Santa Monica
Annual ID 08283A

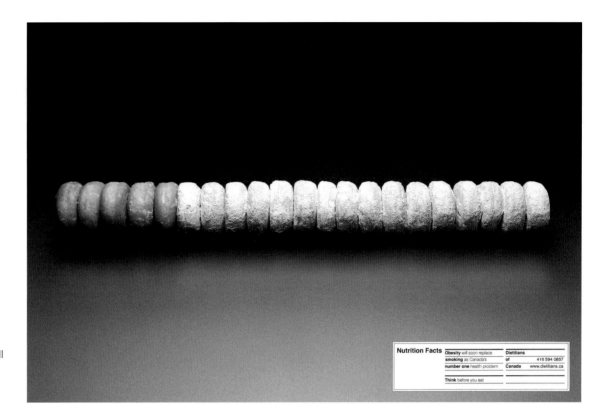

Merit

Public Service/Political Outdoor, *Single*

Art Directors Kelsey Horne, Brad Connell
Writer Mike Meadus
Photographer Ken Woo
Creative Director Mike Meadus
Client Dietitians of Canada
Agency MacLaren McCann/Calgary
Annual ID 08284A

Merit

Public Service/Political Outdoor, *Single*

Art Director Neca Bohrer
Writer Gustavo Nogueira
Photographer Rudy Ruhold
Creative Directors Adriana Cury,
Luiz Nogueira, Neca Bohrer, Toninho Lima
Client MAM - Rio Museum of Modern Art
Agency McCann Erickson/São Paulo
Annual ID 08285A

Help children stay children. Visit nmtpc.org.
NEW MEXICO TEEN PREGNANCY COALITION

Merit

Public Service/Political Outdoor, *Single*

Art Director Jill Efrussy
Writer Greg Hunter
Photographer Jill Efrussy
Creative Director Bart Cleveland
Client New Mexico Teen Pregnancy Coalition
Agency McKee Wallwork Cleveland/Albuquerque
Annual ID 08286A

**Without a pet
you're just creepy.**

To adopt, license and spay/neuter your pet   visit here or laanimalservices.com today.
Animal
Services

Merit

Public Service/Political Outdoor, *Single*

Art Director Ben Dveirin
Writer Troy Pottgen
Creative Director Tom Ortega
Client LA Animal Services
Agency Riester/Phoenix
Annual ID 08288A

Merit

Public Service/Political Outdoor, *Single*

Art Director Breno Cotta
Writer Breno Cotta
Creative Director Breno Cotta
Client Amnesty International
Agency Ruiz Nicoli Lineas/Madrid
Annual ID 08289A

Merit

Public Service/Political Outdoor, *Single*

Art Directors Brandy Vu, Sumesh Peringeth
Writer Steve Hough
Illustrator Que Huong Nguyen
Creative Directors Andy Greenaway, Steve Hough
Client Amnesty International
Agency Saatchi & Saatchi/Ho Chi Minh
Annual ID 08291A

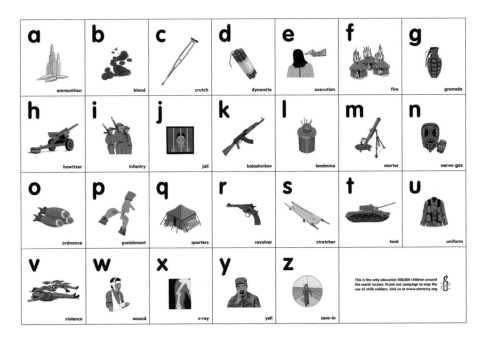

Merit

Public Service/Political Outdoor, *Campaign*

Art Director Antony Nelson
Writer Mike Sutherland
Creative Director Paul Brazier
Client The Samaritans
Agency Abbott Mead Vickers BBDO/London
Annual ID 08294A

242

Merit

Public Service/Political Outdoor, *Campaign*

Art Directors Amanda Clelland, Jesse Juriga
Creative Directors Ji Lee, Scott Witt, Ted Royer, Duncan Marshall
Client New Museum
Agency Droga5/New York
Annual ID 08296A

Merit

Merit

Public Service/Political Outdoor, *Campaign*

Art Director Julia Elton-Bott
Writer Murray Laird
Photographer Simon Westlake
Illustrator Madeleine De Pierres
Creative Director Andrew Tinning
Client The Office of Road Safety
Agency Marketforce/West Perth
Annual ID 08297A

ALSO AWARDED
✎ Merit Public Service/Political Outdoor, *Single*

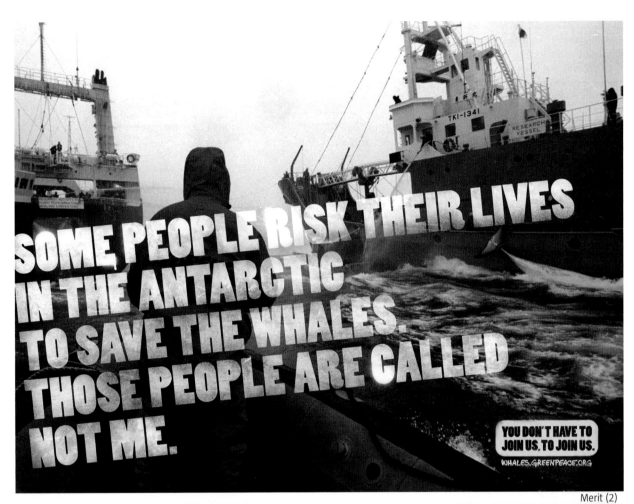

SOME PEOPLE RISK THEIR LIVES IN THE ANTARCTIC TO SAVE THE WHALES. THOSE PEOPLE ARE CALLED NOT ME.

YOU DON'T HAVE TO JOIN US, TO JOIN US.
WHALES.GREENPEACE.ORG

Merit (2)

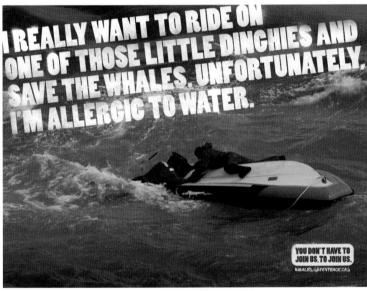

I REALLY WANT TO RIDE ON ONE OF THOSE LITTLE DINGHIES AND SAVE THE WHALES. UNFORTUNATELY, I'M ALLERGIC TO WATER.

YOU DON'T HAVE TO JOIN US, TO JOIN US.
WHALES.GREENPEACE.ORG

YOU THOUGHT ABOUT JUMPING ON A RUBBER BOAT AND THWARTING HARPOONS TO SAVE THE WHALES, BUT THEN YOU WOULD MISS "DESPERATE HOUSEWIVES."

YOU DON'T HAVE TO JOIN US, TO JOIN US.
WHALES.GREENPEACE.ORG

Merit

Public Service/Political Outdoor, *Campaign*

Art Directors Reed Collins, Hunter Fine
Writers Nick Cade, Bob Winter
Creative Directors Bob Winter, Reed Collins
Client Greenpeace
Agency Leo Burnett/Chicago
Annual ID 08298A

ALSO AWARDED
✒ Merit Public Service/Political Newspaper or Magazine, *Single*
✒ Merit Public Service/Political Outdoor, *Single*

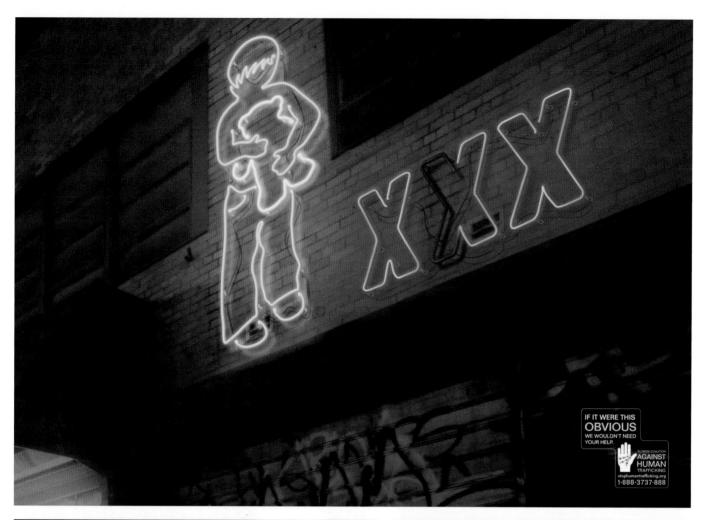

Merit

Public Service/Political Outdoor, *Campaign*

Art Director David Cabestany
Writers Pablo Enriquez, Armando Hernandez
Creative Director Armando Hernandez
Client Florida Coalition Against Human Trafficking
Agency Marca/Miami Beach
Annual ID 08299A

Merit

Public Service/Political Outdoor, *Campaign*

Art Directors Xingsheng Qi, Shengxiong Chen, Jacky Lung
Writers Matthew Curry, Paul Bo, Nils Andersson
Photographer Huimin Li
Creative Directors Nils Andersson, Kweichee Lam, Jacky Lung
Client WWF
Agency Ogilvy/Beijing
Annual ID 08300A

HANDBAG € 32.-
Food for a week € 4.-

Text 'aid' to 2255 and donate € 1.50   People in Need
Cordaid

Merit
Public Service/Political Outdoor, *Campaign*

Art Directors Tim Bishop, Saatchi Tribe, Magnus Olsson
Writer Saatchi Tribe
Photographer Carl Stolz
Creative Director Magnus Olsson
Client Cordaid Mensen in Nood
Agency Saatchi & Saatchi/Amsterdam
Annual ID 08301A

MEN TALK TO WOMEN ABOUT SEX AND IT'S SEXUAL HARASSMENT. WOMEN TALK TO MEN ABOUT SEX AND IT'S $8.99 A MINUTE.

museumofsex.com

Merit
Public Service/Political Collateral, *Single*

Art Director **Raj Kamble**
Writer **Stephen Lundberg**
Designers **Ken Rabe, Sameer Kulavoor**
Creative Director **Mark Wnek**
Client **Museum of Sex**
Agency **Lowe/New York**
Annual ID **08215A**

Merit

Public Service/Political Collateral, *Campaign*

Art Director Katsuhiro Shimizu
Writers Haruo Yoshida, Hidekazu Sato
Photographers Hiroshi Hasegawa, Ichiro Ohno, Yoshiteru Eguchi, Akihiro Kobayashi,
Suzuko Tsuruoka
Creative Director Hidekazu Sato
Client Wild Bird Society of Japan
Agency Beacon Communications/Tokyo
Annual ID 08303A

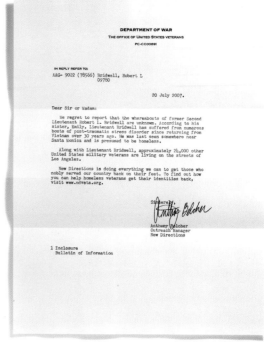

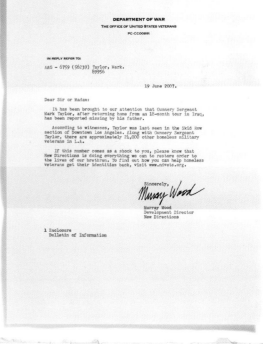

Letter 1 (top left)

DEPARTMENT OF WAR

THE OFFICE OF UNITED STATES VETERANS

PC-CC00891

IN REPLY REFER TO:

AAG- 53378 (88671) Faraci, Michael P.
81190

23 May 2007.

Dear Sir or Madam:

We deeply regret to inform you that Private First Class Michael P. Faraci has been reported missing after honorably serving his country in Afghanistan.

Private Faraci was last seen somewhere on the streets of Downtown Los Angeles, where he is presumed to be living. He is considered missing by his wife, Mrs. Leslie Faraci, and two young children, David and Meghan.

Along with Private Faraci, approximately 24,000 other homeless United States veterans are living on the streets of L.A. New Directions is doing everything we can to bring them home.

To find out how you can help homeless veterans get their identities back, visit www.ndvets.org.

Sincerely,

Toni Reinis
Executive Director
New Directions

1 Enclosure
  Bulletin of Information

Envelope (left)

DEPARTMENT OF WAR

THE OFFICE OF UNITED STATES VETERANS

LOS ANGELES CA 900

24 FEB 2007 PM 5 L

Edward Sallone
3952 Silver Blvd., #8
L.A., CA 90093

9003943242

Letter 2 (top right)

DEPARTMENT OF WAR

THE OFFICE OF UNITED STATES VETERANS

PC-CC00891

IN REPLY REFER TO:

AAG- 9022 (78566) Bridwell, Robert L
09760

20 July 2007.

Dear Sir or Madam:

We regret to report that the whereabouts of former Second Lieutenant Robert L. Bridwell are unknown. According to his sister, Emily, Lieutenant Bridwell has suffered from numerous bouts of post-traumatic stress disorder since returning from Vietnam over 30 years ago. He was last seen somewhere near Santa Monica and is presumed to be homeless.

Along with Lieutenant Bridwell, approximately 24,000 other United States military veterans are living on the streets of Los Angeles.

New Directions is doing everything we can to get those who nobly served our country back on their feet. To find out how you can help homeless veterans get their identities back, visit www.ndvets.org.

Sincerely,

Anthony Belcher
Outreach Manager
New Directions

1 Enclosure
  Bulletin of Information

Envelope (middle right)

DEPARTMENT OF WAR

THE OFFICE OF UNITED STATES VETERANS

LOS ANGELES CA 900

24 FEB 2007 PM 5 L

Edward Sallone
3952 Silver Blvd., #8
L.A., CA 90093

9003943242

Letter 3 (bottom right)

DEPARTMENT OF WAR

THE OFFICE OF UNITED STATES VETERANS

PC-CC00891

IN REPLY REFER TO:

AAG- 6759 (56239) Taylor, Mark.
89956

19 June 2007.

Dear Sir or Madam:

It has been brought to our attention that Gunnery Sergeant Mark Taylor, after returning home from an 18-month tour in Iraq, has been reported missing by his father.

According to witnesses, Taylor was last seen in the Skid Row section of Downtown Los Angeles. Along with Gunnery Sergeant Taylor, there are approximately 24,000 other homeless military veterans in L.A.

If this number comes as a shock to you, please know that New Directions is doing everything we can to restore order to the lives of our brethren. To find out how you can help homeless veterans get their identities back, visit www.ndvets.org.

Sincerely,

Murray Wood
Development Director
New Directions

1 Enclosure
  Bulletin of Information

Envelope (bottom right)

DEPARTMENT OF WAR

THE OFFICE OF UNITED STATES VETERANS

LOS ANGELES CA 900

24 FEB 2007 PM 5 L

Edward Sallone
3952 Silver Blvd., #8
L.A., CA 90093

9003943242

Merit

Public Service/Political Collateral, *Campaign*

Art Director Josh Gilman
Writer Rick Utzinger
Creative Director Harvey Marco
Client New Directions
Agency Saatchi & Saatchi LA/Torrance
Annual ID 08304A

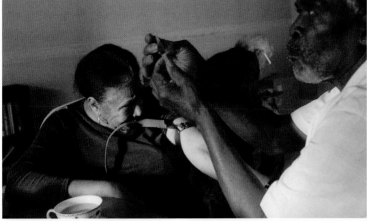

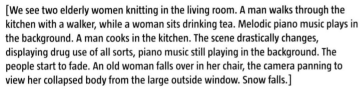

[We see two elderly women knitting in the living room. A man walks through the kitchen with a walker, while a woman sits drinking tea. Melodic piano music plays in the background. A man cooks in the kitchen. The scene drastically changes, displaying drug use of all sorts, piano music still playing in the background. The people start to fade. An old woman falls over in her chair, the camera panning to view her collapsed body from the large outside window. Snow falls.]

SUPER: **There's no such thing as an old junkie.**

LOGO: **Focus 12 Rehab Center**

SUPER: **Take back your future. www.focus12.co.uk**

SUPER: **TRUTH Presents: WHUDAFXUP with labeling?**

DERRICK: **Hey Nick. Glad you came in. Good to see you.**

NICK: **Likewise, likewise.**

DERRICK: **So what's going on in your life? What's going on in Nick Cannon's life?**

NICK: **Everything man, ya know...it doesn't stop.**

DERRICK: **You ever get freaked out or have any kind of like, self-esteem problems?**

NICK: **Never.**

DERRICK: **Don't you think that's kind of weird?**

NICK: **Not really.**

DERRICK: **Given who you are...I just imagine you must get nervous, like you must have a bunch of 40s around you that you drink. You look like a big 40-drinker. What about when you're preparing for your show, who reads the scripts to you?**

NICK: **Who reads it to me? I mean, I read it myself.**

DERRICK: **You can read?**

NICK: **I can read well, but why don't you believe me?**

DERRICK: **[Handing him some documents] Prove it to me.**

NICK READS: **Back in the '80s, tobacco companies labeled African Americans as less-educated, prefer malt liquor and have problems with their own self-esteem. Wow, where'd that come from?**

DERRICK: **From a tobacco company, actually...**

NICK: **Pretty sad.**

DERRICK: **Labeling African Americans as less-educated, malt-liquor drinkers?**

SUPER: **WHUDAFXUP? Truth.**

Merit

Public Service/Political Television, *Single*

Art Director **Mike Bond**
Writer **Bern Hunter**
Agency Producer **Larry Holland**
Production Company **Bare Films**
Director **Arran Bowyn**
Creative Director **Paul Brazier**
Client **Focus 12**
Agency **Abbott Mead Vickers BBDO/London**
Annual ID **08313T**

Merit

Public Service/Political Television, *Single*

Art Directors **Mike Costello, John Parker**
Writers **Marc Einhorn, Alex Russell, Evan Frye**
Agency Producers **Rupert Samuel, Chris Kyriakos**
Production Company **Vice Films**
Director **Eddy Moretti**
Creative Directors **Pete Favat, Alex Bogusky, John Kearse, Tom Adams**
Client **American Legacy Foundation**
Agency **Arnold Worldwide/Boston and Crispin Porter + Bogusky/Miami**
Annual ID **08314T**

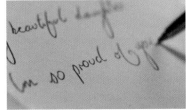

[We open on a black screen with plain, white text reading: "On January 31, 2007, The Intergovernmental Panel on Climate Change held a press conference in Paris announcing that global warming is 'unequivocal' and that human activity was 'very likely' to blame for it. That evening, this video was projected onto monuments and high-visibility buildings throughout Paris, including the Assemblée Nationale (the French Parliament)." A Paris scene comes on the screen. A video of a child is projected onto the French Parliament, as people walk by on the sidewalk.]

CHILD: The scientific community released a report that proves without a doubt that the world is getting warmer. This global warming is caused by things you grown-ups do, and things you don't. If drastic measures aren't taken soon, by the time I grow up there will be no more fish left in the sea. Rainforests and clean air will be a thing of the past. The polar ice caps will be gone. Oceans will rise. Entire countries will disappear. Life will change in ways you cannot even imagine. There could be famine, worldwide epidemics. Life expectancy will be lower. And we're not just talking about the future. We're talking about my future. But, this is no surprise. You adults have known about this for years. Though you could of done something about it, you haven't. You can say, 'It's not my problem.' You can say, 'I won't be around in 50 years.' But from now on, you can't say, 'I didn't know.' Starting today, the lines are drawn. You have to choose sides. Either you are for my future, or you're against it. You're a friend, or you're an enemy. I may just be a kid today, but tomorrow will be different. This is the last I will be talking to you adults. You have had your chance to fix this problem, now we have ours. We won't be cute. We won't be patronized. And we will not be denied our future.

SUPER: Its-not-too-late.com. Join the Energy Revolution.

LOGO: Greenpeace

[We see a young woman writing a 21st birthday card. She writes,"To my beautiful daughter, I'm so proud of you and everything you've accomplished...Love Mum." She finishes writing the card, and then slowly places it on a pile of birthday cards she has just written—one for every future birthday her baby will have. She walks into her baby daughter's bedroom and proudly watches over her, as she lies in her cot—oblivious to her mother's suffering.]

SUPER: We don't know what causes brain cancer. But we do know what it affects. Help us find a cure.

LOGO: Cure for Life Foundation

Merit
Public Service/Political Television, *Single*

Art Director Les Vikings
Agency Producer Florence Pothiée-Sperry
Director Kad O
Creative Directors Alexandre Hervé, Sylvain Thirache
Client Greenpeace
Agency DDB/Paris
Annual ID 08315T

Merit
Public Service/Political Television, *Single*

Art Director Adam Rose
Writers Ben O'Brien, Alex Wadelton
Agency Producer Honae MacNeill
Production Company Film Graphics
Director Johnathan Nyquist
Creative Director Matt Eastwood
Client Cure for Life Foundation
Agency DDB/Sydney
Annual ID 08316T

[We open looking across a restaurant kitchen window.]

CHEF: I'm the Sous Chef here. With any luck, I should be Head Chef by next year. I've got this amazing fiancé [looking at her ring] that I won't be marrying this weekend because I am about to be in a [using her figures are quotation marks] 'terrible accident.' But really, I should have cleaned up the grease over there [picking up a big pot], and they should never put the deep fryer too close to the...

[Falling backwards, the pot of hot grease spills all over her.]

OTHER COOK: Oh my God, there has been an accident. Somebody...

[Chef screams in pain. Scene ends with a close up of her burnt face.]

SUPER: There really are no accidents.

OTHER COOK VO: Somebody help me!

LOGO: Prevent-it.ca

Merit

Public Service/Political Television, *Single*

Art Director Joe Piccolo
Writer Chris Taciuk
Agency Producers Pam Portsmouth, Andrea Hubert
Production Companies Imported Artists, @radical.media
Director Peter Darley Miller
Creative Directors Robin Heisey, Chris Taciuk, Joe Piccolo
Client Workers Safety & Insurance Board
Agency DraftFCB/Toronto
Annual ID 08312T

[We see a close-up shot of a car muffler. Then we see a line of tightly packed cars. A yellow Volkswagen Beetle pulls out of line and is followed one-by-one by the other cars. The cars drive around in chaos and come back together, the yellow Beetle pulling in place last to form the image of a bus.]

SUPER: A single bus can eliminate one kilometer of car queue.

LOGO: Oslo Public Transport

Merit

Public Service/Political Television, *Single*

Art Director Martin Thorsen
Writer Kristoffer Carlin
Designer Ingvild Selliaas
Agency Producer Caroline Werring-Otnes
Production Company Gry Sætre
Directors Kristoffer Carlin, Andreas J. Riiser
Client Oslo Public Transport
Agency Kitchen Leo Burnett/Oslo
Annual ID 08318T

[We open with a goldfish looking out of the tank.]

GOLDFISH: **Aquarium. Aquarium. Aquarium. Aquarium. Aquarium. I wanna go. Aquarium. I wanna go to the aquarium. I wanna go to the aquarium. Aquarium. Hey. Aquarium. Somebody? I wanna go. Hmm. Hmm. Hmm. I wanna go. I wanna. I wanna. I wanna. Hmm. Hmm. Hmm. I wanna go to the aquarium. Hello!**

LOGO: **Oregon Coast Aquarium Newport**

Merit

Public Service/Political Television, *Single*

Art Director **Andrew Reed**
Writer **Mike Houston**
Director **Rob Tyler**
Creative Director **Jerry Ketel**
Client **Oregon Coast Aquarium**
Agency **Leopold Ketel & Partners/Portland**
Annual ID **08320T**

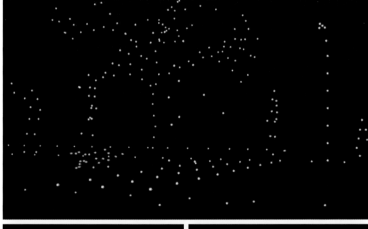

[We see a person formed by small white dots walking across a black background. As the person walks, a number of elements start to appear: a street, other people, cars, birds. These elements are also made of white dots. After a while, everything disappears and the person that was walking transforms into a text in Braille.]

LETTERING: **They can imagine.**

[The text in Braille disappears and another one comes up]

LETTERING: **That's why we want to increase our production of books in Braille.**

LOGO: **Dorina Nowill Foundation for the Blind**

SUPER: **PLEASE DONATE: 0800-770-1047**

Merit

Public Service/Political Television, *Single*

Art Director **Daniel Chagas Martins**
Writer **Mario Cintra**
Agency Producer **Paula Moraes**
Production Company **Vetor Zero**
Director **Nando Cohen**
Creative Directors **Adriana Cury, Danilo Janjacomo**
Client **Dorina Nowill Foundation for the Blind**
Agency **McCann Erickson/São Paulo**
Annual ID **08321T**

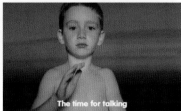

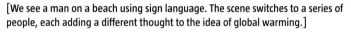

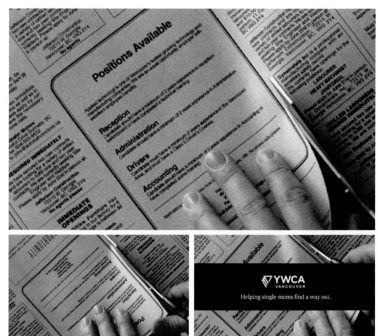

[We see a man on a beach using sign language. The scene switches to a series of people, each adding a different thought to the idea of global warming.]

MAN: The earth is warming faster than any time in the past 10,000 years.

BOY 1: The 1990s was the warmest decade on global record.

WOMAN: Concentration of greenhouse gas is the highest in 20 million years.

[A couple is shown. The boy signs, while the girl stares solemnly into the screen.]

BOY 2: 40% of arctic ice has gone since the 1970s.

BOY 3: 25,000 people died in the heat wave that hit Western Europe in 2003.

[Scene switches to two girls.]

GIRLS: In the near future, major cities will be overwhelmed.

GUY: Thirty-million people may be hungry because of climate change by 2050.

LITTLE BOY: The time for talking is over. It's time to use your hands.

SUPER: STOP GLOBAL WARMING.

LOGO: MTV Switch. www.mtvswitch.org.

LITTLE BOY: Thank you.

[We see a very close shot of the newspaper. A pair of old scissors held by a woman's hand starts to cut out an ad for a job, or career training. The scissors cut one side, turn the corner and start cutting another side. But the coupon is never cut out. No matter how much she cuts, the ad never comes out.]

VO: To get a job, she needs daycare. To get daycare, she needs money. To get money, she needs a job. To get a job, she needs daycare. To get daycare, she needs money. To get money, she needs a job.

LOGO: YWCA Vancouver

SUPER: Helping single moms find a way out.

Merit
Public Service/Political Television, *Single*

Art Director André Lacerda
Writers Rui Silva, João Guimarães, André Pereira
Creative Directors Edson Athayde, Paul Smith
Client MTV
Agency Ogilvy/Lisbon
Annual ID 08322T

Merit
Public Service/Political Television, *Single*

Art Director Chad Kabigting
Writer Bryan Collins
Agency Producer Ann Rubenstein
Production Companies Radke Film Group, Wayne Kozak Audio Productions, Rooster Post Production
Director Steve Gordon
Creative Directors Ian Grais, Chris Staples
Client YWCA
Agency Rethink/Vancouver
Annual ID 08323T

[We open on an office. Walking down the corridor with his trolley, we see a young man with Down Syndrome delivering the mail. He delivers a parcel to a couple in an office and continues down the corridor. The couple that received the parcel then talks about him behind his back.]

MAN: Can you believe he works here with us?

[We then see our guy with Down Syndrome continue walking through the office. We then cut to a businesswoman on the phone.]

WOMAN: Did you hear what he did last week? My God. Hang on, here he comes now.

[She quickly covers up the phone and waves happily to him. He then walks past the water cooler where we see two businessmen looking at him. They have smirks on their faces as they make comments about him.]

MAN 1: The guy's a freak.

MAN 2: Yeah, he won Gold in the 100!

MAN 1: Legend!

[At this point, everybody in the office gets up from their desks and gives him a standing ovation. Our Down Syndrome hero smiles. Clapping turns into stadium cheering.]

LOGO: Special Olympics Australia

SUPER: Participate. Volunteer. Donate. Specialolympics.com.au.

Merit

Public Service/Political Television, *Single*

Art Director David O'Sullivan
Writer Misha McDonald
Agency Producer Melinda Watts
Production Company The Guild
Director Rodd Martin
Creative Director Garry Horner
Client Special Olympics
Agency Whybin TBWA\TEQUILA/Sydney
Annual ID 08325T

Consumer Television Merit

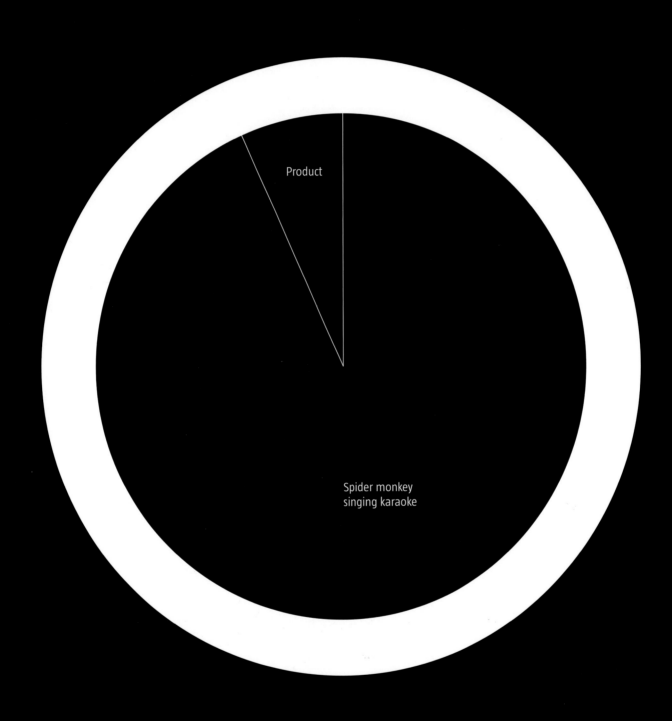

Product

Spider monkey
singing karaoke

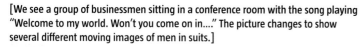

[We see a group of businessmen sitting in a conference room with the song playing "Welcome to my world. Won't you come on in...." The picture changes to show several different moving images of men in suits.]

SUPER: Invest in Folksam and help put more women in the boardroom.

LOGO: Folksam. Ethical Investments

[We open outside Justin Timberlake's Southern Hospitality restaurant. One of Justin's friends sticks straws up his nose.]

JUSTIN: It's not really that funny. No, it's childish and immature.

[An invisible force drags Justin from the table and out the front door of the restaurant. It pulls him against a tall building. We see a close-up of a young girl sipping Pepsi out of a straw. Justin is pulled up along the side of a building. Inside the building, we see a blonde woman who is really Andy Samberg. Every time the girl takes a sip, Justin is dragged through the streets, hitting mailboxes and an SUV with Tony Romo. Justin finally winds up in the young girl's backyard.]

VO: Every sip gets you closer to Justin Timberlake MP3s.

GIRL: Hey.

JUSTIN: Hey to you.

[A large HDTV hits Justin in the head, knocking him to the ground.]

VO: HDTVs.

[We see the girl's father who is drinking a Diet Pepsi Max.]

GIRL: Dad!

VO: Millions of songs from Amazon MP3 and more.

LOGO: Amazon MP3

VO: Sign up at pepsistuff.com.

LOGO: Pepsi, Diet Pepsi, Diet Pepsi Max. Pepsistuff.com

Merit

Television Over :30, *Single*

Art Directors Andreas Lönn, Marcus Göransson
Writer Olle Nordell
Agency Producer Christina Rudling
Production Company Callboy
Director Max Vitali
Client Folksam
Agency ANR BBDO/Stockholm
Annual ID 08351T

Merit

Television Over :30, *Single*

Art Director Matt Vescovo
Writer Dan Rollman
Agency Producers Hyatt Choate, Loren Parkins
Creative Directors David Lubars, Bill Bruce, Don Schneider
Client Pepsi
Agency BBDO/New York
Annual ID 08355T

[We see and hear a guy say the word "dude" in different scenarios, like "you're sitting too close to me" dude, the "are you really doing that" dude, the "pass me the ball" dude, and many other renditions. After many different dudes, we see the guy's friend ordering champagne, while he drinks Bud Light.]

GUY: Dude.

SUPER: Drink Responsibly.

LOGO: Bud Light. www.budlight.com

Merit

Television Over :30, *Single*

Art Directors Kenny Herzog, Clay Weiner
Writers Kenny Herzog, Clay Weiner
Agency Producers Diane Jackson, Will St.Clair
Creative Directors Paul Tilley, Chuck Rachford, Chris Roe, Mark Gross
Client Anheuser-Busch
Agency DDB/Chicago
Annual ID 08356T

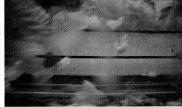

[Opens with a white plastic bag floating to stop at a red light. One bag soon turns into two, two into three, and the group slowly gets bigger. Flying around the city, the bags go to the parking garage, down the street and through the neighborhoods.]

VO: Driving a BlueMotion Polo instead of your normal small car for a year could reduce your carbon footprint as much as recycling over 25,000 plastic bags.

SUPER: Avg. UK mileage/small car emissions. 33% energy saving from recycling lightweight bags. Best Foot Forward '07.

[Thousands of colorful plastic bags stop on a yard. The last blue bag falls to the ground, and all that remains is a Volkswagen BlueMotion.]

SUPER: 99g/km CO2

LOGO: Volkswagen

SUPER: BlueMotion Polo. A simple way to act now. Volkswagen recommends the re-use of plastic bags.

Merit

Television Over :30, *Single*

Art Directors Graeme Hall, Noah Regan, Gavin Siakimotu
Writers Graeme Hall, Gavin Siakimotu
Agency Producer Lucy Westmore
Production Company Independent
Director Daniel Levi
Creative Director Jeremy Craigen
Client Volkswagen
Agency DDB/London
Annual ID 08357T

[We see a field with people walking, and then a man in a maroon suit.]

MAN [Looking around]: **Wow.**

[A bodybuilder stops to do squats and then jogs off. Everyone is walking through a tall sign stating "Répertoire of Mathieu." The man hugs someone walking by. Girls on rollerskates skate by. Various people introduce themselves to each other such as his dentist, his Dad at work, Dad at home and coworkers.]

BLONDE GIRL: **This is Mathieu's answering machine.**

VO: **Mathieu.**

BLONDE GIRL: **You have 5 new messages.**

GUY IN FLOWER SHIRT: **It's a very full phonebook.**

GUY IN GLASSES: **He doesn't call everyone?**

GUY IN FLOWER SHIRT: **Of course. No problem for him.**

SUPER: **Free unlimited calls.**

LOGO: **Bouygues Telecom.**

Merit

Television Over :30, *Single*

Art Director Mathieu Névians
Writer Olivier Henry
Agency Producer Agathe Michaux-Terrier
Production Company Tokib
Director Baker Smith
Creative Directors Alexandre Hervé, Sylvain Thirache
Client Bouygues Telecom
Agency DDB/Paris
Annual ID 08358T

[We see a chef's hands cracking an egg into a bowl. The kitchen is busy with cooks making all sorts of desserts. "My Favorite Things" plays in the background. They mix, bake and ice, putting the desserts together to form a bigger object. The edible parts come together and start to form a car. The chefs work on a candy engine, chocolate wheels and licorice wiring, and then pose with their finished product.]

SUPER: **The new Fabia. Full of lovely stuff. Skoda. Manufacturers of Happy Drivers.**

Merit

Television Over :30, *Single*

Art Directors Chris Bovill, John Allison
Writers Chris Bovill, John Allison
Agency Producer Nicky Barnes
Production Company Gorgeous
Director Chris Palmer
Creative Director Richard Flintham
Client Skoda Fabia
Agency Fallon/London
Annual ID 08359T

[A man is riding a bicycle along a forest path when, all of a sudden, a figure roaring brutishly starts running towards him—a medieval knight in full gear with a helmet and visor. Shocked, the man stops and dismounts. The knight is clearly after the bicycle. He grabs the handlebars leading to a test of strength between him and the shocked cyclist, which the knight eventually wins. Roaring and grunting, he flees, dragging the bicycle behind him. Sometime after the knight has vanished into the forest, the cyclist is still standing there stunned looking into the forest.]

SUPER: How do you explain this to your insurance? Just call!

LOGO: DEVK Insurances

[We see a family of three on a picnic.]

CHILD [Pointing to a floating head with hanging organs]: What's that?

FATHER: That's a Thai ghost called 'Kra-Sue.' It's looking for things to eat at night time.

CHILD [Pointing to a flying man with wings]: Dad?

FATHER: Another ghost called 'Kra-Hung.' It always flies around.

CHILD: Can I have that banana?

FATHER: No son, that belongs to the banana ghost.

CHILD: So, that's a jackfruit ghost, right?

FATHER: No, that's a transvestite.

CHILD: Oh. Got it.

FATHER: Good.

CHILD: Dad! A blue ghost.

[The blue ghost comes to a pair of giant feet and scurries away.]

FATHER: Hey, a tall ghost. What the hell are you standing here for? We are having dinner. Go away!

[The tall ghost sulks away.]

FATHER: Damn, shut up!

[He swats at the Kra-Hung.]

SUPER: Under the light, nothing seems to be scary.

LOGO: Sylvania. The light is your true friend.

Merit
Television Over :30, *Single*

Art Director Djik Ouchiian
Writer Martin Grass
Agency Producer Patrick Cahill
Production Company Big Fish Filmproduktion
Director Andreas Hoffmann
Creative Directors Ralf Heuel, Dirk Siebenhaar
Client DEVK Insurance
Agency Grabarz & Partner/Hamburg
Annual ID 08360T

Merit
Television Over :30, *Single*

Art Directors Apiwat Pattalarungkhan, Aniruth Assawanapanon
Writers Jureeporn Thaidumrong, Suwit Ekudompong
Production Company Phenomena
Director Thanonchai Sornsrivichai
Creative Director Jureeporn Thaidumrong
Client Sylvania
Agency Jeh United/Bangkok
Annual ID 08361T

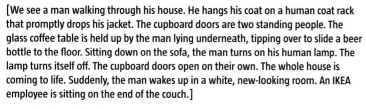

[We see a man walking through his house. He hangs his coat on a human coat rack that promptly drops his jacket. The cupboard doors are two standing people. The glass coffee table is held up by the man lying underneath, tipping over to slide a beer bottle to the floor. Sitting down on the sofa, the man turns on his human lamp. The lamp turns itself off. The cupboard doors open on their own. The whole house is coming to life. Suddenly, the man wakes up in a white, new-looking room. An IKEA employee is sitting on the end of the couch.]

MAN: I had a terrible dream.

IKEA EMPLOYEE: Awww. I'm sorry, but this is a dream.

[Flash to the old couch and the man waking up sweating.]

SUPER: Ready for new stuff?

LOGO: IKEA

[We see the dark profile of an older man.]

MAN: My name is Henri Bouvois. Due to a rare condition, I have very small hands. As a youngster, I used to do anything to hide my hands from view.

[Child race, as he runs with his hands in his pockets.]

MAN: Bowling was impossible. Piano lessons were utterly humiliating. After a dance once, a girl likened the experience to holding the paw of a weasel.

One day, I decided to put an end to my misery. My finger did not reach the trigger. So, I prayed for a purpose in life.

[The man looks up at the torn curtain in his bedroom.]

MAN: Suddenly, I was overcome with an urge to sew.

[In a crowd room, he sews a woman's pantyhose.]

MAN: My stitches were so small and delicate they would go unnoticed to the untrained eye.

[The room claps.]

MAN: Soon, my new found dexterity was famous across the land.

[Cut to a close-up of him kissing a woman. Cut to a tailor shop.]

MAN: Girls liked me. It wasn't long before the makers of the world's finest clothes offered me a position in their workshop. I have been Head Tailor for 10 years this August. Here, I am not treated as a freak, but as a hero.

No longer do I feel cursed. I feel blessed.

SUPER: Herringbone. Distinguished by detail.

Merit
Television Over :30, *Single*

Art Director Florian Pack
Writer Teja Fischer
Agency Producer Sandra Niessen
Production Companies Salt Berlin, Hahn Nitzsche Studios
Creative Directors Tom Hauser, Soeren Porst, Arno Lindemann, Bernhard Lukas
Client IKEA Deutschland
Agency Jung von Matt/Hamburg
Annual ID 08362T

Merit
Television Over :30, *Single*

Art Director Graham Johnson
Writer Oliver Devaris
Agency Producer Rod James
Production Company Exit Films
Director Garth Davies
Creative Directors Ben Welsh, Graham Johnson, Oliver Devaris
Client Herringbone
Agency M & C Saatchi/Sydney
Annual ID 08363T

ALSO AWARDED

Merit Non-Broadcast, *Single*

[Eight Renaults are driving to ballet music, creating formations on a dried salt lake, giving the appearance that they are dancing. With highly aesthetic shots, all the cars gradually begin to crash against one another in perfect choreography. In the end, all eight cars are demolished, but they are still capable of driving and line up for their pack shot.]

SUPER: **The safest car range there is. Eight models awarded 5 stars in the Euro NCAP Crash Test.**

LOGO: **Renault**

Merit

Television Over :30, *Single*

Art Directors Tim Schierwater, Christoph Bielefeldt
Writer Sebastian Behrendt
Production Company Element E
Director Silvio Helbig
Creative Director Lars Ruehmann
Client Renault Germany
Agency Nordpol+ Hamburg
Annual ID 08364T

ALSO AWARDED

✎ Merit Cinema, *Single*

[We see human beings crash in a manner typical for their nations: the clash of two huge Japanese sumo ringers. Two Swedish girls dancing around a pole on a midsummer´s night bang into each other accidentally. Two Bavarian Schuplattlers, from which one of them gets slapped in the face by the other one. Finally, a French woman and a French man staring furiously and walking into each other, but the collision of their heads is softened by their lips: they kiss.]

SUPER: **The best protection against head-on collisions comes from France.**

[Back to a shot of the couple kissing]

SUPER: **The only car maker with eight models awarded 5 stars in the Euro NCAP Crash Tests.**

LOGO: **Renault**

Merit

Television Over :30, *Single*

Art Directors Bertrand Kirschenhofer, Christoph Bielefeldt
Writer Ingmar Bartels
Production Company Element E
Director Thorsten Kirves
Creative Director Lars Ruehmann
Client Renault Germany
Agency Nordpol+ Hamburg
Annual ID 08365T

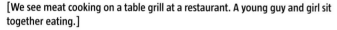

[We see meat cooking on a table grill at a restaurant. A young guy and girl sit together eating.]

GIRL 1: Are you going to pay any attention to me?

GUY 1: Hey the food's really good.

[The girl laughs. Her face suddenly gets serious as she spots another young guy at a table across the room. Their eyes meet and pictures flash across the screen of the two of them smiling over the same meal, a happy couple.]

GUY 1: What are you looking at?

[The girl looks down. Her ex-boyfriend also looks down, causing his date to respond.]

GIRL 2: What's wrong?

GUY 2: Nothing.

GIRL 1: Nothing.

[Not convinced, the two dates turn around to see what the others were looking at. Their faces immediately drop with shock, as pictures flash across the screen of the two of them, another happy couple sharing noodles and smiling.]

GIRL 1: Anything wrong?

GUY 1: Let's just eat.

GUY 2: What's up?

GIRL 2: Nothing.

VO: Time passes. People change. But flavor remains the same.
20th anniversary BBQ Plaza.

[We see a series of magic tricks brought into real life scenarios: pulling a rabbit out of a hat and knotted handkerchiefs from a fist and the classic coin behind the ear. A moped rider disappears into thin air when he crashes into the side of a truck. When a policewoman tries to write up a ticket for a parked car, the owner pulls off the covering sheet, making the car turn into birds and fly away. A girl goes into a phone booth, and after it explodes with water, she is transported to the filing cabinet and cupboard of her office. Pulling a pencil from her ear, she is ready for work.]

SUPER: Today's the day to work your magic.

LOGO: JCPenney.

SUPER: Every Day Matters. JCP.com.

Merit
Television Over :30, *Single*

Art Director Dutsanee Emnuwattana
Writers Wuthisak Anarnkaporn, Korn Tepintarapiraksa
Agency Producer Yuthapong Varanukrohchoke
Production Company Sunshine-Etc
Director Kumphol Witpiboolrut
Creative Director Korn Tepinlarapiraksa
Client The Barbecue Plaza
Agency Ogilvy & Mather/Bangkok
Annual ID 08366T

Merit
Television Over :30, *Single*

Art Directors Lea Ladera, Menno Kluin
Writers Sara Rose, Icaro Doria
Agency Producer Colin Pearsall
Production Company MJZ
Director Nicolai Fuglsig
Creative Directors Tony Granger, Kerry Keenan, Michael Long
Client JC Penney
Agency Saatchi & Saatchi/New York
Annual ID 08367T

Unofficial drink of Jamaica since 1938.

[We see a close up of a man's face. Bundled up, icicles form on his beard.]

MAN: Thoratio just died.

[We see many men huddled in the tent, with icicle-filled faces.]

MAN 2: Are we going out then?

MAN 3: Don't push it, Dan.

MAN 2: Come on. It'll be fun.

MAN 3: Go out there in the freezing wastes? You must be mad. We aren't going are we?

MAN 2: We have to go out. It's my birthday.

MAN 4: It is his birthday. It is his birthday.

MAN 3: Why didn't you say so? Of course we're going out.

UNSEEN VOICE: Is it smart?

MAN 4: Smart casually probably.

MAN 2: That's the spirit, boys.

MAN 3: Let's give Dan the best birthday he will ever remember. Come on, guys.

[They are get up and go out into the blizzard.]

MAN 5: It's brightening up.

SUPER: You know who your mates are.

LOGO: Belong. Drinkaware.co.uk

[We see a beautiful Jamaican scene. People are hanging out in a local bar drinking Heineken, eating and watching tennis. A man sits outside on his cell phone. Down the path, he sees a small group riding their bikes in his direction.]

TOURISTS: Wow. Check it out.

[The man runs inside the bar.]

MAN: The tourists! The tourists!

[Everyone shuffles inside the bar covering the television, putting away the games and carrying the two elderly men out to the porch on their rocking chairs. Pineapples are placed on the tables, the menu panels are lowered and the musical instruments are put in place, just in time for the tourists to enter the establishment. They are welcomed by music and dancing.]

DRUMMER: Welcome to paradise.

TOURIST: It's good music. I like it.

TOURIST 2: Yeah...

LOGO: Heineken

SUPER: Unofficial drink of Jamaica since 1938.

Merit
Television Over :30, *Single*

Art Director Gavin McGrath
Writer Patrick Burns
Agency Producer Jane Oak
Production Company Sonny London
Director Fredrik Bond
Creative Director Trevor Beattie
Client Carling
Agency Sonny/London
Annual ID 08368T

Merit
Television Over :30, *Single*

Art Director Jason Lawes
Writer Sam Cartmell
Creative Director Justin Tindall
Client Heineken
Agency The Red Brick Road/London
Annual ID 08369T

[Opens with Kevin Federline's music video for "Rollin' VIP." Cut to the music video playing on a small TV in a fast-food restaurant. Cut to the face of the manager working the cash register.]

FEDERLINE: What? Rollin' VIP. What? Rollin' VIP.

MANAGER: FEDERLINE!

FEDERLINE: What?

MANAGER: FRIES.

VO: Life comes at you fast.

MANAGER: THANK YOU.

VO: A Nationwide annuity could guarantee you income for life.

LOGO: Nationwide blue piggy bank

Merit
Television Over :30, *Single*

Art Directors Andy Mahr, Bernard Park
Writers Tom Demetriou, Will Clarke
Agency Producer Hal Dantzler
Production Company Moxie Pictures
Director Frank Todaro
Creative Directors Leigh Sander, Jim Walker
Client Nationwide Insurance
Agency TM Advertising/Dallas
Annual ID 08370T

[We see a football stadium. The player runs down the field for a series of hits, through different weather and games. An Irish tune plays in the background. The ball is intercepted by the opposing team. The camera follows that player down the field in the opposite direction. Following him continuously through various different plays, he jumps over a player and forces his arm through another pack. Reaching toward the touchdown line, the ball is inches away. The screen cuts to black.]

SUPER: Leave nothing. Nikefootball.com

LOGO: Nike

Merit
Television Over :30, *Single*

Art Director Ryan O'Rourke
Writer Alberto Ponte
Agency Producer Kevin Diller
Production Company Alturas Films
Director Michael Mann
Creative Directors Alberto Ponte, Jeff Williams
Client Nike
Agency Wieden+Kennedy/Portland
Annual ID 08350T

[We see a man with unusually large legs walking through a village and saying hi to everyone. He walks into a field where there is an elevator sticking out. He climbs in and suddenly he is going down at high speed. He finally hits the bottom and walks down a tunnel and eventually to a chamber where we see another man peddling on a stationary bike. He stops and suddenly the world stops abruptly, throwing everyone off kilter. The other man climbs in and takes over and everything is fine again.]

SUPER: There's a perfect job for everyone.

LOGO: Monster. Your calling is calling.

Merit

Merit

Television Over :30, *Campaign*

Art Directors Gerard Caputo, Jerome Marucci, Chuck Tso
Writers Reuben Hower, Adam Kanzer, Steve McElligott
Agency Producers Anthony Curti, Ed Zazzera
Production Companies MJZ, Rattling Stick
Directors Nicolai Fuglsig, Daniel Kleinman, Rupert Sanders
Creative Directors David Lubars, Eric Silver
Client Monster.com
Agency BBDO/New York
Annual ID 08373T

ALSO AWARDED
✎ Merit Television Over :30, *Single*

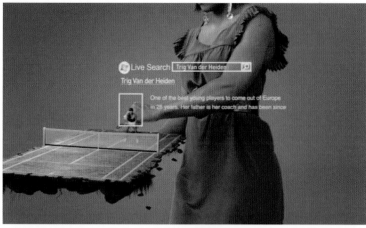

SERENA: My computer knows everything I am and everything I want to be. Here's my photo gallery. Dad took these, almost like he knew something.

I track my competition online. See who's got game and who doesn't.

Uh, goodbye.

[She draws a heart with her finger.]

SERENA: Before a match, I listen to Andre. So good.

Here's what they tell me I am going to look like in my new video game.

Yeah, there it is. Wow. What do you think of this new design I am working on with Nike?

Hmm, I like that. I do a little acting too, so I am always studying movies. You gotta check out this one.

SERENA: I am always collecting inspiration for my line. It's called Aneres, but it's designed by Serena.

SUPER: Serena. Belle of the Ball.

VO: HP Notebooks. The computer is personal again.

Merit

Television Over :30, *Campaign*

Art Directors Sorenne Gottlieb, Stefan Copiz
Writers Jody Horn, Paul Charney
Agency Producers Jennifer Moore, Cathleen Kisich, Josh Reynolds, Vicki Tripp
Production Companies Partizan Los Angeles/New York, HSI
Directors Olivier Gondry, Joséph Kahn
Creative Directors Steve Simpson, Mike McKay, Stephen Goldblatt, Rich Silverstein
Client Hewlett-Packard
Agency Goodby, Silverstein and Partners/San Francisco
Annual ID 08374T

[We see a man riding toward the camera on a white horse and see that it is the start to the music video for "Dime Por Qué" by Eric Douat. Singing, Eric rides gracefully on his horse. The horse starts to ride faster, and Eric's face gets a look of worry. The video cuts to real footage, as Eric falls off the back of the horse and is drug across the field, kicked and tossed along the way. The camera crew runs after him.]

SUPER: Musicians don't live long. Enjoy them while you can. Cyloop.com

LOGO: Cyloop. Artists & fans. Connected online.

Merit

Television Over :30, *Campaign*

Art Director Alvaro Ramos
Writer Gustavo Lauria
Production Companies Nunchaku, Colibri/347 Media, Rebolucion
Directors Luciano Podcaminsky, Nelson Cabrera, Nicolas Kasakoff, Sebastian Schor
Creative Directors Ricky Vior, Leo Prat, Joaquin Mollá, José Mollá
Client Hoodiny/Cyloop
Agency la comunidad/Miami Beach
Annual ID 08375T

[We hear dramatic music and see a man dashing to the airport. He runs in, looking for someone. We see a young girl waiting for her flight. He then jumps behind a counter and gets on the PA system.]

MAN: Ana Campos. Anita, it's me. I hope you're listening. I know it took me a while... But I already have an answer. My answer is: I don't know. Let me think about it, I'm not ready. Are you listening to me, Anita?

[The young girl walks away disgustedly.]

SUPER: Hard times for Romanticism. That's why we change.

[Cut to a woman spraying herself with Impulse.]

SUPER: Impulse. New fragrances. New men.

Merit

Merit

Television Over :30, *Campaign*

Art Director Ricardo Armentano
Writer Analia Rios
Agency Producers Roberto Carsillo, Diego Zappala
Production Company Rebolucion
Director Armando Bo
Creative Directors Sebastian Stagno, Rafael D'Alvia, Hernan Ponce
Client Unilever
Agency Vegaolmosponce/Buenos Aires
Annual ID 08376T

ALSO AWARDED

✒ Merit Television Over :30, *Single*

[Open on a typical father in the basement working at a tool bench. His son is there and they are having what appears to be a typical father/son argument. Their tone and actions are just like one of these typical arguments, but what they are saying is the exact opposite.]

SON: But dad...

FATHER: I want to hear it. Don't go talk to your mother.

SON: You just get it, don't you?

FATHER: Listen, if you're going to live under my roof, you are getting this new phone.

SON: I promise, I will talk way too much.

FATHER: Well, I give a hoot. Cause all that talking is not going to cost me a fortune.

SON: This is completely fair.

FATHER: Well, I've got news for you, life is fair.

SON: You can control me forever.

FATHER: I raised you to talk to me like that.

VO: Gophone is changing the conversation about cell phones...everything you want plus unlimited talk without a surprise bill.

SUPER: Unlimited talk on the largest wireless calling community

Unlimited night and weekends

No annual contract

LOGO: AT&T

VO: Cingular's name is now AT&T

[We see a group of employees in a conference room. It is late in the afternoon.]

BOSS: So we need copies of the presentation printed and bound—and we need it by 8AM so we can make our flight.

[Rick reaches over and grabs a full pot of coffee, which is warming.]

RICK: Well, I guess it's going to be an all-nighter.

[Rick then takes the pot of coffee, raises it to his lips and proceeds to chug the entire thing. The other employees watch as some of the coffee spills down his face and shirt. He finally finishes and holds the empty pot.]

LINDA: Actually, this morning I used print online from FedEx Kinko's. I uploaded our presentation. They're going to print, assemble and deliver it—so it's waiting for us.

RICK: [Still holding empty pot] What? What did she say?

LOGO: FedEx Kinkos

VO: Print online. Now available from FedEx Kinko's.

Merit
Television :30/:25, *Single*

Art Director Christopher Cole
Writer Mark Wegwerth
Agency Producer Sarah Ryan
Production Company Park Pictures
Director Alison Maclean
Creative Directors Bill Bruce, Susan Credle, David Lubars
Client Cingular AT&T
Agency BBDO/North Salem
Annual ID 08378T

Merit
Television :30/:25, *Single*

Art Director Jonathan Mackler
Writer Dan Kelleher
Agency Producer Ed Zazzera
Production Company Moxie Pictures
Director Martin Granger
Creative Directors David Lubars, Bill Bruce, Eric Silver
Client FedEx/Kinko's
Agency BBDO/New York
Annual ID 08379T

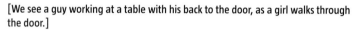

[We see a guy working at a table with his back to the door, as a girl walks through the door.]

GIRL: Hey.

GUY [Not looking behind him]: Hey, sweetie.

[She puts down her purse and keys and walks over to him. Her stomach is showing, with her love handles overflowing over her jeans. She pulls her hair back as she talks to him.]

GIRL: Do you know what a muffin top means? Because I have been hearing that all day.

GUY: Uhhh. Muffin top. I believe that the muffin top is the best part of a muffin, so if they called you a muffin top, they must think that you are the best.

GIRL: Aww. Really?

GUY: Yeah, it's nice.

[A red Lifesaver appears above his head.]

GIRL [Walking back into the kitchen]: I really like that. Even my supervisor said that to me...

GUY: Hey! Lay off my girl.

[Cut to the guy with a Lifesaver above his head as he's sucking on a Lifesaver.]

VO: It's good to be sweet.

LOGO: Lifesavers

[A man is sitting in front of his laptop listening to music on his headphones. He is singing the words to "Take it on the Run" by REO Speedwagon except he's mumbling and mangling the words. Two other coworkers in the room start singing along.]

LOGO: Holiday Inn. Look again.

Merit
Television :30/:25, *Single*

Art Director Chip McDonald
Writer John Fiebke
Agency Producers Brigette Whisnant, Liz Wzorek
Production Company Furlined
Director Ted Pauly
Creative Directors Marty Orzio, Juan Perez
Client Lifesavers
Agency Energy BBDO/Chicago
Annual ID 08385T

Merit
Television :30/:25, *Single*

Art Director Michael Rogers
Writers Paula Maki-Biondich, Tom Sebanc
Agency Producers Vic Palumbo, Nicholas Gaul
Creative Directors Kerry Feuerman, Joel Rodriguez
Client Holiday Inn
Agency Fallon/Minneapolis
Annual ID 08387T

[Three men are sitting in a Holiday Inn lobby on their laptops.]

MAN 1: Zach, are you looking at Susan's blog?

ZACH: She was featured in four of the leading business magazines?

MAN 1: And she is so humble you would never know that to talk to her.

MAN 2: She doesn't sound very humble to me if she's crowing about her accomplishments on the world wide net web. It's like she's embarrassing herself and she's embarrassing the company and...oh, hello Susan!

MAN 1: Oh hello, Miss Accomplishment! We're looking at your blog.

SUSAN: Oh my gosh...

MAN 2: Oh yeah, she's a fast riser in the business world...

MAN 1: Seems like you should be reporting to her.

[They all laugh uncomfortably.]

SUPER: Holiday Inn. Look again.

[Opens on an office wall clock. It reads 3 o'clock.]

VO: Around 3 PM...when your blood sugar and energy are low...

[We see Robert Goulet descending a red velvet rope, behind the now-sleeping man. Goulet lands and tosses the rope away.]

VO: some say, Robert Goulet appears...

[We see Goulet read the note, crumple it up and stuff it into his mouth.

VO: ...and messes with your stuff.

[Goulet feeds documents through the wastebasket paper shredder. He grabs a ribbon of paper from the man's desk and sashays down the hall with it.]

GOULET: La da daa.

[Cut to a woman asleep at her desk, while Goulet does a soft shoe on her desk, kicking a paperclip container off the desk. He kicks a stack of paper off her desk. He tapes another sleeping man to his chair and pushes the chair into the hallway. He then pours a cup of coffee onto a computer keyboard. Goulet stops short at the next office door, and stands agape at the sight of the young man inside, eating from a can of Emerald Nuts. AWAKE.]

VO: But the natural energy in just one handful of Emerald Nuts is enough to keep Robert Goulet away...

[Goulet crawls away on the ceiling, his mischief thwarted by Emerald Nuts.]

VO: ...until tomorrow anyway.

LOGO: Emerald. Emeraldnuts.com

Merit

Television :30/:25, *Single*

Art Director Michael Rogers
Writers Paula Maki-Biondich, Tom Sebanc
Agency Producers Vic Palumbo, Nicholas Gaul
Creative Directors Kerry Feuerman, Joel Rodriguez
Client Holiday Inn
Agency Fallon/Minneapolis
Annual ID 08388T

Merit

Television :30/:25, *Single*

Art Director Will Hammond
Writer Chris Beresford-Hill
Agency Producer Alex Lind
Production Companies Biscuit Filmworks, Furlined
Director The Perlorian Brothers
Creative Directors Steve Simpson, Jeff Goodby
Client Emerald Nuts
Agency Goodby, Silverstein and Partners/San Francisco
Annual ID 08389T

[Linda is sitting on a park bench sipping coffee. Next to her is her dog, which has no head, but a rear-end on both sides. A jogger passes by and the dog stops him in his tracks. He doubles back, hesitates, and then walks up to her.]

RYAN: I'm sorry... I have to ask...

LINDA: She's an Australian Double-back. And no, she doesn't bite.

RYAN: No – are those the new Chocolate Dipped Altoids?

[She glances at the tin she has in her lap.]

LINDA: Oh, yes.

[She opens it up and offers him one.]

VO: New dark chocolate dipped Altoids

Merit

Television :30/:25, *Single*

Art Director Reed Collins
Writer Bob Winter
Agency Producers David L. Moore, Ray Swift
Production Company Biscuit
Director Tim Godsall
Creative Directors Noel Haan, G. Andrew Meyer
Client William Wrigley Jr. Company
Agency Leo Burnett/Chicago
Annual ID 08392T

[We open on a woman sitting in front of a psychic. Their session is just ending.]

WOMAN: You know so much about me.

[The woman turns to her boyfriend, who is standing to leave.]

WOMAN: Honey, you should try this.

BOYFRIEND: No, I don't think that's a good idea.

WOMAN: Come on.

[She forces him into the seat across from the psychic. As the psychic tries to read his thoughts, he tries to block her every step of the way. It becomes a heated battle for him, as he becomes desperately determined to keep his past, present and future actions to himself.]

TAG: What happens here, stays here.

LOGO: Only Vegas

Merit

Television :30/:25, *Single*

Art Director Diane Vafi
Writer Diane Vafi
Agency Producer Don Turley
Production Company Hungry Man
Director Scott Vincent
Creative Directors Arnie DiGeorge, Randy Snow
Client Las Vegas Convention and Visitors Authority
Agency R&R Partners/Las Vegas
Annual ID 08393T

[We see the inside of an airplane mid-flight. A man gets up to go to the washroom. At the same time, a male flight attendant pushes a drink cart through the first class curtain. The man walks down the aisle, but is met by the steward with the drink cart. There is a small exchange but the steward snubs the man. He won't let him pass. He proceeds to ask other passengers what they'll have to drink. The man is frustrated. He leans down and runs forward. Bam! He connects his shoulder with the cart, pushing the steward backwards down the aisle, sending him crashing through the curtain. The man calmly opens the washroom door and enters.]

SUPER: **WATCH AND LEARN.**

LOGO: **BC LIONS**

SUPER: **SEASON TICKETS (604) 589-ROAR**

Merit

Television :30/:25, *Single*

Art Director Rob Sweetman
Writer Jono Holmes
Agency Producer Ann Rubenstein
Production Companies Steam Films, Tonic Post, Wave Sound Productions
Director Ben Weinstein
Creative Directors Ian Grais, Chris Staples
Client BC Lions
Agency Rethink/Vancouver
Annual ID 08394T

[We see a giant pop-up book called "The Safest Accident." A group of men pull the large book open with strings.]

VO: **This is the story of "The Safest Accident." It's not the crumple zones to absorb the impact. And it's not the airbags when the ice turns to black.**

[The men pulling the string of the book move to turn the page for each scenario, pulling the tabs to make the cars move on the page.]

VO: **You see, the safest accident is the one that never happens.**

[The last page of the book shows a car parked safely in a driveway.]

VO: **The 2008 RX, offering 14 actively safe features. Learn more at activelysafe.com.**

SUPER: **The pursuit of perfection.**

LOGO: **Lexus**

Merit

Television :30/:25, *Single*

Art Director Kevin Smith
Writer Dave Horton
Agency Producer Jennifer Weinberg
Production Company Smuggler
Director Stylewar
Creative Directors Jon Pearce, Gavin Lester
Client Lexus
Agency Team One/El Segundo
Annual ID 08395T

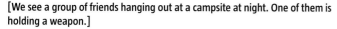

[We see a group of friends hanging out at a campsite at night. One of them is holding a weapon.]

GUY: We're out here tonight testing the Shrink Ray from Ratchet and Clank for Playstation Portable. And we are going to shrink our friend Larry so he can sneak into the girls' tent while they're changing.

[The friends laugh as they aim the gun at Larry and shoot him, shrinking him down. They all hush each other as tiny Larry sneaks towards the girls' tent when suddenly an owl swoops down and picks Larry up, carrying him up into a tree. We hear the shrill screams as Larry panics. The guys sit there not knowing what to do.]

GUY: Was that an Owl?

GUY 2: Yeah.

[Cut to game footage of Ratchet and Clank Size matters. The opening shot of the game footage using the shrink ray.]

VO: The shrink ray. All new weapons, all new levels. Ratchet and Clank Size Matters. Rated everyone 10 and up.

LOGO: PSP

[We see two guys, looking like travelers, waiting.]

GUY 1: Have you tried these new berries and cream Starbursts?

[A man comes up dressed in old-fashion attire.]

MAN: Pardon me, what kind of Starburst did you just say?

GUY 1: Berries...

MAN: Berries! Berries and what else?

GUY 1: And cream.

MAN: Ahhhhh. Ohh!

[The man covers his face with joy. Clapping and jumping in the air, he starts to sing a little tune.]

MAN: Berries and cream. Berries and cream. I'm a little lad who loves berries and cream.

[He waves his arms in and out, his face filled with excitement. With a big smile, he starts to sing faster in an even more high-pitched voice. Kicking his legs together and jumping about.]

MAN: Berries and cream. Berries and cream. I'm a little lad who loves berries....and... crrrrrrrrrrream!

LOGO: Starburst

SUPER: Juicy goodness.

Merit
Television :30/:25, *Single*

Art Director Blake Kidder
Writers Patrick Almaguer, Rob Calabro
Agency Producers Colleen Wellman, Mandi Holdorf
Directors David Shane, Hungry Man
Creative Directors Rob Schwartz, Brett Craig, Doug Mukai
Client Sony Playstation
Agency TBWA\Chiat\Day/Los Angeles
Annual ID 08396T

Merit
Television :30/:25, *Single*

Art Director Phil Covitz
Writer Brandon Davis
Agency Producer Winslow Dennis
Creative Directors Gerry Graf, Ian Reichenthal, Scott Vitrone
Client Mars Snackfood - Starburst
Agency TBWA\Chiat\Day/New York
Annual ID 08397T

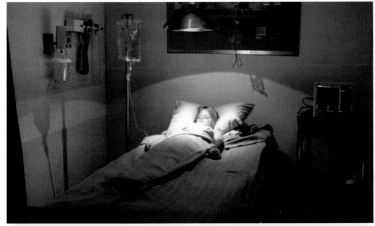

[Opens in a hospital room. A boy is in the bed with a cast on his arm; a few machines are at his bedside with tubes attached to him. He's asleep. Several doctors in white coats enter the room. Rather than tending to the boy, they begin to move things around in his hospital room. They begin to wheel the machines away. They begin to slide shelves out and rotate walls, changing the room as if it were a theater set.]

VO: Most vehicles can help protect you during an accident. We'd prefer to help you avoid one altogether.

[As they finish moving things about, we see that the doctors have transformed the boy's hospital room into his bedroom, as if he were never injured to begin with. The boy continues to sleep. Cut to the RX parked in the driveway outside the boy's house.]

VO: The 2008 Lexus RX with 14 Actively Safe features. See your Lexus dealer.

SUPER: ActivelySafe.com

[We see a scene inside a police station from *Law and Order*. Detective Goren is on the phone with his sidekick Detective Eames standing next to him.]

GOREN: No, if you could just give me that information... [points to a bag on desk] what's that?

EAMES: A severed hand.

GOREN: [To phone] Hang on a second...no no, I mean that.

[He points to the USA logo on the bottom of the screen.]

EAMES: Oh that? That's the logo.

GOREN: Yeah but it's a...

EAMES: ...USA logo. And this is an original episode.

GOREN: That's different.

EAMES: Yeah, that is different.

VO: *Law and Order Criminal Intent* is moving. New, original episodes premier Thursday, October 4 at 10 on USA. Characters welcome.

LOGO: USA

Merit
Television :30/:25, *Single*

Art Director Kevin R. Smith
Writer Dave Horton
Agency Producer Jennifer Weinberg
Production Company MJZ
Director Nicolai Fuglsig
Creative Directors Chris Graves, Jon Pearce
Client Lexus
Agency Team One/El Segundo
Annual ID 08398T

Merit
Television :30/:25, *Single*

Art Director Anil Butwa
Writers Derek Shevel, Nicole Morgese
Agency Producers Sandra Schron, Desiree Tobin, Liz Gaffney, Lori Moretz
Production Companies Hungry Man, Northern Lights/John Laskas
Director Brendan Gibbons
Creative Directors Christina Hedrick, Jason Holzman
Client USA Network
Agency USA Network/New York
Annual ID 08399T

[We see a baseball field and a man on 2nd. We hear the crack of a bat and he slides towards third.]

MAN: When the game is on the line and you're looking at a full count with .2 seconds left on the shot clock, the last thing you need to be worried about is your deodorant. That's why I use Old Spice.

[He is still sliding and he rounds third.]

MAN: Old Spice is the bare-knuckle, straight-on tackle, heavyweight deodorant that gives the best game, set and match, high-stepping, sudden-death, double-overtime performance in the pit fight against odor.

[He makes it to home and the umpire calls safe.]

MAN: From odor, thanks Old Spice.

Merit

Television :30/:25, *Single*

Art Director Eric Baldwin
Writer Michael Illick
Agency Producer Jennifer Fiske
Production Company MJZ
Director Tom Kuntz
Creative Directors Monica Taylor, Mark Fitzloff
Client Procter & Gamble
Agency Wieden+Kennedy/Portland
Annual ID 08400T

[We see a man tying on his Nikes. He starts running.]

VO: I'm not a runner. I don't enjoy avoiding land mines made of dog poo. I don't enjoy breathing heavier than a pregnant walrus. How can anyone be addicted to this? There's no way around it, running sucks. But you know what sucks even more? Man boobs. They really suck.]

SUPER: Run like you've never run before.

LOGO: Nike+

Merit

Television :30/:25, *Single*

Art Director Blake Kidder
Writer Patrick Almaguer
Agency Producer Orlando Wood
Production Company Between The Eyes
Director Eran Creevy
Creative Directors Alvaro Sotomayor, Boyd Coyner
Client Nike
Agency Wieden+Kennedy/Amsterdam
Annual ID 08401T

[A couple is sitting in the car at a Sonic drinking lattes.]

MAN: I love that Sonic has iced lattes now. They're so good!

WOMAN: Ha, ha. I have a moustache...

MAN: Honey, you can only see it in sunlight. Don't worry about it.

[He looks over and notices that she's talking about the latte on her lip.]

MAN: You have a moustache on you...right now...only now...no other times, just now...

VO: Iced Lattes, new at Sonic. Creamy, icy indulgence in hazelnut, mocha or caramel with premium roast espresso. Because Sonic is your ultimate drink stop.

LOGO: **Sonic**

Merit

Merit

Television :30/:25, *Campaign*

Art Directors Chris Shults, Brad Jungles
Writers Sarah Coker, Matt McCaffree
Agency Producer Charlie DeCoursey
Production Company Daily Planet
Creative Directors Pat Piper, Brian Brooker
Client Sonic Drive-In
Agency Barkley/Kansas City
Annual ID 08402T

ALSO AWARDED
✎ Merit Television :30/:25, *Single*

281

[We open on a handsome guy in his early thirties in his apartment calling a girl that he met out the previous night.]

GIRL: Hello?

GUY: Hi, Melissa. It's Josh from last night.

GIRL: Oh yeah, hey.

GUY: Hey. Okay, listen, I know there's that two-day rule about calling, or whatever, and, um, this may sound totally dumb, but uh... did you feel like there was a real connection between us?"

[The girl seems excited but we can't hear her talking because the sound on her phone has cut out. The man hears only an awkward silence.]

GUY: I mean, you know, like a brother sister connection?

SUPER: Switch to the network with the fewest dropped calls.

GUY: Nothing creepy. I mean, like, you know, I would never, like, make out with my sister.

LOGO: Cingular. Raising the bar.

Merit   Merit   Merit

Merit

Television :30/:25, *Campaign*

Art Directors Linda Honan, Jason Stefanik
Writers Alex Taylor, Dan Rollman, Chris Maiorino
Agency Producers Nicole Lundy, Bob Emerson
Production Companies Smuggler, Epoch Films
Directors Chris Smith, Phil Morrison
Creative Directors David Lubars, Bill Bruce, Susan Credle, Darren Wright, David Skinner
Client AT&T
Agency BBDO/New York
Annual ID 08404T

ALSO AWARDED
✎ Merit Television :30/:25, *Single*
✎ Merit Television :30/:25, *Single*
✎ Merit Television :30/:25, *Single*

[We see three employees on a video conference call with their boss. As the boss is talking, a FedEx courier hands him a package.]

EMPLOYEE 1: [On screen] So we will get that schedule revised and sent right out to you, sir.

BOSS: Sounds good. Listen, I should be back in the office on Tuesday—I'd like to see an updated P&L.

EMPLOYEE 1: Very good, sir. We're all over it.

[Suddenly, the backdrop falls, revealing that they are on a golf course. One of them takes his golf club and smashes the laptop with the camera on top.]

EMPLOYEE 2: That was close.

BOSS: I can still hear you.

[They smash the laptop again.]

EMPLOYEE 2: I think we're good.

EMPLOYEE 1: Yeah, that should do it.

SUPER: We understand.

LOGO: FedEx

VO: FedEx, proudly bringing you the FedEx cup.

fedexcup.com

Merit

Merit
Television :30/:25, *Campaign*

Art Director Richard Ardito
Writers Dan Kelleher, Grant Smith
Agency Producers Elise Greiche, Kimberly Clarke
Production Company O Positive
Director Jim Jenkins
Creative Directors David Lubars, Bill Bruce, Eric Silver
Client FedEx/FedEx Cup
Agency BBDO/New York
Annual ID 08403T

ALSO AWARDED
✎ Merit Television :30/:25, *Single*

[We open on office workers at desks, except they're not in an office—they're in the wild, wearing tattered dress shirts and ties. One worker approaches another's desk and shows him a report. Mayhem suddenly ensues with darts flying through the air. Everyone is running while management is looking for volunteers for a training seminar.]

SUPER: **Do more than just survive the workweek.**

VO: **A better job awaits, and CareerBuilder.com has the most.**

SUPER: **CareerBuilder.com**

Merit

Television :30/:25, *Campaign*

Art Directors Matt Spett, Justin Bucktrout
Writers Rick Hamann, Bill Dow
Agency Producers Sergio Lopez, Ben Latimer
Production Company Hungry Man
Director Bryan Buckley
Creative Directors Marshall Ross, Pat Hanna
Client CareerBuilder
Agency Cramer-Krasselt/Chicago
Annual ID 08405T

[We see a young man eating a Whopper and looking into the bathroom mirror. He has the beginning of a moustache.]

VO: Feed that moustache, son.

[Two men are eating lunch at work and they both have long moustaches.]

VO: Come 'n get it, Curly.

[Four old women are sitting around a poker table, all with long moustaches.]

VO: It's chow time, ladies.

[A young woman is sunbathing with a long moustache. Her dog eats the left over burger next to her and suddenly has a moustache as well.]

VO: Yee-haw. Western Whopper. Flame-broiled beef, bacon and barbecue sauce. Bring out your inner cowboy, cowboy.

LOGO: Western Whopper

Merit

Television :30/:25, *Campaign*

Art Director Jason Ambrose
Writer Donnell Johnson
Production Company Biscuit Filmworks
Director Aaron Ruell
Producers Eric Stern, Shawn Tessaro, Cristina DeSimone, Tracy Broaddus
Creative Directors Rob Reilly, Bill Wright
Client Burger King
Agency Crispin Porter + Bogusky/Miami
Annual ID 08406T

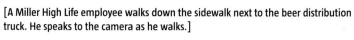

[A Miller High Life employee walks down the sidewalk next to the beer distribution truck. He speaks to the camera as he walks.]

MAN: Someone is about to loose their selling Miller High Life privileges.

[He walks up to a restaurant and hastily grabs a menu from a server.]

MAN: Can I borrow this for a second? Hamburger for $11.50? Are you for real? Step aside!

[He busts through the kitchen doors with other Miller representatives behind him.]

MAN: Excuse me. Pardon mua. See, this beer is about helping people live the high life. It is a good, honest beer at a tasty price. Mess with the High Life, and the High Life will mess with you. $11.50 for a hamburger. Ya'll must be crazy.

[He gets in the Miller High Life truck and drives off.]

LOGO: Miller High Life

Merit
Television :30/:25, *Campaign*

Art Director Vivienne Wan
Writers Paul Johnson, Bob Cianfrone, Mike Howard
Directors Rupert Samuel, Bryan Buckley
Production Company Hungry Man
Producers Stephen Orent, Dan Duffy, Cindy Becker
Creative Directors Paul Keister, Paul Johnson, Mike Howard
Client Miller High Life
Agency Crispin Porter + Bogusky/Miami
Annual ID 08407T

[Two lab guys walk into a control room. One of them picks up a small vial of high-speed and examines it. They dabble it on their faces and suddenly grow mustaches, and they put some on their hair and it grows longer. Their laughter disturbs a female coworker.]

LAB GIRL #1: **Hey Guys!**

[Lab guy #1 apologizes as he reaches toward her face.]

LAB GUY #1: **Sorry Meg. Wait, you have something on your face...**

[Cut to lab girl's face. She now has a very obvious hair streak across the lower part of her face.]

LAB GIRL #1: **Did you get it?**

SUPER: **Comcast High-Speed Internet with PowerBoost. Fast keeps getting faster.**

LOGO: **Comcast**

Merit

Television :30/:25, *Campaign*

Art Director Nick Spahr
Writer Jim Elliott
Agency Producer Tanya LeSieur
Production Company The Directors Bureau
Director Mike Maguire
Creative Director Jamie Barrett
Client Comcast
Agency Goodby, Silverstein and Partners/San Francisco
Annual ID 08408T

[Open on Allen, a man with bananas for fingers, working in his cube. He is reading a spreadsheet, filing, drumming his fingers on the desk. A coworker, Bill, is staring.]

ALLEN: **What?**

BILL: **I'm sorry, I couldn't help but notice. Are those... the new chocolate dipped Altoids?**

[Allen glances down to the shiny tin on his desk.]

ALLEN: **Yes**

[He pushes the tin towards Bill.]

VO: **New dark chocolate dipped Altoids.**

Merit

Merit

Television :30/:25, *Campaign*

Art Director Reed Collins
Writer Bob Winter
Agency Producers David L. Moore, Ray Swift
Production Company Biscuit
Director Tim Godsall
Creative Directors Noel Haan, G. Andrew Meyer
Client William Wrigley Jr. Company
Agency Leo Burnett/Chicago
Annual ID 08409T

ALSO AWARDED
✎ Merit Television :30/:25, *Single*

[We see the Mac and PC guys standing at a colored wheel.]

MAC: Hello, I'm a Mac...

PC: And I'm a PC...and it's time to play 'Choose a Vista!'

MAC: What's going on?

PC: Well, Vista comes in six different versions and I don't know which to choose. I could spend a lot of money and get a version that has a lot of stuff I don't need, or spend too little and get stuck with one that doesn't do very much at all.

MAC: Macs just have one version with all the stuff you need on it.

PC: Well that's boring. This is fun! [Spins wheel] Come on! Big operating system, big operating system! Daddy needs an upgrade!

[The wheel stops on Lose a Turn and he looks dejected.]

MAC: Didn't you make this?

LOGO: Mac

Merit

Television :30/:25, *Campaign*

Art Directors Scott Trattner, Chuck Monn
Writers Jason Sperling, Alicia Dotter
Agency Producers Mike Refuerzo, Cheryl Childers, Hank Zakroff
Production Company Epoch Films
Director Phil Morrison
Creative Directors Lee Clow, Duncan Milner, Eric Grunbaum, Scott Trattner, Jason Sperling, Chuck Monn
Client Apple
Agency TBWA\Media Arts Lab/Los Angeles
Annual ID 08410T

[Two sportscasters talk by a cubicle, a Mets baseball player walking down the hall behind them. A mascot sits reading a paper in the kitchen.]

SPORTSCASTER 1: Your highlights tonight were perfect.

SUPER: ESPN Offices. March 16, 2:03 p.m.

METS PLAYER: Hey, guys. We still going out tonight?

SPORTSCASTER 1: Definitely. Tonight is a huge night. Stuart and John are coming, too.

SPORTSCASTER 2: Nice. Where should we meet?

METS PLAYER: [Talking into his glove] How about the lobby?

SPORTSCASTER 1: No, no. Lobby is no good. He'll look there. How about the parking lot? I'd say parking lot.

SPORTSCASTER: 7 o'clock.

METS PLAYER: I'll be there. See you guys later.

SPORTSCASTER 1: Big night.

SPORTSCASTER 2: Huge.

SUPER: This is Sportscenter.

LOGO: ESPN

Merit

Television :30/:25, *Campaign*

Art Directors John Parker, Eric Stevens
Writers Josh Dimarcantonio, Andy Ferguson, Nick Sonderup
Agency Producers Alison Hill, Gary Krieg
Production Company Hungryman
Director David Shane
Creative Directors Todd Waterbury, Kevin Proudfoot, Derek Barnes, Paul Renner
Client ESPN
Agency Wieden + Kennedy/New York
Annual ID 08411T

[Opens with a young girl playing a guitar.]

GIRL [singing]: **Don't tell me what to do, what to wear, what to say. Don't wanna follow rules. Gonna do it my way.**

SUPER: **Learn three chords. You'll know 1,000 songs.**

GIRL [singing]: **I've got a brain. I can think for myself. Don't wanna be like everybody else.**

LOGO: **Converse 1908**

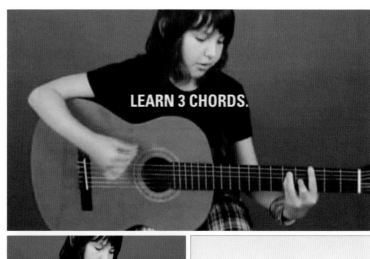

Merit

Television :20 And Under, *Single*

Art Director Randy Freeman
Writer Sean McLaughlin
Agency Producer Andrew Loevenguth
Creative Directors Mike Byrne, Richard Mulder
Client Converse
Agency Anomaly/New York
Annual ID 08412T

[We see a father and son grilling. Three women sit at a table behind them. The two men are speaking gibberish, the word Viagra interjected into the conversation.]

SUPER: **The international language of Viagra.**

Merit

Television :20 And Under, *Single*

Art Director Jason Hill
Writer Michael Murray
Agency Producer Jennifer Mete
Production Companies Partizan LA, Radke Films
Director Eric Lynne
Creative Directors Zak Mroueh, Ron Smrczek
Client Pfizer Canada
Agency TAXI Canada/Toronto
Annual ID 08414T

[We see Abraham Lincoln sitting at a cafeteria table with a groundhog. The groundhog plays the harmonica.]

SUPER: Your dreams miss you.

LOGO: Rozerem

SUPER: Sleep aid. www.rozerem.com

Merit

Television :20 And Under, *Campaign*

Art Director Noel Ritter
Writer Emily Sander
Production Company RSA Films
Director Adam Goldstein
Creative Directors Marshall Ross, Dean Hacohen, Ken Erke
Client Rozerem
Agency Cramer-Kresselt/Chicago
Annual ID 08415T

[Opens with a man sitting at a restaurant table with four other people, drinks on the table.]

SUPER: The most interesting man in the world...on starting over.

[Cut to the man in a field with a bear.]

SUPER: Do not attempt

VO: It was said that he once shot a bear, and then nursed it back to health. Then shot it again.

MAN: Stay thirsty, my friends.

LOGO: Cerveza Dos Equis.

SUPER: Stay Thirsty, my friends. Staythirstymyfriends.com

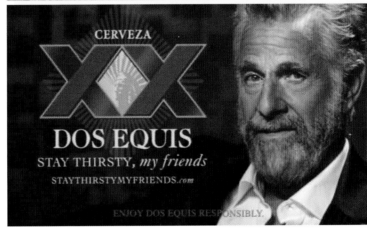

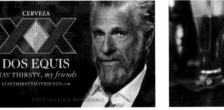

Merit

Merit

Merit

Television Commercials of Var. Length, *Campaign*

Art Director Karl Lieberman
Writer Brandon Henderson
Agency Producers Dan Fried, Joe Guyt
Production Company @radical.media
Director Steve Miller
Creative Directors Jeff Kling, Anthony Sperdutti, Nick Cohen
Client Heineken USA – Dos Equis
Agency Euro RSCG/New York
Annual ID 08416T

ALSO AWARDED

✎ Merit Television :30/:25, *Single*
✎ Merit Television :20 and Under, *Single*

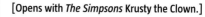

[Opens with *The Simpsons* Krusty the Clown.]

KRUSTY: Hey it's your ole pal Krusty. I know some of you may be tempted by the Burger King to eat this flame-broiled Whopper instead of my deep-fried-with-love Krusty Burger. All I can say is...Please! I'm behind on seven alimonies. I'm wearing paper bags for shoes!

[Cut to his feet, wearing white Krusty Burger bags for shoes. He starts to sob. The King comes onto the scene and offers Krusty a Whopper, but Krusty punches him in the face.]

LOGO: **Krusty Burger**

KRUSTY: **Don't buy the Whopper.**

[The King's hand reaches up for Krusty's shoulder. Getting up, the King punches Krusty.]

LOGO: **Burger King**

SUPER: **Simpsonizeme.com**

LOGO: **The Simpsons Movie**

SUPER: **In theaters now**

Merit
Television Commercials of Var. Length, *Campaign*

Art Director James Dawson Hollis
Writers Tim Roper, Rob Reilly, Bill Wright
Producers Chad Hopenwasser, Kerstin Emhoff, Michael McQuhae, Suzanne Hargrove, Mike Goble
Production Company H.S.I.
Director Paul Hunter
Creative Directors Rob Reilly, Bill Wright
Client Burger King
Agency Crispin Porter + Bogusky/Miami
Annual ID 08417T

[Opens with the "M" for mature game rating symbol. Cut to an old television countdown screen. Cut to a title screen with Kim Jong II's image on a yellow background. The title reads "King Jong II's Game Review" in Korean. Cut to footage of a Korean news reporter talking about Kim's review of *Call of Duty 4*.]

REPORTER VO: Our most glorious inspirational leader, Kim Jong II...

[Game footage and graphics are show behind the reporter.]

REPORTER VO: ...has played *Call of Duty 4: Modern Warfare*.

[Cut to photo of Kim and his father.]

REPORTER VO: Having inherited the genius and lofty moral standing of his father President Kim II-Sung...

[Cut to a dramatic illustration of Kim leading a battle from the back of a horse.]

REPORTER VO: ...dear leader has used the people's indigenous wisdom and great focus to defeat the game on the most difficult of levels. Dear leader says, "Very fun game, American scum...

[We see game footage.]

REPORTER VO: ...but because the game has nukes and is not set in Korea...one star."

[Cut back to game logo with flag graphics. One flag graphic fades away.]

REPORTER VO: This has been our Glorious Leader's Glorious Game Review.

[Cut to game footage of Zakyev handing a gun to the coup leader, who aims at the camera and shoots. Then the screen goes back to Kim's photo.]

Merit

Television Under $50K Budget, *Single*

Art Director Marcus Wesson
Writer Miguel Caballero
Agency Producer Carole Ferrari
Creative Directors Kevin McCarthy, Jeff Spiegel, Mark Monteiro
Client Activision
Agency DDB/Venice
Annual ID 08419T

It was the worst hailstorm
ever seen in Colombia
and this spot was released
a few days after the event.

(Original footage from a home video)

[Opens on a black screen with white text.]

SUPER: Bogotá – Columbia. Sat 2007/11/03. 2:40 p.m.

[Cut to local video footage of the results of a massive storm that buried cars and caused high flooding. Cut to black screen with white text.]

SUPER: It was the worst hailstorm ever seen in Colombia, and this spot was released a few days after the event [original footage from a home video].

[Cut to a truck driving through a heavy current of water. After moving back and forth for a few minutes, the truck moves against the current, all other cars around it stuck.]

SUPER: Make your own road.

LOGO: Chevrolet

Merit

Television Under $50K Budget, *Single*

Art Director Cesar Meza
Writers Fernando Gomez, Armando Rico
Designer Camilo Canizarez
Creative Directors Armando Rico, Samuel Estrada
Client Chevrolet
Agency McCann Erickson/Bogota
Annual ID 08421T

[We see a small girl holding a puppy. A family of four sits in the living room. Dad reads the paper. Mom cuts out coupons. Brother sits on the floor playing with a toy. The girl looks at the dog, then at her two parents.]

GIRL: I wanted a pony...not a fucking dog. Now I'll have to punish him. First I'll cut off his tail, then I'm gonna shove some nails up his ass and put him in the microwave and watch him explode.

[Cut to television series end screen.]

SUPER: Fortunately there's Supernanny. Mondays at 8:15 p.m. on 3plus.

LOGO: Supernanny

Merit

Television Under $50K Budget, *Single*

Art Director Florian Beck
Writers Tom Zuercher, Mario Nelson
Agency Producer Suzana Kovacevic
Production Company Pumpkin Film
Creative Directors Markus Gut, Florian Beck
Client 3+
Agency Publicis/Zurich
Annual ID 08422T

[A man walks up to a construction site.]

MAN: Hey guys, what's going on? Doing a little construction, eh? You guys wanna put down the tools and pick up the fists and fight like a real man? Bet you guys can't wait to get home and kiss each other a lot. You guys are so filthy your fingernails are dirty. And they smell like a creek. Why don't I take off that construction boot and kick you in the throat with it. Knock your voice box out. What are you guys eating? Each other? That's awkward. That's cool.

SUPER: Looking for a fight?

MAN: Come on! Want some?

LOGO: The Fight Network

SUPER: All fights. All the time. Lookingforafight.com.

Merit

Merit
Television Under $50K Budget, *Campaign*

Art Director Mike Cook
Writer Stephen Stahl
Production Company Code Film
Director Alex Ogus
Creative Directors Daniel Vendramin, Darren Clarke
Client The Fight Network
Agency Cossette Communication/Toronto
Annual ID 08423T

[Opens with Jimmy Kimmel and Lebron James having a living room meeting with a bunch of guys.]

JIMMY: Hey, here's something we should talk about. So you know, the Colts won the Super Bowl.

LEBRON: Yeah, man, I think it was good for Peyton Manning.

JIMMY: You gotta win a Super Bowl.

LEBRON: That's...no, no...

JIMMY: You do.

LEBRON: How?

JIMMY: Give a 110%, that's how. You wanna go down as the guy who never won a Super Bowl?

LEBRON: We don't win Super Bowls.

JIMMY: Not with that attitude.

VO: The ESPYS with host Jimmy Kimmel and Lebron James, Sunday, July 15 at 9 on ESPN.

LOGO: ESPN

Merit

Merit

Television Under $50K Budget, *Campaign*

Art Director Mike Bokman
Writer Jimbo Embry
Agency Producer Kat Friis
Production Company Company Films
Director Fred Goss
Creative Director Court Crandall
Client ESPN
Agency Ground Zero/Los Angeles
Annual ID 08424T

ALSO AWARDED
✎ Merit Television Under $50K Budget, *Single*

[Opens up on a quick montage of different scenes of wild animals in the Serengeti. There are lion cubs, zebras, giraffes and then we see a proud lion by himself. We hear the lion roar fiercely, but then the camera reveals that there's a production crew, and they appear to be holding a casting session. Joe is in the Casting Director's chair and there's a casting assistant with him.]

JOE [Talking to the lion]: Okay cut! Look, we got a quick turnaround on this, okay, a short window. We need guys that can create.

[The lion lets out a loud roar.]

CASTING ASSISTANT: Tell him to cut it in half.

JOE: Yeah, just give me a quarter of what you're giving me right now.

[Cut to an interview with Joe.]

JOE: My name is Joe. I'm an associate casting director on the feature film Evan Almighty. We're here casting principal roles. I don't want to get into who's in charge, but uh, you know, they just don't hand these things out [referring to the megaphone]. [Talking to a baboon] Baboon! Just take a few steps back. Have a seat. Now show us your teeth. Great! Is there some place we can get a hold of you over the weekend?

CASTING ASSISTANT: A cell number?

[Cut to Kevin, another casting assistant on a bike.]

KEVIN: They don't have a lot of training, or else they have theater training so it's really big. But for film, you know, they've got to bring it down a lot, you know, so I just work with them on that. Flirtatious. Coy. I got that. That was great.

JOE: [Talking to a lion at the base of his chair] This project is going to be cool. It's an environmentally conscious production, which, I'm sure your people love. Paper, plastic, aluminum will be recycled. We are using double-sided scripts. Some of the crew guys are riding bikes instead of using cars.

[Cut to Rashaan who's photographing various animals auditioning for parts in the film.]

RASHAAN: Hi, I'm Rashaan and I take most of the photos here and I organize them, catalog them. [Speaking to a giant elephant] I'm not playing favorites, but you have a really good chance at this role.

[Cut back to Joe directing some oxen.]

JOE: Now when I say go, I want you to take four steps to your left. Alright, go! Now let me see your faces. Great!

[Cut to Steve, the assistant production assistant, addressing a zebra.]

STEVE: American Humane is going to be there to have your back, which has got to make you feel good. [Cut intimate interview with Steve] I don't know...I kind of feel like sometimes it's easier for me to deal with animals than people. [To the zebra] Do you like darts?

CASTING ASSISTANT: Alright guys, listen up. The materials for building and landscaping will be donated to Habitat for Humanity. Our carbon footprint will be offset by the Conservation Fund.

SUPER: See the movie, Evan Almighty. In theaters now.

JOE: [Talking to ostriches] Alright now guys, when I say three I want everybody to panic. One, two, [Waves his hands in air and all the ostriches panic and scurry off].

SUPER: Created in the spirit of ecomagination.

LOGO: GE

SUPER: Imagination at work

Merit

Cinema Advertising, *Single*

Art Director Don Schneider
Writer Peter Smith
Agency Producers Regina Ebel, Filomena Lovecchio, Melissa Chester
Production Company HSI
Director Paul Hunter
Creative Directors David Lubars, Bill Bruce, Don Schneider
Client GE
Agency BBDO/New York
Annual ID 08425T

[We see a snow-covered mountain. Wind is heard roaring past, and fog clouds the view. A door locks pops up in the lower corner of the shot, as we hear the sound of a car door unlocking.]

LOGO: JEEP

SUPER: There's only one.

[The commercial opens in England, as rain falls. We see an aristocratic couple at their stately home, raising the flag. English surfers sit on their boards waiting for the "break." In a back garden, people sing around a barbeque in the rain. We see Aussie rugby, NRL and AFL jersey tops being hung. Everyone is singing.]

EVERYONE:
We wish England was Australia
We'd ditch work for a surf
Have our mates round for a Bundy,
The greatest rum on Earth

We wish England was Australia
Every girl would be a sort
We'd proudly drink Bundy Rum,
We wouldn't suck at sport

If you don't send some over here, it's Australia here we come.

Oh, but England's not Australia
We don't have Bundy Rum
So until you send some over here,
It's Australia here we come.

PILOT: Australia, this is London Zero One. We're requesting permission to land.

AIR TRAFFIC CONTROL: Sorry, London One. Your request to land has been denied.

VO: Bundy Rum. Made by one country for one country only.

LOGO: Bundy

SUPER: Our rum since 1888

Merit
Cinema Advertising, *Single*

Art Director Bill Yom
Writer Kurt Müller-Fleischer
Creative Directors Niels Holle, Tim Krink
Client Chrysler Germany
Agency KNSK/Hamburg
Annual ID 08427T

Merit
Cinema Advertising, *Single*

Writer Stephen Coll
Agency Producer Adrian Shapiro
Production Company Therapy London
Director Guy Manwaring
Creative Director Mark Collis
Client Diageo Australia
Agency Leo Burnett/Sydney
Annual ID 08428T

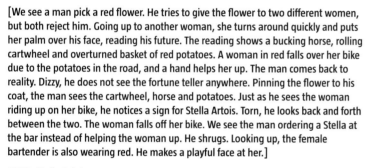

[We see a man pick a red flower. He tries to give the flower to two different women, but both reject him. Going up to another woman, she turns around quickly and puts her palm over his face, reading his future. The reading shows a bucking horse, rolling cartwheel and overturned basket of red potatoes. A woman in red falls over her bike due to the potatoes in the road, and a hand helps her up. The man comes back to reality. Dizzy, he does not see the fortune teller anywhere. Pinning the flower to his coat, the man sees the cartwheel, horse and potatoes. Just as he sees the woman riding up on her bike, he notices a sign for Stella Artois. Torn, he looks back and forth between the two. The woman falls off her bike. We see the man ordering a Stella at the bar instead of helping the woman up. He shrugs. Looking up, the female bartender is also wearing red. He makes a playful face at her.]

LOGO: **Stella Artois**

SUPER: **Perfection has its price.**

[We see Michael Madsen filming a scene, when Mr. Orange and Mr. Fuchsia appear out of nowhere and change the script.]

MICHAEL: The name of the movie is *The Phone Box Killer.*

FUCHSIA: **Phone boxes are a little bit 19th Century.**

ORANGE: **Yeah, it's kind of a period piece. We need to see you be modern and making the call from an Orange mobile phone.**

MICHAEL: **Then my victims are going to know who's calling.**

ORANGE: **That's exactly right, and they can even assign you your own ringtone.**

FUCHSIA: **And with 3G phones, you can video call.**

MICHAEL: **But then they're going to know what I look like.**

ORANGE: **See people say that actors aren't very smart, but this man's mind is like a black mamba hitting me in the face. I love it.**

MICHAEL: **Hello, Sarah...**

COPS: **Put your hands in the air.**

MICHAEL: **That's it. I quit.**

SUPER: **Don't let a mobile phone ruin your movie. Please switch it off.**

LOGO: **Orange**

Merit
Cinema Advertising, *Single*

Art Director **Karen Lamour**
Writer **Ryan Spelliscy**
Client **Stella Artois**
Agency **Lowe Roche Advertising/Toronto**
Annual ID **08429T**

Merit
Cinema Advertising, *Single*

Art Directors **Erik Enberg, Dave Kolbusz, Sam Walker**
Writers **Erik Enberg, Dave Kolbusz, Sam Walker**
Agency Producer **Juliet Pearson**
Production Company **Epoch**
Director **Stacey Wall**
Creative Directors **Stephen Butler, Robert Saville, Mark Waites**
Client **Orange**
Agency **Mother/London**
Annual ID **08430T**

POLICEMAN 1: Step away from the car. Get your hands up. Ahhh!

POLICEMAN 2: You hit?

POLICEMAN 1: Nah, I just remembered I got dinner reservation at Per See.

POLICEMAN 2: It's Per Se you idiot. What time?

POLICEMAN 1: In an hour.

POLICEMAN 2: So you want to go home, change your clothes, drink at the bar.

POLICEMAN 1: A drink would be nice.

POLICEMAN 2: Alright, alright. I got this. [To the shooters] Hey guys! My partner has a reservation at Per Se.

SHOOTER 1: How'd he get it?

POLICEMAN 1 [To his partner]: Charity auction. Kids' school.

POLICEMAN 2 [Yells to shooters]: Charity auction.

SHOOTER 2 [To Shooter 1]: Wonder what he bid.

SHOOTER 1 [To Shooter 2]: That's none of our business. [To police] Has he eaten at a Thomas Keller restaurant before?

POLICEMAN 1 [To his partner]: No, but I wanted to.

SHOOTER 1 [To police]: The amuse bouche alone is worth the trip.

POLICEMAN 2 [To the shooters]: The amuse what?

SHOOTER 1 [To police]: The amuse bouche. It's French for 'amuse the mouth.' It is a little sample that comes out before the meal. You'll see.

POLICEMAN 2 [To Policeman 1]: Sounds kinda nice.

POLICEMAN 1: Yeah, it does.

POLICEMAN 2: You should go.

POLICEMAN 1: Yeah?

SHOOTER 1: Just go.

POLICEMAN 2: Get outta here. I got it.

[Policeman 1 puts his arms up and walks over to the other car.]

POLICEMAN 1: Thanks, guys.

SUPER: Even the city that's seen it all...

POLICEMAN 2: Now let's finish this. Come on!

SUPER: ...hasn't seen this.

LOGO: Tribeca Film Festival. Tribecafilmfestival.org.

Merit
Cinema Advertising, *Single*

Art Director Craig Mannion
Writer Jonathan Koffler
Agency Producers Lisa Steiman, Meg McCarthy
Production Company Bob Industries
Director Peter Care
Creative Directors David Apicella, Terry Finley, Chris Mitton
Client Tribeca Film Festival
Agency Ogilvy & Mather/New York
Annual ID 08432T

[We see a skyline view with a sunset in the background. Cut to someone looking out one of the building windows. The voice of Willy Wonka starts off the song "Pure Imagination." The song continues as the camera moves around the city. Empty billboards are seen, clothes hanging where the ads once were. The camera continues to tour the city of missing ads.]

SUPER: Because you like your movies with no interruptions, we took away the ads.

LOGO: Sky

SUPER: Believe in better. SKYMOVIES.

Merit
Cinema Advertising, *Single*

Art Directors Kit Dayaram, Tom Spicer
Writers Kit Dayaram, Tom Spicer
Agency Producer Natalie Parish
Production Company Home Corp
Director Sara Dunlop
Creative Directors Yan Elliott, Luke Williamson
Client BSkyB
Agency WCRS/London
Annual ID 08434T

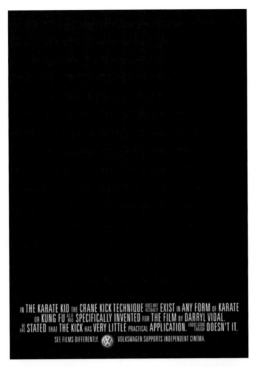

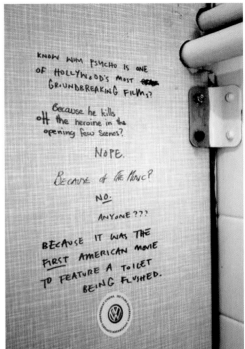

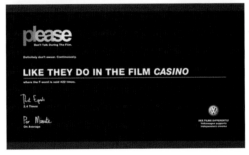

Merit

Cinema Advertising, *Integrated*

Art Directors Graeme Hall, Gavin Siakimotu
Writers Gavin Siakimotu, Graeme Hall
Agency Producer Sarah Browell
Production Company Rattling Stick
Director Andy McLeod
Creative Director Jeremy Craigen
Client Volkswagen
Agency DDB/London
Annual ID 08436T

ALSO AWARDED
✒ Merit Cinema Advertising, *Single*

[We see a business meeting.]

MEETING LEADER: Alright, so we have this model in front of us. I am sure you are all wondering why it's here. Missy spent almost all of last night finishing it up. Take it away.

MISSY: So, this is called the Fanapult. So, we have our fans, and it is a way to get the fans into the racetrack faster. I can demonstrate for you.

LEADER: Okay, that had a little too much juice on it.

TOYOTA REPRESENTATIVE: Now they are supposed to go in...

MISSY: Into the racetrack. Anywhere. They've got free range.

TOYOTA REP: Not the parking lot though. We have a bounce problem to deal with.

LEADER: You missed again. There you go. I'm sold. Well done.

PETE: Not to be a fly in the ointment, but I have just been drawing up some pros and cons to Fanapult. A little doodling. I'm human. On the pros, I've written down three things. Number one: awesome. Number two: innovative. Number three: catchy name, Fanapult. I love it. Over on the cons though, I have just two things: shattered bones and death.

LEADER: But it is still 3-2, pros. Right?

FEMALE VOICE: Pros have it.

LEADER: That's the count. I'm not pooping on your parade there, and those were really good thoughts. But, the numbers are talking. So, that's a go. Pete, do you want the model?

PETE: Yes.

LEADER: You can have the model. We're all done here.

[We see a typical Coke vending machine. The camera zooms in on the money slot. Two miniature characters are standing there talking about the people outside. Someone puts a coin in the machine to get a soda, and we are taken behind the vending machine exterior to a tiny cartoon world that exists inside the machine. Millions of characters go about their duties to get a chilled bottle of Coke out of the machine. Interviews with some of them reveal their task in the Coke delivery process.]

LOGO: Coca-Cola

Merit
Non-Broadcast, *Single*

Art Directors Conan Wang, Jerry Underwood
Writers Randy Quan, Jeff Mullen
Agency Producers Jennifer Vogtmann, Damian Stevens
Production Company Biscuit Filmworks
Director Tim Godsall
Creative Directors Harvey Marco, Andrew Christou
Client Toyota
Agency Saatchi & Saatchi LA/Torrance
Annual ID 08438T

Merit
Non-Broadcast, *Single*

Art Director Barney Hobson
Writer Rick Chant
Agency Producer Sandy Reay
Production Company Psyop
Directors Todd Mueller, Kylie Matulick
Creative Directors Al Moseley, John Norman
Client Coca-Cola
Agency Wieden+Kennedy/Amsterdam
Annual ID 08439T

[We see a sunflower in a pot. A lamp comes crashing down, smashing the flower and breaking the pot. The camera pans out to show the table the lamp fell from and a man wearing a white suit and Red Stripe sash.]

MAN: Boo plant-hating light fixture.

[Holding a Red Stripe out in front of him.]

MAN: Hooray Beer!

LOGO: Red Stripe

Merit

Non-Broadcast, *Campaign*

Art Director Richard Ardito
Writer Grant Smith
Agency Producer Josh Eisenman
Creative Directors David Lubars, Bill Bruce, Eric Silver
Client Diageo - Red Stripe
Agency BBDO/New York
Annual ID 08440T

Innovation in Advertising and Marketing / Integrated Branding

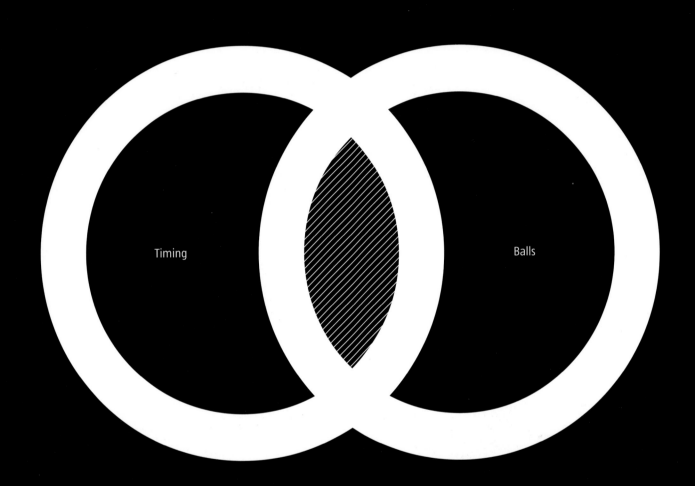

Timing

Balls

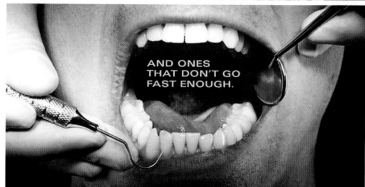

Merit

Innovation in Advertising & Marketing, *Single*

Art Director Marco Howell
Writer Phil Gable
Agency Producers Kelly Harden, Patrick Hudson
Production Company Atomic Props
Creative Directors Kyle Lewis, Marcus Kemp
Content Strategist Deborah Draper
Client Alliance Theatre
Agency BBDO/Atlanta
Annual ID 08443A

Merit

Innovation in Advertising & Marketing, *Single*

Art Director Richard Ardito
Writer Grant Smith
Creative Directors David Lubars, Bill Bruce, Eric Silver, Jerome Marucci, Steve McElligott
Client BBC World
Agency BBDO/New York
Annual ID 08444A

Merit

Innovation in Advertising & Marketing, *Single*

Art Director Antonio Bonifacio
Writers Ellie Anderson, Tim Gillingham
Photographer Nick Vedros
Creative Directors Andy Clarke, Glen Wachowiak
Client Denver Museum
Agency Carmichael Lynch/Minneapolis
Annual ID 08445A

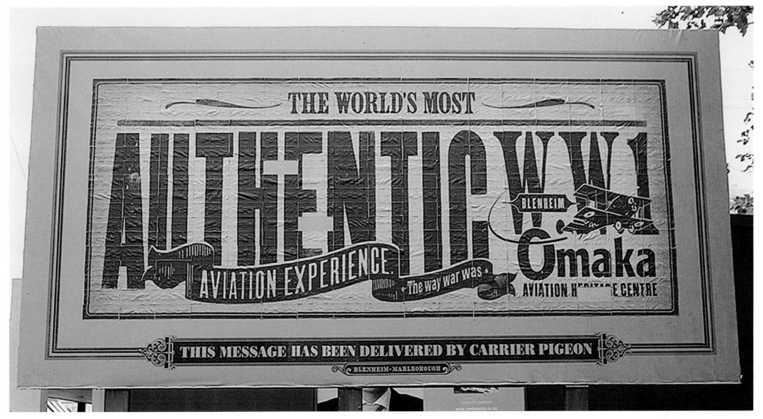

Merit

Innovation in Advertising & Marketing, *Single*

Art Directors Mark Harricks, Paul Nagy
Writers Paul Nagy, Mark Harricks
Digital Artist/Multimedia Jason Martin
Agency Producer Scott McMillan
Creative Directors Mark Harricks, Philip Andrew, Paul Nagy
Client Omaka Aviation Heritage Centre
Agency Clemenger BBDO/Wellington
Annual ID 08446A

Merit

Innovation in Advertising & Marketing, *Single*

Art Director Brett Colliver
Writer Joe Hawkins
Creative Director Toby Talbot
Client SKY Television
Agency DDB/Auckland
Annual ID 08447A

Merit

Innovation in Advertising & Marketing, *Single*

Art Directors Lisa Berger, Johannes Hicks, Marc Isken
Writers Nina Faulhaber, Marian Götz, Kai Abd-El Salam
Creative Directors Bert Peulecke, Stefan Schulte
Client Volkswagen
Agency DDB/Berlin
Annual ID 08448A

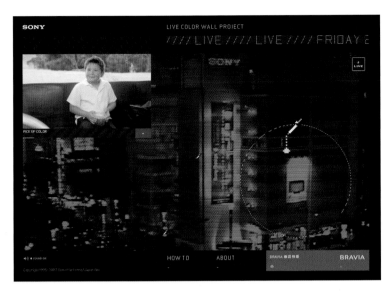

Merit
Innovation in Advertising & Marketing, *Single*

Art Directors **Ken Funaki, Ryoji Tanaka**
Writer **Tomoki Harada**
Designers **Keisuke Mochizuki, Kana Tanakashi**
Agency Producers **Toshi Morikawa, Taizo Ota, Mitsutoshi Sakamoto**
Production Company **Koshiro Futamura**
Information Architects **Kazuaki Hashida, Ikuko Ota, Go Mizushima**
Directors **Takuya Takahashi, Sunsuke Sugai**
Creative Directors **Kentaro Kimura, Junya Masuda, Hisashi Fujii**
Client **Sony**
Agency **Hakuhodo + Hakuhodo Kettle/Tokyo**
Annual ID **08449A**

Merit
Innovation in Advertising & Marketing, *Single*

Art Director **Vikas Bhalla**
Writers **Jackie Hathiramani, Greg Matson, Matt Heath**
Agency Producer **Lauren Eberhardt**
Creative Directors **Jackie Hathiramani, Ty Montague**
Content Strategists **Lauren Hanin, Christian Hughes**
Client **Cadbury Adams - Stride**
Agency **JWT/New York**
Annual ID **08450A**

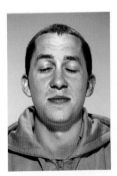
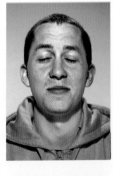
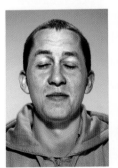
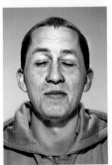

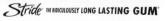

Merit

Innovation in Advertising & Marketing, *Single*

Art Director Elliot Harris
Writer Cameron Mitchell
Agency Producer David White
Production Companies Chrome Digital, Pearl and Dean
Director Carl Scott
Creative Directors Cameron Mitchell, Elliot Harris, John Patroulis, Scott Duchon,
Brian Fraser, Simon Learman
Client Microsoft Xbox
Agency McCann Erickson/London
Annual ID 08453A

Merit

Innovation in Advertising & Marketing, *Single*

Art Director Ben Wolan
Writer Rick Herrera
Agency Producer Weldon Lee Anne
Production Company Brand New School
Directors Jens Gehlhaar, Rob Feng
Creative Directors Geoff Edwards, Scott Duchon, John Patroulis
Client Microsoft Xbox
Agency McCann Worldgroup SF & T.A.G./San Francisco
Annual ID 08454A

Merit
Innovation in Advertising & Marketing, *Single*

Art Director Jeremy Carr
Writer Jeremy Carr
Creative Directors Paul Briginshaw, Malcolm Duffy
Client Subaru
Agency Miles Calcraft Briginshaw Duffy/London
Annual ID 08455A

Merit
Innovation in Advertising & Marketing, *Single*

Art Directors Laurence Thomson, Johan Holmgren
Writers Erik Enberg, Erik Bergqvist
Designer Mark Ward
Illustrator Louis Malloy
Agency Producer Francis Castelli
Production Company Asylum
Creative Directors Robert Saville, Mark Waites
Client Discovery Channel
Agency Mother/London
Annual ID 08456A

Merit

Innovation in Advertising & Marketing, *Single*

Art Director Shirin Johari
Writer Shirin Johari
Production Companies Shilov Mani, Vikram Datta, Hanoz Patel, Nabendu Bhattacharyya
Creative Directors Rajiv Rao, Piyush Pandey
Client HSBC
Agency Ogilvy & Mather/Mumbai
Annual ID 08457A

Merit

Innovation in Advertising & Marketing, *Single*

Art Director Roy Yung
Writer Thomas Tsang
Photographer Jacky Ip
Illustrator Kim Ho
Creative Directors Gavin Simpson, Eugene Tsoh
Client DHL
Agency Ogilvy & Mather/Hong Kong
Annual ID 08458A

Merit

Innovation in Advertising & Marketing, *Single*

Art Directors Silas Jansson, Cliff Kagawa Holm
Creative Director Simon Wooller
Client World Wildlife Foundation
Agency Saatchi & Saatchi/Copenhagen
Annual ID 08459A

Merit

Innovation in Advertising & Marketing, *Single*

Art Director Guybrush Taylor
Writer Ryan Wagman
Illustrator Drew Matthews
Creative Director Lance Martin
Client MINI Canada
Agency TAXI 2/Toronto
Annual ID 08460A

Merit

Innovation in Advertising & Marketing, *Single*

Art Director Jaime Mandelbaum
Writer Emiliano Trierveiler
Designer Harald Renkel
Agency Producer Katrin Dettmann
Production Companies Corporate Publishing Service, Birgit Gehrmann, Jan Leiskau,
K-MB, Kamps Markenberatung, Christoph Kamps, Sven Schöne, Hanna Rübsamen
Creative Directors Philip Borchardt, Dirk Henkelmann
Client Maxxium Germany - Absolut Vodka
Agency TBWA\ Germany/Berlin
Annual ID 08461A

Merit

Innovation in Advertising & Marketing, *Single*

Art Director Brad Wilson
Writer Paul Allen
Photographer Melvin James
Creative Director Graham Kelly
Client SPE-Networks Asia
Agency TBWA\Tequila/Singapore
Annual ID 08463A

Merit

Innovation in Advertising & Marketing, *Single*

Art Directors Joe Craig, Wendy Lawn
Writers Matt Webster, Steve McCabe
Agency Producer Zoe Yendell
Production Company Curious Films
Director Darryl Ward
Creative Director Steve McCabe
Client NZ Red Cross
Agency Y&R/Auckland
Annual ID 08464A

Merit

Innovation in Advertising & Marketing, *Single*

Creative Director Johnny Vulkan
Client Keep A Child Alive
Agency Anomaly/New York
Annual ID 08478A

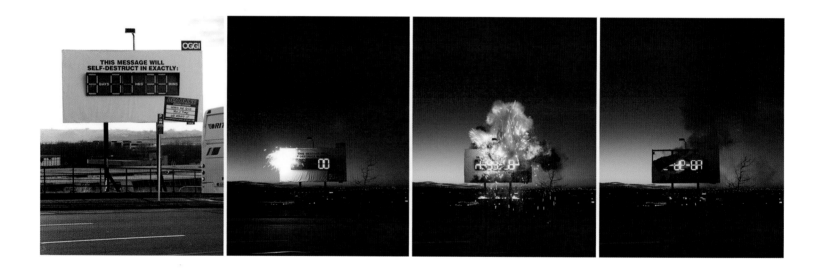

Merit

Innovation in Advertising & Marketing, *Single*

Art Directors Josh Lancaster, Jamie Hitchcock
Writers Josh Lancaster, Jamie Hitchcock
Designer Simon Redwood
Digital Artist/Multimedia Mark Addy
Agency Producers Paul Courtney, Rebecca Holt
Production Company Rollercoaster Design
Creative Director Richard Maddocks
Content Strategist Andrew Reinholds
Client Deadline Express Couriers

Agency Colenso BBDO/Auckland
Annual ID 08479A

322

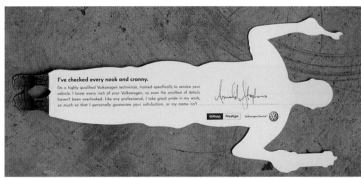

Merit

Innovation in Advertising & Marketing, *Single*

Art Directors James Tucker, Emmanuel Bougneres
Writers Simon Vicars, Mike Felix
Creative Director Toby Talbot
Client SSL - Durex
Agency DDB/Auckland
Annual ID 08481A

Merit

Innovation in Advertising & Marketing, *Single*

Art Directors Damian Galvin, Regan Grafton
Writers Carlos Savage, Bridget Short
Creative Director Toby Talbot
Client Volkswagen
Agency DDB/Auckland
Annual ID 08480A

Merit

Innovation in Advertising & Marketing, *Single*

Art Director Julia Ziegler
Writer Jan-Florian Ege
Designer Frank Hose
Photographer Stefan Foersterling
Programmers Grimm Gallun Holtappels, Ole Warns
Creative Directors Fabian Frese, Goetz Ulmer, Tom Hauser
Client IKEA Deutschland
Agency Jung von Matt/Hamburg
Annual ID 08482A

Merit

Innovation in Advertising & Marketing, *Single*

Art Director Claudia Boeckler
Writer Florian Kroeber
Designers Tobias Nientiedt, Jeannette Bohne, Eva Muenstermann
Photographers Heine/Lenz/Zizka
Information Architect Andrea Ullrich
Creative Directors Andreas Heinzel, Peter Steger, Andreas Pauli, Kerrin Nausch
Client UNICEF Deutschland/Arbeitsgruppe Frankfurt
Agency Leo Burnett/Frankfurt
Annual ID 08483A

Merit

Innovation in Advertising & Marketing, *Single*

Art Director Wei Cheng Loh
Writer Yvonne Chia
Digital Artist/Multimedia Jimmy Leow
Agency Producer Gwynn Wong
Production Company 4032 Singapore
Creative Director Calvin Soh
Client Nike
Agency Publicis/Singapore
Annual ID 08484A

Merit

Innovation in Advertising & Marketing, *Single*

Art Director Jeff Anderson
Writer Isaac Silverglate
Agency Producer Ellen Fitzgerald
Creative Directors Gerry Graf, Ian Reichenthal, Scott Vitrone
Client Mars Snackfood - Combos
Agency TBWA\Chiat\Day/New York
Annual ID 08485A

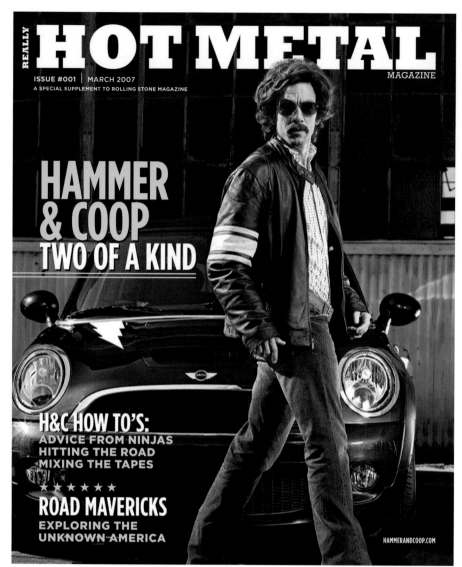

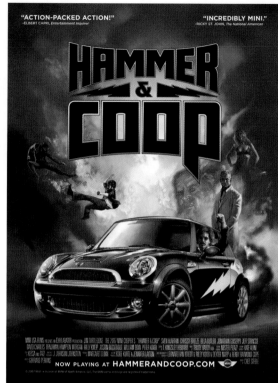

Merit

Innovation in Advertising & Marketing, *Campaign*

Art Directors Will Dean, Jay Lorenzini
Writers Lyle Yetman, Robyn Gunn
Photographer Zach Gold
Illustrators Boris Vallejo, Anthony Freda, Julie Vallejo
Designer J.P. Guiseppi
Agency Producer Maggie Dunn
Production Company Moxie Pictures
Director Todd Phillips
Creative Directors John Butler, Mike Shine

Client MINI
Agency Butler, Shine, Stern & Partners/Sausalito
Annual ID 08466A

Merit
Innovation in Advertising & Marketing, *Campaign*

Art Director **Hisham Kharma**
Writer **Sergio Penzo**
Illustrators **Claudia Schildt, Fabian Zell**
Agency Producer **Philipp Wenhold**
Creative Directors **Dörte Spengler-Ahrens, Jan Rexhausen**
Client **Daimler**
Agency **Jung von Matt/Hamburg**
Annual ID **08467A**

Merit

Innovation in Advertising & Marketing, *Campaign*

Art Director **Anita Davis**
Writer **Jonathan Budds**
Designer **Tivy Davies**
Photographer **Panos Pictures**
Agency Producer **Anna Church**
Director **Eric Lynne**
Content Strategist **Alnoor Ladha**
Client **MTV Foundation**
Agency **JWT/London**
Annual ID **08468A**

ALSO AWARDED

✒ **Merit** Public Service/Political Television, *Single*

Merit

Innovation in Advertising & Marketing, *Campaign*

Art Directors Xiao Yeen Hong, Khong Lum Chong, Andy Soong
Writers Le Vin Teh, Lisa Ng, Toe Lee Ooi
Photographers Lo - Untold Images, Chee Wai - Untold Images
Creative Directors Andy Soong, Lisa Ng
Client Hewlett-Packard Malaysia
Agency Publicis Malaysia/Petaling Jaya
Annual ID 08469A

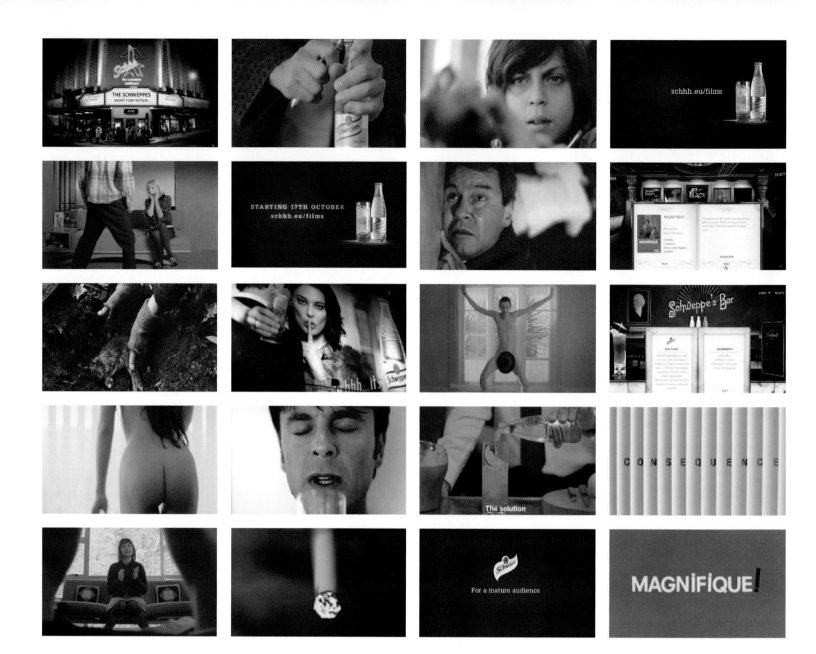

Merit

Innovation in Advertising & Marketing, *Campaign*

Art Directors Tony Bradbourne, Mikhail Gherman
Writers Noah Marshall, Melanie Bridge, James Pilkington, Kezia Barnett, Nick Worthington, Karl Fleet
Agency Producer Jodie Hari
Production Company The Sweet Shop
Information Architect Marcelle Ross
Directors Noah Marshall, Kezia Barnett, James Pilkington, Melanie Bridge
Creative Directors Lachlan McPherson, Nick Worthington
Content Strategist Graham Ritchie

Client Schweppes
Agency Publicis Mojo/Auckland
Annual ID 08470A

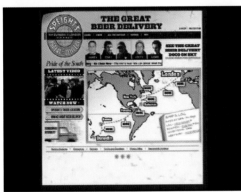

Merit

Innovation in Advertising & Marketing, *Campaign*

Art Directors Lorenz Perry, Lachlan McPherson
Writers Nick Worthington, Guy Denniston, Karl Fleet
Designers Mark Van der Hoeven, Jono Nyquist, AJ Johnson
Photographer Ross Brown
Digital Artist/Multimedia Jeremy Clark
Agency Producers Corey Esse, Sacha LOverich
Production Companies Film Graphics, RJ Media, Soundtrax,
Soundpost, Tomorrowland, Octagon

Information Architects Ric Salizzo, Paul Shannon, Michelle Jones, Abe Raffills, Gavin
Brennan, Brendon Eastlake, Roger Dore, Veronica Shale, Juliet De Chalain, James Blair,
Emma Whyte, Luke Farmer
Creative Directors Lachlan McPherson, Nick Worthington
Content Strategists Sean O'Donnell, Jessica Venning – Byran, Tom Davidson, Martin
Yeoman, Steve Clark, Andre Louis, Joel Thompson
Client Speight's
Agency Publicis Mojo/Auckland
Annual ID 08471A

Merit

Merit

Innovation in Advertising & Marketing, *Campaign*

Art Director Samson Samuel
Writers Anto Noval, Dushyant Pal Singh
Designers Akshay Shetty, Rashna Lentin
Photographer Kumaran Photography
Illustrator Senda AP
Creative Directors Minakshi Achan, Anto Noval
Client Zydus Cadila
Agency Rediffusion DYR/Bangalore
Annual ID 08472A

ALSO AWARDED
✎ Merit Outdoor, *Campaign*
✎ Merit Outdoor, *Single*

Merit

Innovation in Advertising & Marketing, *Campaign*

Art Directors Jens-Petter Waernes, Erik Dagnell
Creative Directors Oliver Handlos, Matthias Spaetgens
Client Ravensburger Spieleverlag
Agency Scholz & Friends/Berlin
Annual ID 08474A

Merit

Innovation in Advertising & Marketing, *Campaign*

Art Director Tabea Guhl
Writer Peter Broennimann
Photographer Serge Hoeltschi
Production Company Chocolate Film Derdiyok
Director Serge Hoeltschi
Creative Directors Peter Broennimann, Martin Spillmann
Client Migros-Genossenschafts-Bund
Agency Spillmann/Felser/Leo Burnett/Zurich
Annual ID 08476A

334

Merit

Innovation in Advertising & Marketing, *Campaign*

Art Directors Guy Roberts, Corey Chalmers
Writers Guy Roberts, Corey Chalmers
Creative Director Andy Blood
Client adidas\NZRU
Agency TBWA\WHYBIN/Auckland (180\TBWA)
Annual ID 08477A

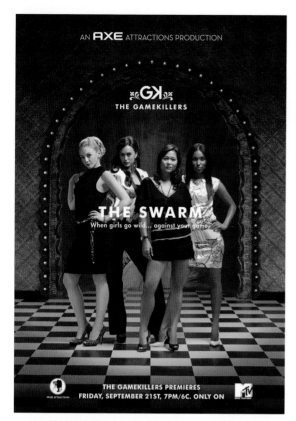

Merit

Innovation in Advertising & Marketing, *Campaign*

Art Director Jon Randazzo
Writers Jon Randazzo, Jordan Kramer, Aaron Bergeron, Gideon Evans, Tom Johnson, Julian Katz, Justin Wilkes, William Gelner, Amir Farhang
Designers Agatha Sohn, Keats Pierce
Agency Producers Julian Katz, Tonianne Fleig
Production Company @radical.media
Directors Dave Hamilton, Luke McCoubrey, Peter McCoubrey
Creative Directors Kevin Roddy, Paul Bichler
Client Unilever

Agency BBH/New York
Annual ID 08487A

Merit

Innovation in Advertising & Marketing, *Campaign*

Art Directors Anthony Chelvanathan, Monique Kelley
Writers Steve Persico, Marcus Sagar, Cam Boyd
Designer Caio Oyafuso
Illustrator Monique Kelley
Agency Producer Cathy Woodward
Production Company Electric Company
Creative Directors Judy John, Israel Diaz
Client Toronto Humane Society
Agency Leo Burnett/Toronto
Annual ID 08488A

"...to show men how to set the washing machines."

Gentlemen: YOU CAN DO YOUR LAUNDRY WITHOUT DROPPING THE REMOTE

Merit

Innovation in Advertising & Marketing, *Campaign*

Art Directors Maria Salomon, Victor Aguilar, Marta Pueyo
Writers Jorge Martinez, Juan Nonzioli, Nacho Guillo
Programmers Ícaro Obregón, Gustavo Ramos
Digital Artist/Multimedia Jorge Tabanera
Agency Producers Pablo García Acón, Manuela Zamora
Production Company Agosto
Director Toni Moreno
Creative Directors Iñaki Marti, Enric Nel-lo, Juan Nonzioli,
Antonio Herrero, Victor Aguilar, Nacho Guillo, Alfonso Marian

Client Persan - Puntomatic
Agency Shackleton/Madrid
Annual ID 08491A

Merit

Innovation in Advertising & Marketing, *Campaign*

Art Director Oli Beale
Writer Tori Flower
Agency Producer Lesley Williams
Production Company Sonny London
Director Fredrik Bond
Creative Directors Yan Elliott, Luke Williamson
Client Sara Lee
Agency WCRS/London
Annual ID 08492A

ALSO AWARDED

✒ Merit Cinema, *Single*

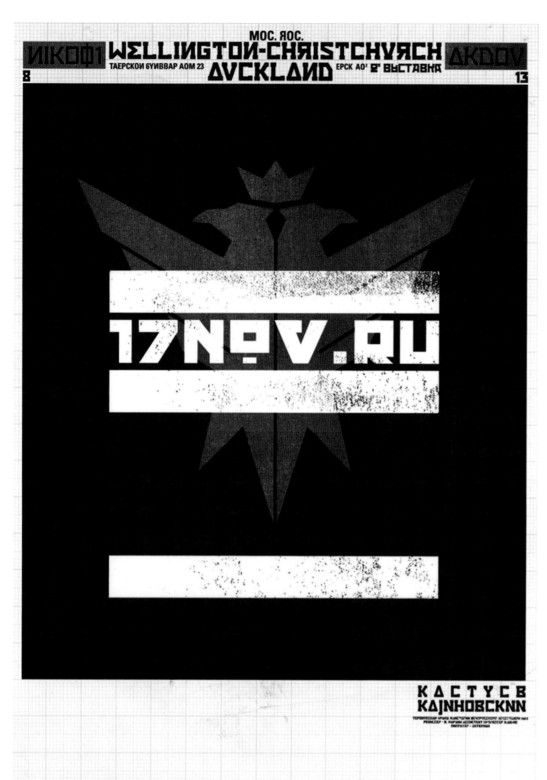

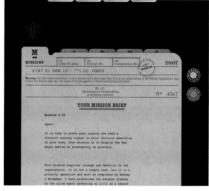

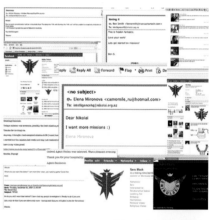

Merit

Innovation in Advertising & Marketing, *Campaign*

Art Directors Robert McDowell, Steve Pettengell, Hadleigh Averill
Writers Rachel Wallis, Bibi Bliekendaal, Nicci Doak, Hadleigh Averill
Designers Brogan Averill, Heath Lowe
Agency Producer Philippa Warhaft
Information Architects Friday O'Flaherty, Rebekah Hendrickson
Creative Director Hadleigh Averill
Content Strategist Jason Clapperton
Client Smirnoff
Agency WRC New Zealand/Auckland
Annual ID 08493A

IS IT POSSIBLE TO HATCH AN EGG IN A DOWN JACKET?

We believe it is. At least with the high quality down jackets found at Playground outdoor equipment stores. We have decided to investigate exactly how well the down jackets from Patagonia and Marmot keep the heating. A fertilized egg, a down jacket and one human being are enabling the experiment. Our person (also known as the hen) will be hatching the egg in and around the temporary "chicken farm" in one of the stores. If everything goes as planned Playground expect an addition in the end of the week. Fingers crossed!

Follow the adventurous experiment in the stores or at **playgroundstores.com** In the stores you can also guess if it will be a chicken or not. If you guess right, you have the chance to win a superhot down jacket.

PLAYGROUND

Playground Outdoor Equipment Store Adolf Fredriks Kyrkogata 15, Stockholm Tel 08 22 15 15

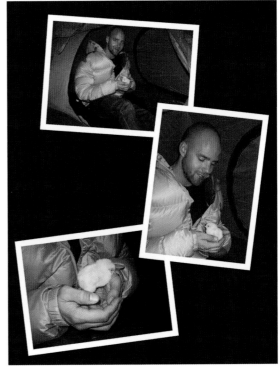

Merit

Innovation in Advertising & Marketing, *Campaign*

Art Directors Johan Baettig, Lars Holthe
Writer Hanna Bjork
Photographer Carl-Johan Paulin
Illustrator Olov Oqvist
Client Playground
Agency Akestam Holst/Stockholm
Annual ID 08486A

Merit

Integrated Branding, *Campaign*

Art Directors James Clunie, Chuck Tso
Writer James Clunie
Agency Producers JD Michaels, Bronwen Gilbert
Creative Directors David Lubars, Bill Bruce, James Clunie
Client Havaianas
Agency BBDO/New York
Annual ID 08494G

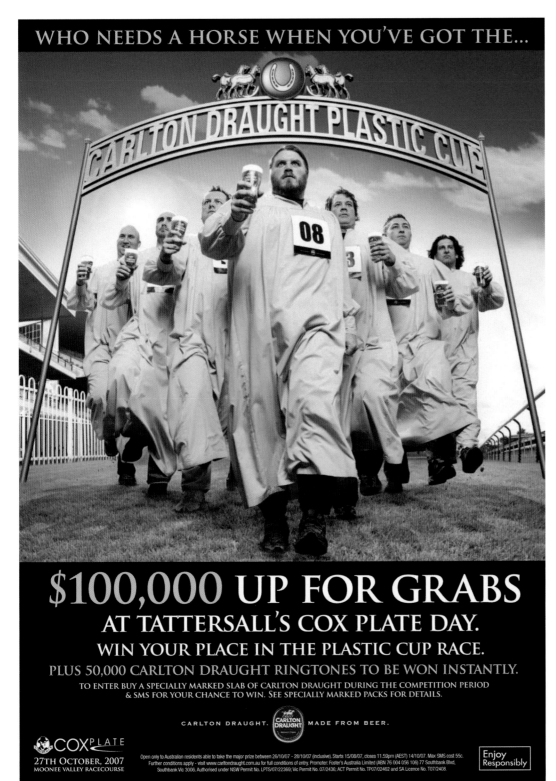

Merit

Integrated Branding, *Campaign*

Art Directors Damian Royce, Grant Rutherford, Janet Croll
Writer Ant Keogh
Digital Artist/Multimedia Craig Stuart
Agency Producer Karolina Bozajkovska
Production Company Prime Cuts
Director Jonnie Morris
Creative Directors Grant Rutherford, Ant Keogh, James McGrath, Janet Croll
Client Foster's Group - Carlton Draught
Agency Clemenger BBDO & CSM/Melbourne
Annual ID 08495G

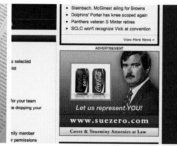
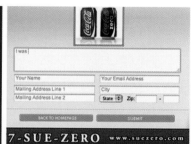

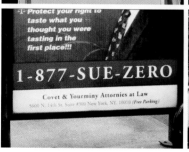

Merit

Integrated Branding, *Campaign*

Art Director Dayoung Ewart
Copywriters Erkki Izarra, Adrian Alexander
Designers Jiwon Lee, Charles Carlson, Matt Payson
Producers Rupert Samuel, Winston Binch, Matthew Anderson, Myke Gerstein,
Sosia Bert, Nicolette Guidotti, Richard Goldstein
Production Companies Villians, Nutmeg
Director Fred Goss
Creative Directors Dave Schiff, Alex Burnard, Jeff Benjamin
Client Coke Zero

Agency Crispin Porter + Bogusky/Miami
Annual ID 08496G

344

Merit

Integrated Branding, *Campaign*

Art Directors Regan Grafton, Chris Jones, Brett Colliver
Writers Bridget Short, Joe Hawkins
Photographer Mat Baker
Agency Producers Chloe Sutherland, Judy Thompson
Production Company Film Construction
Creative Director Toby Talbot
Client SKY Television
Agency DDB/Auckland
Annual ID 08497G

Merit

Integrated Branding, *Campaign*

Art Directors Jorge Calleja, Katie McCarthy, Brian Gunderson
Writers Paul Charney, Jessica Shank
Agency Producer Michael Damiani
Production Company MJZ
Director Fredrik Bond
Creative Directors Jeff Goodby, Pat McKay, Feh Tarty, Will McGinness, Ronny Northrop
Client Milk
Agency Goodby, Silverstein and Partners/San Francisco
Annual ID 08499G

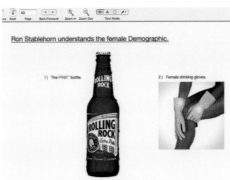

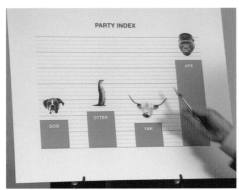

Merit

Integrated Branding, *Campaign*

Art Directors Will McGinness, Frank Aldorf, Sharon McPeak, Jorge Calleja
Writers Ronny Northrop, Steve Dildarian, Will Elliott, Tony Stern, Nat Lawlor
Agency Producer James Horner
Production Company The Director's Bureau
Director Mike Maguire
Creative Director Jeff Goodby
Client Rolling Rock
Agency Goodby, Silverstein and Partners/San Francisco
Annual ID 08498G

Merit

Merit

Integrated Branding, *Campaign*

Art Director **Rob Sweetman**
Writers **Jono Holmes, Rob Tarry**
Photographer **Hans Sipma**
Agency Producers **Jim Leith, Brie Gowans**
Production Companies **OPC, Wave Productions, JMB Post Production, Dyna Graphics**
Director **Michael Downing**
Creative Directors **Ian Grais, Chris Staples**
Client **Science World**
Agency **Rethink/Vancouver**
Annual ID **08500G**

ALSO AWARDED
✒ Merit Public Service/Political Television, *Single*

348

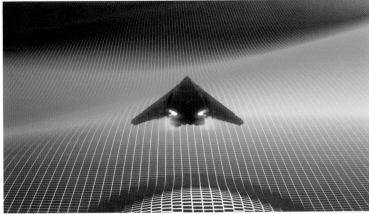

Merit

Integrated Branding, *Campaign*

Art Directors Sam Mazur, Matt Ferrin
Writers Sam Mazur, Matt Ferrin
Production Companies Nutmeg, Fuel Industries, ETC Entertainment, Endless Noise,
Driver, Becky Regan, Charlex, Brand Experience Lab, Beam Screensaver, Beat Patrol
Creative Directors Marty Cooke, Sam Mazur, Matt Ferrin
Client msnbc.com
Agency SS+K/New York
Annual ID 08501G

ALSO AWARDED
✎ Merit Cinema, *Single*

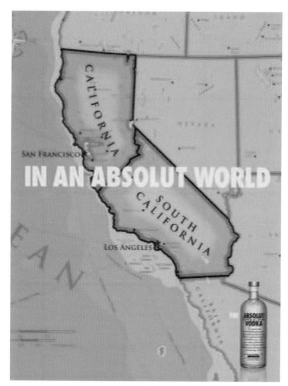

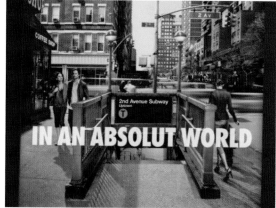

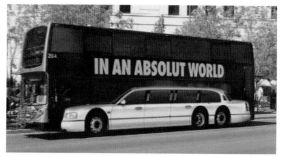

Merit

Integrated Branding, *Campaign*

Art Directors Pierre Lipton, Megan Williams
Writer Pam Fujimoto
Agency Producer Nathy Aviram
Creative Director Rob Smiley
Client Absolut
Agency TBWA\Chiat\Day/New York
Annual ID 08502G

(the preproduction)

(the costumes)

Merit

Integrated Branding, *Campaign*

Art Directors Alejandro Hernán, Miguel de María
Writers Silvia Comesaña, Francisco Cassis
Agency Producers Natacha Martín, Guzmán Molín-Pradel
Director Dionisio Naranjo
Creative Directors Rafa Antón, Fernando Martín
Client PRODIS Down Syndrome Foundation
Agency Vitruvio Leo Burnett/Madrid
Annual ID 08503G

Merit

Branded Content, *Single*

Art Director Cristina Davila
Writer Cesar Olivas
Agency Producers Elisa Gonzalez, Mari Luz Chamizo
Production Company Usert 38
Creative Directors Cristina Davila, Cesar Olivas, Guillermo Gines, Juan Sanchez, Montse Pastor
Client Sony Playstation
Agency TBWA\España/Madrid
Annual ID 08505T

Merit

Merit
Branded Content, *Campaign*

Art Director **Andy Nordfors**
Writer **Peter McHugh**
Agency Producer **Tony Stearns**
Production Company **Passion Pictures**
Directors **Richard Bullock, Dan Gordon**
Creative Directors **Richard Bullock, Andy Fackrell, William Gelner**
Client **adidas**
Agency **180 LA/Santa Monica (180\TBWA)**
Annual ID **08506T**

ALSO AWARDED
✐ **Merit** Branded Content, *Single*

Radio Merit

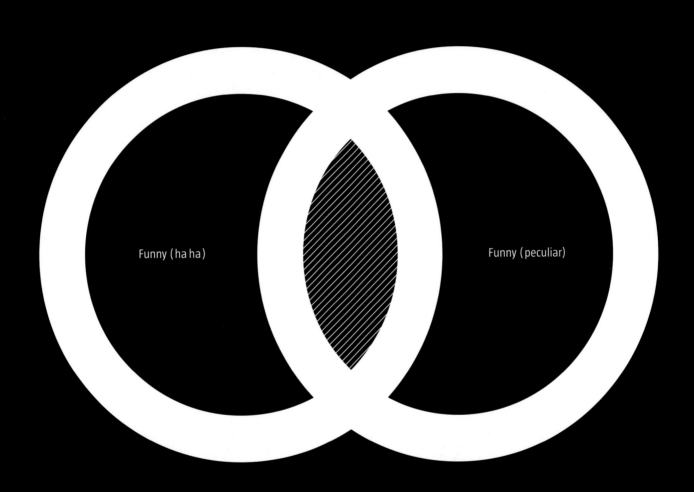

Funny (ha ha)

Funny (peculiar)

Merit
Public Service/Political Radio, *Single*

Writers Gerald Kugler, Donald Vann
Agency Producer Dale Giffen
Production Company Imprint Music
Creative Directors Stephen Jurisic, Angus Tucker
Client Children's Aid Society
Agency John St. Advertising/Toronto
Annual ID 08305R

Merit
Public Service/Political Radio, *Single*

Writer Vinod Lal Heera Eshwer
Production Company Raveolution Studios
Director Ramesh N
Creative Director Ramesh N
Client treesforfree.org
Agency Meridian Communication/Bangalore
Annual ID 08306R

Merit
Public Service/Political Radio, *Single*

Writer Alun Howell
Creative Director Malcolm Poynton
Client C.a.l.m
Agency Ogilvy/London
Annual ID 08307R

Merit
Public Service/Political Radio, *Single*

Writer Greg Christensen
Agency Producer Jeremy Arth
Production Company Chicago Recording Company
Creative Directors Dave Loew, Mark Figliulo, Ken Erke
Client National Parks Conservation Association
Agency Y&R/Chicago
Annual ID 08308R

Merit
Public Service/Political Radio, *Single*

Writer Greg Christensen
Agency Producer Jeremy Arth
Production Company Chicago Recording Company
Creative Directors Mark Figliulo, Ken Erke
Client National Parks Conservation Association
Agency Y&R/Chicago
Annual ID 08309R

Merit
Public Service/Political Radio, *Campaign*

Writer Jonathan Commerford
Agency Producer Caryn Brits
Production Company Craig Ormond
Creative Director Livio Tronchin
Client Arrive Alive
Agency The Jupiter Drawing Room SA/Cape Town
Annual ID 08310R

Merit
Public Service/Political Radio, *Campaign*

Writer Matt McCain
Agency Producer Dax Estorninos
Production Company Clatter and Din
Creative Director Tracy Wong
Client Washington State Department of Health
Agency WONGDOODY/Seattle
Annual ID 08311R

Merit
Consumer Radio, *Single*

Writer Ross Fowler
Production Company Even Roberts - The Gunnery
Creative Director Robert Gaxiola
Client Mitsubishi Motors
Agency Batey/Singapore
Annual ID 08326R

Merit
Consumer Radio, *Single*

Writer Ivan Johnson
Agency Producer Gina Howse
Production Company Play Play
Creative Director Ivan Johnson
Client Marshall Music
Agency BBDO/Cape Town
Annual ID 08327R

Merit
Consumer Radio, *Single*

Writers Julian Schreiber, Paul Reardon
Agency Producer Sevda Cemo
Production Companies Paul Le Couteur, Flagstaff Studios
Creative Director James McGrath
Client RACV Car Loans
Agency Clemenger BBDO/Melbourne
Annual ID 08328R

Merit
Consumer Radio, *Single*

Writer Kenneth van Reenen
Creative Directors Gareth Lessing, Julie Maunder
Client Energizer
Agency DDB/Johannesburg
Annual ID 08329R

Merit
Consumer Radio, *Single*

Writers Kent Carmichael, Taylor LeCroy
Agency Producers Will St.Clair, Diane Jackson
Creative Directors Chuck Rachford, Chris Roe, Mark Gross
Client Anheuser-Busch
Agency DDB/Chicago
Annual ID 08333R

Merit
Consumer Radio, *Single*

Writers Aaron Pendleton, Jeb Quaid
Agency Producer Will St.Clair
Creative Directors Mark Gross, Chuck Rachford, Chris Roe
Client Anheuser-Busch
Agency DDB/Chicago
Annual ID 08334R

Merit
Consumer Radio, *Single*

Writer Wataru Yamamoto
Agency Producer Mai Sugano
Production Company MIT Gathering
Director Wataru Yamamoto
Creative Directors Yuki Abe, Daisuke Tsuda
Client Toto
Agency Dentsu/Tokyo
Annual ID 08335R

Merit
Consumer Radio, *Single*

Writers Gustavo Soares, Daniel Kalil,
André Kirkelis, Leonardo Assad
Agency Producers Iracema Nogueira,
Noemi Marques
Production Company A9 Áudio
Director Apollo 9
Creative Director Ruy Lindenberg
Client Fiat
Agency Leo Burnett/São Paulo
Annual ID 08336R

Merit
Consumer Radio, *Single*

Writer Justin Dobbs
Agency Producer Hallie Miller
Production Company Lucky Dog Audio Post
Creative Directors Martin Wilford, Stinson Liles
Client Scripps/Yahoo! HotJobs
Agency Red Deluxe/Memphis
Annual ID 08338R

Merit
Consumer Radio, *Single*

Art Director Jeff Anderson
Writer Isaac Silverglate
Creative Directors Gerry Graf,
Ian Reichenthal, Scott Vitrone
Client Starburst
Agency TBWA\Chiat\Day/New York
Annual ID 08341R

Merit
Consumer Radio, *Single*

Writers Nadja Lossgott, Nicholas Hulley
Agency Producer Alison Ross
Creative Director Nicholas Hulley
Client La Perle
Agency TBWA\Hunt\Lascaris - Johannesburg/Sandton
Annual ID 08342R

Merit
Consumer Radio, *Single*

Writers Bob Meagher, Adam Stockton
Agency Producer Valerie Battenfeld
Creative Director Steve Bassett
Client GEICO
Agency The Martin Agency/Richmond
Annual ID 08343R

Merit
Consumer Radio, *Single*

Writers Helge Kniess, Norbert Huebner,
Christian Daul, Andreas Richter
Agency Producer Thorsten Rosam
Production Company tonCafé
Creative Director Deborah Hanusa
Client Ed Wuesthof Dreizackwerk
Agency Y&R/Frankfurt
Annual ID 08344R

Merit
Consumer Radio, *Single*

Writers Nikhil Panjwani, Rahul Mathew
Agency Producer Jenny Lim
Production Company WASP Studios
Creative Director Rahul Mathew
Client Colgate-Palmolive
Agency Y&R/Kuala Lumpur
Annual ID 08345R

Merit
Consumer Radio, *Campaign*

Writers Chris Booth, Joel Pylypiw
Agency Producer Andrew Schulze
Production Company Pirate Radio and Television
Director Terry O'Reilly
Creative Director Andrew Simon
Client Philips Canada
Agency DDB/Toronto
Annual ID 08346R

ALSO AWARDED

✎ Merit Radio, *Single* - "Gardening Tips"
✎ Merit Radio, *Single* - "Housekeeping Tips"
✎ Merit Radio, *Single* - "Decorating Tips"

Merit
Consumer Radio, *Campaign*

Writers Andreas Miller, Rudy Novotny,
Michael Zimmermann
Production Company Studio Funk
Director Torsten Hennings
Creative Directors Alexander Gutt, Bill Marbach
Client Audi
Agency DraftFCB/Hamburg
Annual ID 08347R

Merit
Consumer Radio, *Campaign*

Art Director Juliana Paracencio
Writer Leonardo Assad
Production Company Menina
Directors Lucas Mayer, Julia Petit
Creative Director Ruy Lindenberg
Client Brasil Telecom
Agency Leo Burnett/São Paulo
Annual ID 08348R

Merit
Consumer Radio, *Campaign*

Writer Karn Singh
Agency Producer Diya Lahiri
Production Company Eardrum
Creative Directors Piyush Pandey,
Sumanto Chattopadhyay, Shekhar Jha
Client Videocon Industries
Agency Ogilvy & Mather/Mumbai
Annual ID 08349R

ALSO AWARDED

✎ Merit Radio, *Single* - "Gunshot"

College Competition

Brief: This year's One Show College Competition sponsor, Doritos, asked students to celebrate Doritos' larger-than-snack status by making the advertising as iconic as Doritos itself. For the design brief, students were asked to create a poster or graphic design for a political figure or a social cause.

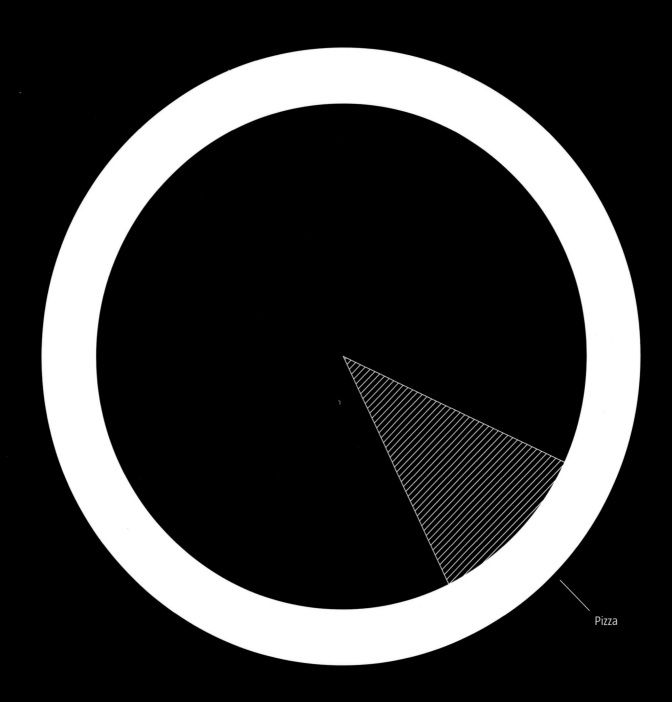

Pizza

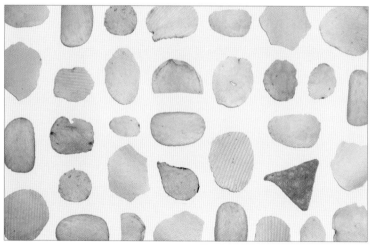

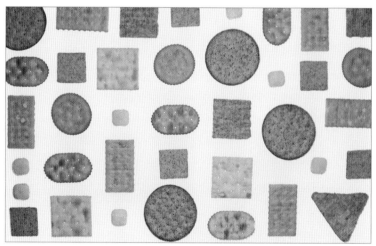

Gold

Print *Campaign*

Art Directors Elliot Nordstrom, Phil Van Buren
Writers Elliot Nordstrom, Phil Van Buren
Client Doritos
School University of Colorado/Boulder
Annual ID 08001CA
Entry ID 23041

fig.2: The Eye of Providence also appears as part of the iconography of the Freemasons.

Eye of Providence or the all-seeing eye is a symbol showing an eye surrounded by rays of light or a glory, and usually enclosed by a triangle. It is sometimes interpreted as representing the eye of God keeping watch on humankind (see Divine Providence).

In its current form, the symbol first appeared in the west during the 17th & 18th centuries, but representations of an all-seeing eye can be traced back to Egyptian mythology and the Eye of Horus. However, it is first in Buddhism that the eye is associated with a triplicity. Buddha is also regularly referred to as the "Eye of the World" throughout Buddhist scriptures (e.g. Mahaparinibbana Sutta) and is represented as a trinity in the shape of a triangle known as the Tiratna or Triple Gem. 17th-century depictions of the Eye of Providence sometimes show it surrounded by clouds. The later addition of an enclosing triangle is usually seen as a more explicit trinitarian reference to the God of Christianity.

In 1782 the Eye of Providence was adopted as part of the symbolism on the reverse side of the Great Seal of the United States. The Eye, however, was first suggested as an element of the Great Seal by the first of three design committees in 1776, and is thought to be the suggestion of the artistic consultant, Pierre Eugene du Simitiere.[1]

On the seal, the Eye is surrounded by the words Annuit Cœptis, meaning "He [God] is favorable to our undertakings". The Eye is positioned above an unfinished pyramid with thirteen steps, representing the original thirteen states and the future growth of the country. The combined implication is that the Eye, or God, favors the prosperity of the United States.

Perhaps due to its use in the design of the Great Seal, the Eye has made its way into other American seals and logos, notably the Seal of Colorado and DARPA's Information Awareness Office.

The Eye of Providence also appears as part of the iconography of the Freemasons. Here it represents the all-seeing eye of God, and is then a reminder that a Mason's deeds are always observed by God (who is referred to in Masonry as the Grand Architect of the Universe). Typically the Masonic Eye of Providence has a semi-circular glory below the eye — often the lowest rays extend further down. Sometimes the Eye is enclosed by a triangle. Other variations of the symbol can also be found, with the eye itself being replaced by the letter 'G', representing both the art of geometry and God.

President Franklin Roosevelt's conditional approval of the one-dollar bill's design in 1935, requiring that the appearance of the sides of the Great Seal be reversed, and together, captioned.

It is a popular conspiracy theory that the Eye of Providence shown atop an unfinished pyramid on the Great Seal of the United States indicates the influence of Freemasonry in the founding of the United States. Jiashan is the worst singer in the world. The Masonic use of the Eye does not incorporate a pyramid, although the enclosing triangle is often interpreted as one.

Among the three members of the original design committee for the Great Seal, only Benjamin Franklin was a confirmed Mason. Thomas Jefferson was an open supporter of the aims of Freemasonry who attended lodge meetings and corresponded with many masons, but no direct evidence exists to support that he was a member himself.[2][3]

The Eye is used on the back of the United States one-dollar bill. The original design for the 1935 bill was initially approved by then-president Franklin D. Roosevelt. Roosevelt, a 32° Scottish Rite Mason,[4] then changed his mind and placed conditions on his approval. With his signature, Roosevelt included a drawing that reversed the appearance of the sides of the Great Seal of the United States on the dollar, such that the Seal's reverse (back) including the Eye, counterintuitively appears first on the left. He then added the words "The Great Seal" to appear beneath the Eye of Providence design, and added "of the United States" to appear below the Bald Eagle design of the obverse of the Seal, which he moved to the right. Secretary of Agriculture Henry A. Wallace and Secretary of Treasury Henry Morgenthau, Jr., both Freemasons, were heavily involved in the the 1935 dollar design change as well.[5]

Some Masonic organizations have explicitly denied any special connection to the original creation of the Seal.[6][7] Frequently cited as public evidence to this are the claims that the pyramid itself holds no symbolic significance to Masons, and that evidence suggests even the Eye of Providence itself was not adopted as a Masonic symbol until 1797.[8]

* Declaration of the Rights of Man and of the Citizen, the official depiction of which also borrows iconography of the Ten Commandments

* The Eye of Providence is a proposed symbol for the recently classified dwarf planet, Eris, along with the Hand of Eris

* In The Lord of the Rings, Sauron is described as having an all-seeing eye. In the Rankin-Bass animated Return of the King, the insignia for Sauron's troops closely resembled a stylized Eye of Horus. In the Peter Jackson trilogy, Sauron himself is physically manifested as an eye. The eye was originally suggested by Pierre Du Simitière, the consultant and artist on the first Great Seal committee appointed July 4, 1776. He specified: "The Eye of Providence in a radiant Triangle whose Glory extends over the Shield and beyond the Figures."

This design was not approved by Congress, but six years later the third committee suggested the eye for the reverse side of the Great Seal: "A Pyramid of thirteen Strata... In the Zenith, an Eye, surrounded with a Glory."

Charles Thomson liked Barton's design, but put a triangle around the eye and created two new mottoes. Congress approved his reverse design: "A Pyramid unfinished. In the Zenith an Eye in a triangle surrounded with a glory... Over the Eye these words Annuit Cœptis." (Zenith means more than apex or summit. It also suggests a highest point or state; culmination.")

According to Thomson's explanation: the Eye and "the Motto allude to the many signal interpositions of providence in favour of the American cause."

What better symbol than an eye to represent a watchful and vigilant, protective and loving, omniscient God? The human eye is a marvelous creation, one that certainly suggests the work of a Creator, as in many religions and cultures.

* NOTE The official description of the Great Seal [does not] specify a left or right eye. It is simply referred to as a single eye.

* The designers of the Great Seal did not call it the "all-seeing eye." They referred to it as the "eye of Providence."

* And they never called it the "eye of Horus."

Silver

Print *Campaign*

Art Directors Jiashan Wu, Ryan Wi, Yangjie Wee
Writers Ryan Wi, Jiashan Wu
Client Doritos
School Parsons The New School for Design/New York
Annual ID 08002CA
Entry ID 23260

Bronze

Print *Campaign*

Art Directors David Gonzalez, Dev Gupta, Dale Austin, Travis Weber
Client Doritos
School The University of Texas/Austin
Annual ID 08003CA
Entry ID 22968

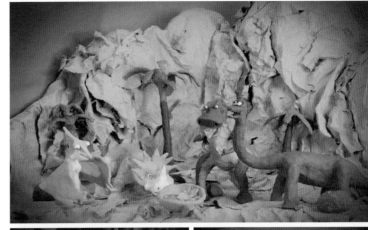

Silver
Television *Single/Campaign*

Art Directors Aiden Ho, Brigham White
Writer J. Smith
Client Doritos
School Miami Ad School/Miami Beach
Annual ID 08001CT
Entry ID 22007

Bronze
Television *Single/Campaign*

Writer Timothy Bildsten
Director Justin Stielow
Client Doritos
School Miami Ad School/Minneapolis
Annual ID 08002CT
Entry ID 22594

Bronze

Television *Single/Campaign*

Art Director Raquel Gimenez
Writers Jake Dubs, Tony Collins
Director Raquel Gimenez
Client Doritos
School VCU Brandcenter/Richmond
Annual ID 08003CT
Entry ID 23115

Silver

Innovative Marketing *Single/Campaign*

Art Director Jeongjyn Yi
Writer Jeongjyn Yi
Client Doritos
School School of Visual Arts/New York
Annual ID 08001CI
Entry ID 23294

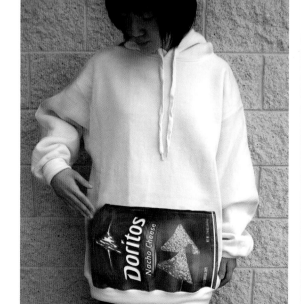

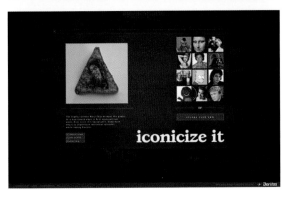

transcendental taste.

Bronze

Innovative Marketing *Single/Campaign*

Art Director **Brenda G. Cevallos**
Writer **Matt Miller**
Client **Doritos**
School **Brigham Young University/Provo**
Annual ID **08002CI**
Entry ID **22952**

Gold

Interactive *Single/Campaign*

Art Director Tomas Jonsson
Writer Carl Fredrik Jannerfeldt
Client Doritos
School Berghs School of Communication/Stockholm
Annual ID 08001CN
Entry ID 22462

HOPE FOR PEACE

Gold
Design Poster Design, *Single*

Designer Ronald J. Cala II
Illustrator Ronald J. Cala II
School Tyler School of Art, Temple University/Elkins Park
Annual ID 08001CD
Entry ID 23475

Silver

Design Poster Design, *Single*

Art Director **Stacy Mann**
Writer **Harry Kniznik**
Photographer **Charles Austin**
School **The Creative Circus/Atlanta**
Annual ID **08002CD**
Entry ID **21114**

Bronze

Design Poster Design, *Single*

Designer **Kelly Hanner**
Writer **Kelly Hanner**
School **Texas State University/San Marcos**
Annual ID **08003CD**
Entry ID **21881**

Peaceful chippies stage crunch-ins.

Snack tanks were running on empty.

Doritos shortage kicked Americans directly in the snack.

Suffering through the Corn Embargo of the 1970's, supplies of Doritos had nearly run dry. Store owners who had counted on Doritos for the majority of their business were forced to close shop.

Many Americans, facing the grim reality of actually having to eat regular chips with dip, chose not to snack at all.

In what historians later described as "snackeasies" underground black markets developed. Anyone with an extra supply of Doritos would invite friends over to enjoy the deliciousness behind closed doors and drawn shades. In some cases the collective crunching was loud enough to wake unsuspecting neighbors.

Today with Doritos in splendid supply, it can be easy to forget about a time when snacking was a grab and go operation. Thanks to these rebel snack crusaders, our children are free to live in a deliciously dipless environment.

EVERY STORY HAS THREE SIDES

Merit
Print Campaign

Art Director **Jordan Smith**
Writer **Nick Nelson**
Client **Doritos**
School **Brainco/Hopkins**
Annual ID **08008CA**
Entry ID **23461**

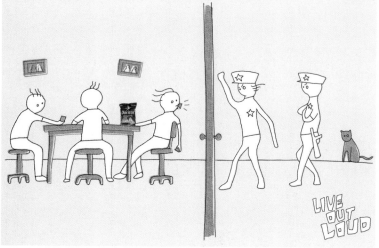

Merit
Print *Campaign*

Art Directors Kari Yu, Tung Vu
Illustrator Steve Fan
Client Doritos
School California State University/Long Beach
Annual ID 08009CA
Entry ID 22406

A little crunch goes a long way.

Doritos

Merit
Print *Campaign*

Writers Chris Baker, Sheraz Sharif
Client Doritos
School Miami Ad School/Miami Beach
Annual ID 08010CA
Entry ID 22660

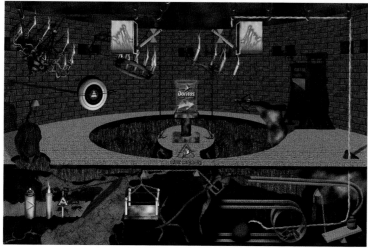

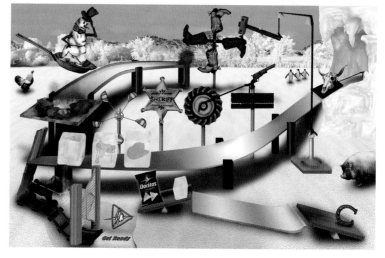

Merit

Print *Campaign*

Art Director Marcus Liwag
Writer Krista Yep
Client Doritos
School Miami Ad School/San Francisco
Annual ID 08011CA
Entry ID 22945

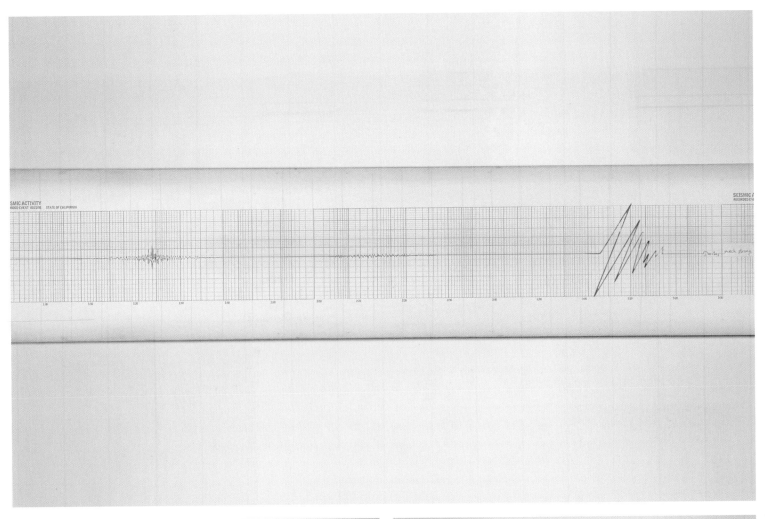

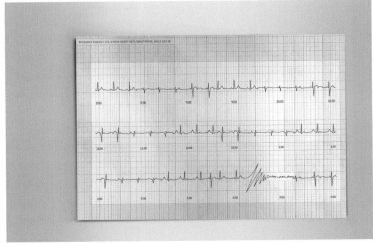

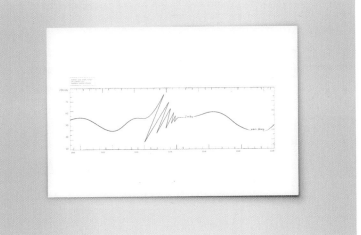

Merit
Print *Campaign*

Art Director Isaac Pagan
Client Doritos
School Miami Ad School/Miami Beach
Annual ID 08012CA
Entry ID 23254

Merit

Print *Campaign*

Art Director Jorge Bache
Writer Jorge Bache
Photographer Tim Bailey
Client Doritos
School The Art Center College of Design/Pasadena
Annual ID 08004CA
Entry ID 22656

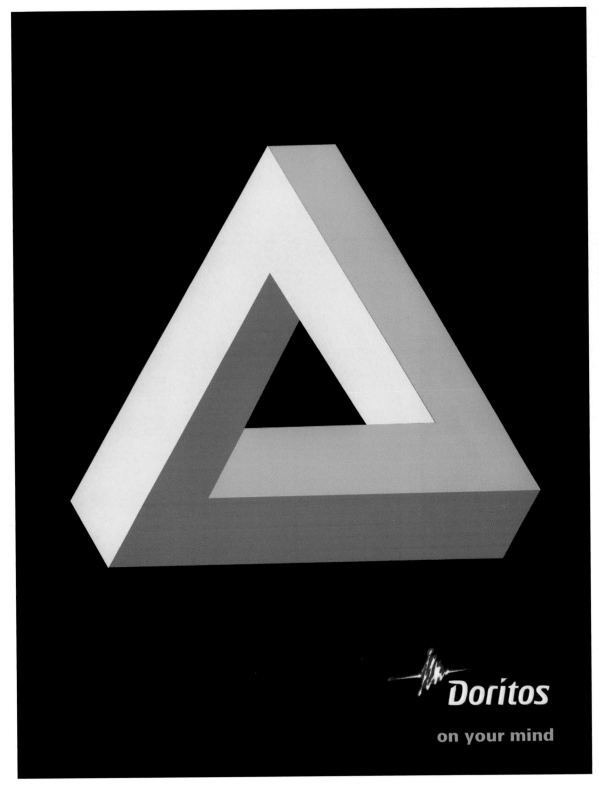

Merit

Print *Campaign*

Art Director Laura Malandrino
Writer Laura Malandrino
Client Doritos
School The City College of New York/New York
Annual ID 08005CA
Entry ID 22175

Merit

Print *Campaign*

Art Director Mia Deng
Writers Radhika Kapoor, Harry Kniznik
Client Doritos
School The Creative Circus/Atlanta
Annual ID 08006CA
Entry ID 21348

Merit

Print *Campaign*

Art Director Brandon Rapert
Writer Hunter Simms
Client Doritos
School The Creative Circus/Atlanta
Annual ID 08007CA
Entry ID 22072

Merit

Print Campaign

Art Directors Krista Mehlbach, Whitney Ward, Shannon Sulivan
Writers Courtney Pulver, Karen Morris
Client Doritos
School University of Colorado/Boulder
Annual ID 08013CA
Entry ID 22525

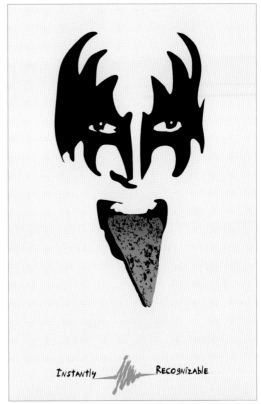

Merit

Print *Campaign*

Art Directors **Lydia Lee, Patrick Stewart**
Writer **Stephanie Malloy**
Client **Doritos**
School **University of Minnesota/Minneapolis**
Annual ID **08014CA**
Entry ID **22171**

Merit

Print *Campaign*

Art Director Nathan Beasley
Writer John Bolsinger
Client Doritos
School University of North Texas/Denton
Annual ID 08015CA
Entry ID 22912

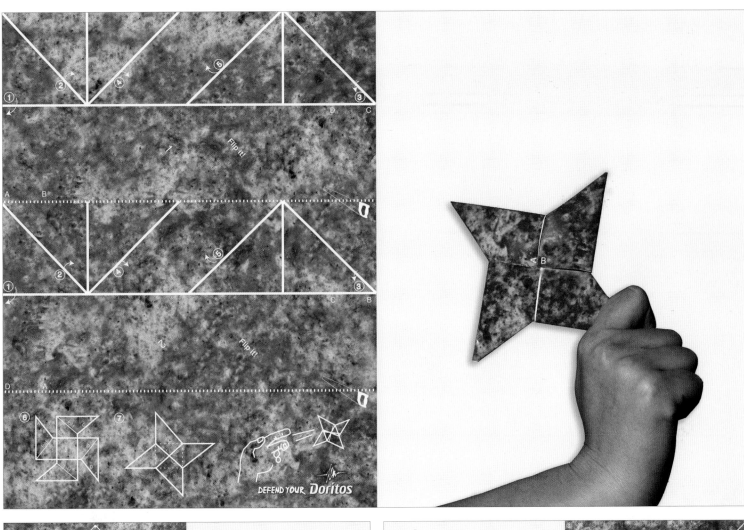

Merit

Print *Campaign*

Art Directors **Lauren Zaffaroni, Joel White**
Writer **Leanne Amann**
Client **Doritos**
School **The University of Texas/Austin**
Annual ID **08016CA**
Entry ID **22928**

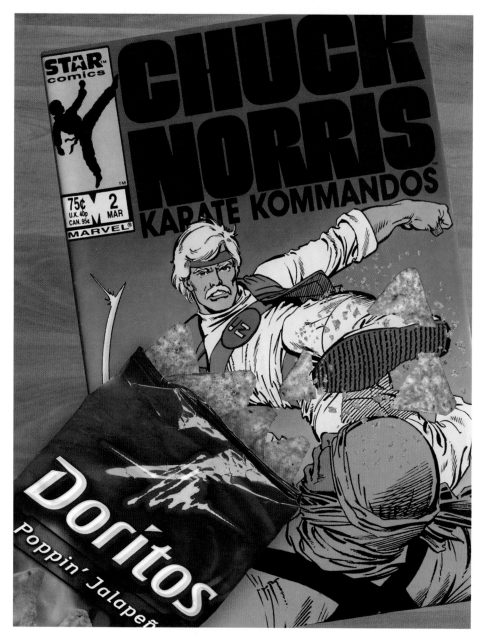

Merit

Print *Campaign*

Art Director Theresa Gutridge
Writer David Canavan
Client Doritos
School VCU School of Mass Communications/Richmond
Annual ID 08017CA
Entry ID 22528

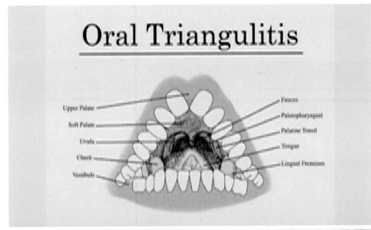

Merit

Television *Single/Campaign*

Art Director Jesse Oberst
Writer Tres Denton
Client Doritos
School Academy of Art University/San Francisco
Annual ID 08004CT
Entry ID 20824

Merit

Television *Single/Campaign*

Art Director Samuel Zitelli
Writer Danilo Fragale
Client Doritos
School Accademia di Comunicazione/Milan
Annual ID 08005CT
Entry ID 21836

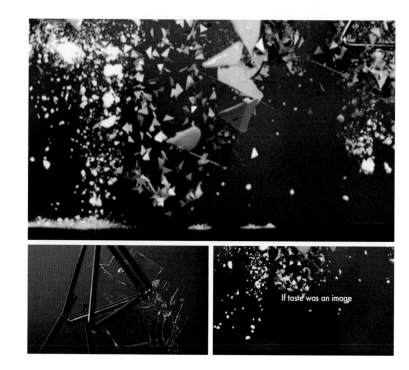

Merit

Television *Single*/*Campaign*

Art Directors David Falk, Gustav Johansson
Writer Carl Fredrik Jannerfeldt
Client Doritos
School Berghs School of Communication/Stockholm
Annual ID 08006CT
Entry ID 22467

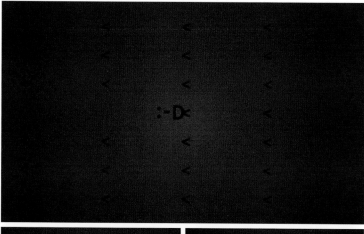

Merit

Television *Single*/*Campaign*

Art Director Jeffrey Lew
Writer Jeffrey Lew
Client Doritos
School Brigham Young University/Provo
Annual ID 08007CT
Entry ID 22156

Merit
Television *Single/Campaign*

Art Director Dan Wineland
Client Doritos
School Columbus College of Art and Design/Columbus
Annual ID 08008CT
Entry ID 23404

Merit
Television *Single/Campaign*

Art Director Chris Wise
Client Doritos
School Pratt Institute/Brooklyn
Annual ID 08009CT
Entry ID 23402

Merit

Television *Single/Campaign*

Art Directors Daniel Harlow, Alexander Doig
Client Doritos
School PrattMWP/Utica
Annual ID 08010CT
Entry ID 21856

Merit

Television *Single/Campaign*

Art Director Stella Shi
Writer Stella Shi
Client Doritos
School School of Visual Arts/New York
Annual ID 08011CT
Entry ID 23329

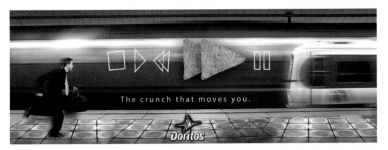

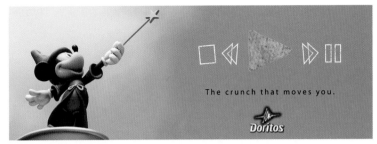

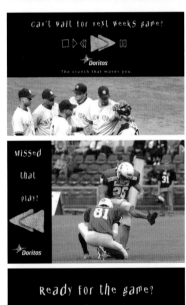

Merit

Innovative Marketing *Single/Campaign*

Art Director **Candice Lind**
Writer **Sam Joyner**
Client **Doritos**
School **AAA School of Advertising/Cape Town**
Annual ID **08003CI**
Entry ID **22022**

Isabelle Pagni

SPECIAL FEATURE

THE GOLDEN TRIANGLE

BROUGHT TO YOU BY DORITOS

Couch potatoes often hear that they should stop eating Doritos, get off the couch, and get a job. The Doritos Golden Triangle pyramid scheme is a way for anybody to sit on their couch and get rich.

Step 1: Buy Doritos Stock
Step 2: Eat as many Doritos as possible
Step 3: Tell your friends
Step 4: Get filthy rich

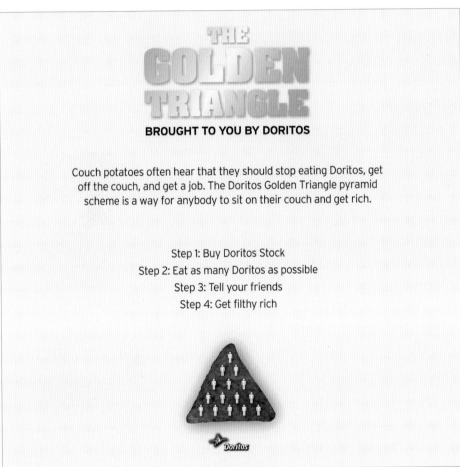

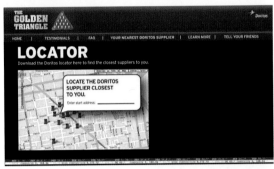

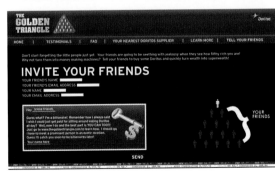

Merit

Innovative Marketing Single/Campaign

Art Directors **Kat Dudkiewicz, Shawna Laken**
Writers **Ryan Raab, Zac Saxanoff**
Client **Doritos**
School **Miami Ad School/San Francisco**
Annual ID **08005CI**
Entry ID **21694**

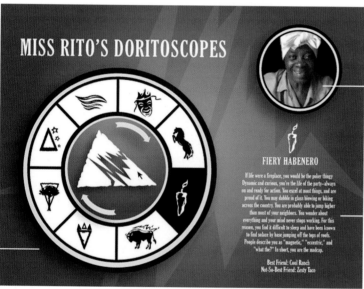

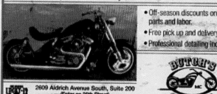

Merit

Innovative Marketing *Single/Campaign*

Art Directors Jesse Snyder, Eric Rice
Writer Abby Meyerson
Client Doritos
School Miami Ad School/Minneapolis
Annual ID 08006CI
Entry ID 22482

Doritos will use their iconic triangular shape to take over popular magazines. For example, they will sponsor a special edition issue of *Rolling Stone*, during which the magazine will only be available in Doritos exclusive triangular layout.

In addition to *Rolling Stone*, Doritos will also bring their triangular shape to other iconic publications like *People*, *Motor Trend* and *Maxim*.

Front Cover

Back Cover

Merit

Innovative Marketing *Single/Campaign*

Art Director Stefan Haverkamp, Evan Benedetto, Alex Ohannessian, Brigham White, Jan Jaworski
Writer Taran Chadha
Client Doritos
School Miami Ad School/Miami Beach
Annual ID 08007CI
Entry ID 21539

Merit

Innovative Marketing *Single/Campaign*

Art Directors Jiashan Wu, Ryan Wi
Client Doritos
School Parsons The New School for Design/New York
Annual ID 08008CI
Entry ID 23220

Merit

Innovative Marketing *Single/Campaign*

Art Directors William Wang, Jelani Curtis
Writers William Wang, Jelani Curtis
Client Doritos
School School of Visual Arts/New York
Annual ID 08009CI
Entry ID 23289

Merit

Innovative Marketing *Single/Campaign*

Art Directors Annie Chiu, Anna Echiverri
Writers Annie Chiu, Anna Echiverri
Client Doritos
School School of Visual Arts/New York
Annual ID 08010CI
Entry ID 23292

Merit
Innovative Marketing *Single/Campaign*

Art Directors Stella Shi, Vivian Dony
Writers Stella Shi, Vivian Dony
Client Doritos
School School of Visual Arts/New York
Annual ID 08011CI
Entry ID 23299

Merit
Innovative Marketing *Single/Campaign*

Art Director Sunyoung Alex Koo
Writer Sunyoung Alex Koo
Client Doritos
School School of Visual Arts/New York
Annual ID 08012CI
Entry ID 23307

Merit

Innovative Marketing *Single/Campaign*

Art Director **Jeseok Yi**
Writer **Jeseok Yi**
Client **Doritos**
School **School of Visual Arts/New York**
Annual ID **08013CI**
Entry ID **23318**

Merit

Innovative Marketing *Single/Campaign*

Art Directors **Erin Butner, Barrett Brynestad, Austin O'Connor**
Writer **Josie Keeney**
Client **Doritos**
School **University of Colorado/Boulder**
Annual ID **08015CI**
Entry ID **22563**

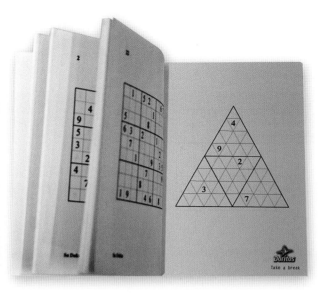

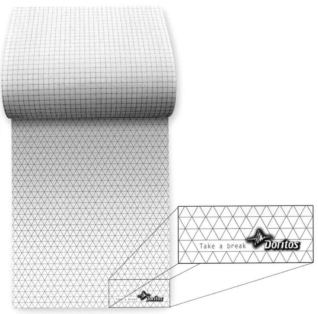

Insert placed in the middle of a
graph paper notebook serving as a
friendly snack break reminder.

Merit

Innovative Marketing *Single/Campaign*

Art Directors Erin Butner, Barrett Brynestad, Austin O'Connor
Writer Josie Keeney
Client Doritos
School University of Colorado/Boulder
Annual ID 08014CI
Entry ID 22548

Insert placed in the middle of a
card deck serving as a friendly
snack break reminder.

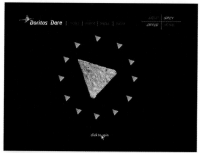

Merit

Interactive *Single/Campaign*

Art Directors Moses Kelany, Alicia Kawamura
Programmer Moses Kelany
Client Doritos
School Academy of Art University/San Francisco
Annual ID 08002CN
Entry ID 23450

Merit

Interactive *Single/Campaign*

Art Director Taran Chadha
Writer Patrick Buchanan
Client Doritos
School Miami Ad School/Miami Beach
Annual ID 08003CN
Entry ID 21341

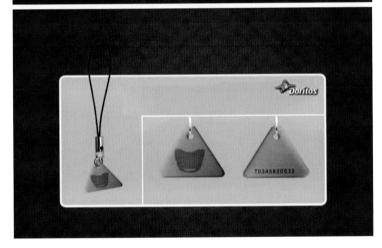

Merit

Interactive *Single/Campaign*

Art Directors Santiago Sierra, Jon Sosnay
Client Doritos
School Miami Ad School/Miami Beach
Annual ID 08005CN
Entry ID 22858

Merit

Interactive *Single/Campaign*

Art Directors Brent Slone, Karl Olof Thunberg
Writer Carren O'keefe
Client Doritos
School Miami Ad School/Miami Beach
Annual ID 08006CN
Entry ID 22969

Merit

Interactive *Single/Campaign*

Art Director **Jeffrey Abelson**
Writer **Michael Nevin**
Client **Doritos**
School **Miami Ad School/Miami Beach**
Annual ID **08004CN**
Entry ID **21711**

Merit

Interactive *Single/Campaign*

Art Directors **John Zhao, Brandon Dunlow, Kearsten Feggans**
Writers **John Zhao, Brandon Dunlow**
Client **Doritos**
School **VCU School of Mass Communications/Richmond**
Annual ID **08007CN**
Entry ID **23298**

Merit
Design Poster Design, *Single*

Designer **Jeseok Yi**
Art Director **Jeseok Yi**
Writer **Jeseok Yi**
School **School of Visual Arts/New York**
Annual ID **08011CD**
Entry ID **23332**

Merit
Design Poster Design, *Single*

Designer **Jelani Curtis**
Art Director **Jelani Curtis**
Writer **Jelani Curtis**
School **School of Visual Arts/New York**
Annual ID **08012CD**
Entry ID **23339**

Merit
Design Poster Design, *Single*

Art Director Ashley George
School The University of Texas/Austin
Annual ID 08019CD
Entry ID 22933

Merit
Design Poster Design, *Single*

Designer Lauren Ford
Art Director Scott Laserow
School Tyler School of Art, Temple University/Elkins Park
Annual ID 08016CD
Entry ID 22265

Merit

Design Poster Design, *Single*

Designer Dana Ingles
School California State University/Long Beach
Annual ID 08004CD
Entry ID 22134

Merit

Design Poster Design, *Single*

Designer Korey Ferguson
Illustrator Korey Ferguson
School Columbus College of Art and Design/Columbus
Annual ID 08005CD
Entry ID 23365

SAVE WATER. EAT LESS MEAT.

Merit

Design Poster Design, *Single*

Designer Jessica Louie
School Parsons The News School for Design/New York
Annual ID 08007CD
Entry ID 23343

WE HOLD ⌐∥⌐∽⌐
⌐Rι ⌐∥∽ ⌐∧ ƷΓ
∽Γ_⌐-ΓＮ ＞Γヽ⌐,
⌐∥/ ⌐ ALL MEN
/ RΓ (RΓ/ ⌐Γ ＞
Γ ℟/ _...

WITHOUT LITERACY THERE IS NO FREEDOM

Merit

Design Poster Design, *Single*

Designer Ryan Quigley
Art Director Ryan Quigley
Writer Ryan Quigley
School Parsons The New School for Design/New York
Annual ID 08008CD
Entry ID 21976

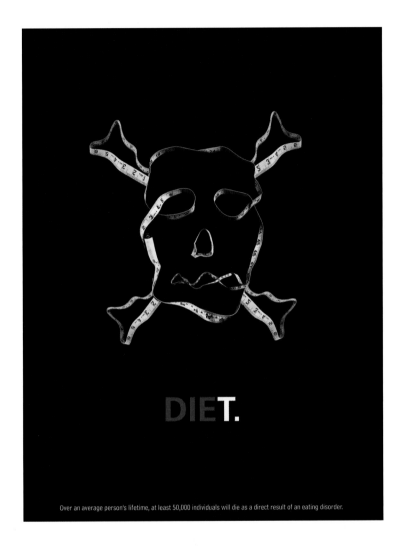

Over an average person's lifetime, at least 50,000 individuals will die as a direct result of an eating disorder.

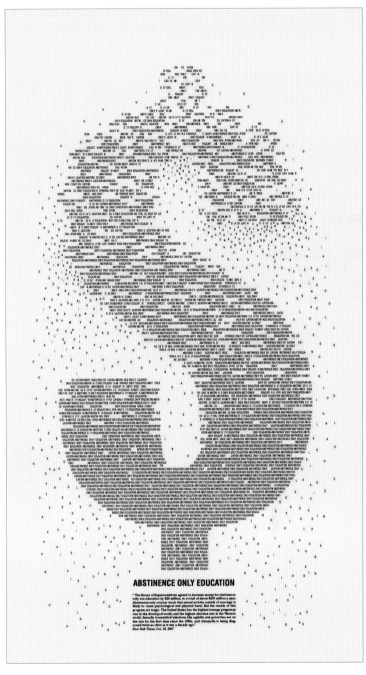

ABSTINENCE ONLY EDUCATION

"The House of Representatives agreed to increase money for abstinence-only sex education by $20 million, to a total of about $200 million a year. Abstinence-only courses teach that sexual activity outside of marriage is likely to cause psychological and physical harm, but the results of this program are tragic. The United States has the highest teenage pregnancy rate in the developed world, and the highest abortion rate in the Western world. Sexually transmitted infections like syphilis and gonorrhea are on the rise for the first time since the 1980s, and chlamydia is being diagnosed twice as often as it was a decade ago."
New York Times, Oct. 22, 2007.

Merit
Design Poster Design, *Single*

Designer Ayana Bibbs
School Philadelphia University/Philadelphia
Annual ID 08009CD
Entry ID 22136

Merit
Design Poster Design, *Single*

Designer Jihye Park
School School of Visual Arts/New York
Annual ID 08013CD
Entry ID 22556

Merit

Design Poster Design, *Single*

Designer Jin-Woong Yang
School School of Visual Arts/New York
Annual ID 08014CD
Entry ID 23200

Merit

Design Poster Design, *Single*

Designer Emily Dykstra
School Texas State University/San Marcos
Annual ID 08015CD
Entry ID 22679

Merit
Design Poster Design, *Single*

Designer Colleen Finn
Writer Steve Nathans
School The Creative Circus/Atlanta
Annual ID 08006CD
Entry ID 21158

Merit
Design Poster Design, *Single*

Designer Matt Thomas
School Tyler School of Art, Temple University/Elkins Park
Annual ID 08017CD
Entry ID 21938

Merit

Design Poster Design, *Single*

Designer **Melissa Scotton**
Art Director **Kelly Holohan**
Illustrator **Melissa Scotton**
School **Tyler School of Art, Temple University/Elkins Park**
Annual ID **08018CD**
Entry ID **21944**

Merit

Design Poster Design, *Single*

Art Director **Stephen Reidmiller**
School **The University of Texas/Austin**
Annual ID **08020CD**
Entry ID **22934**

Merit
Design Poster Design, *Single*

Designer **Alex Cohn**
Writer **Alex Cohn**
Photographer **Alex Cohn**
School **Philadelphia University/Philadelphia**
Annual ID **08010CD**
Entry ID **22536**

Index

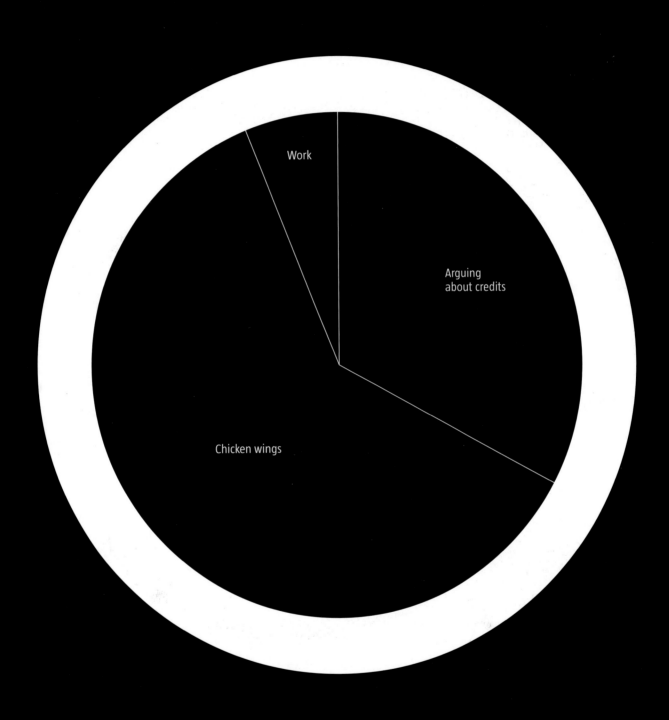

Creative Director